T

Nancy Drew® Mysteries

This *Nancy Drew* Three-in-One
was first published in the UK in 1992.
This edition published in 1994 by Diamond Books,
77–85 Fulham Palace Road, Hammersmith,
London W6 8JB.

Nancy Drew®
in

The Triple Hoax

The Flying Saucer Mystery

The Secret in the Old Lace

by Carolyn Keene

The Triple Hoax was first published
in the UK in a single volume in 1981 by
William Collins Sons & Co. Ltd.

1

A Sudden Trip

"Dad! Aunt Eloise wants me to come to New York immediately to solve a mystery!" eighteen-year-old Nancy Drew called out excitedly.

Carson Drew, a well-known attorney in River Heights, looked fondly at his attractive, titian-haired daughter as she returned to the breakfast table. "What kind of mystery?"

Nancy waved a special delivery letter that the mailman had brought. "Listen to this. I'll read it to you.

> "Dear Nancy,
> A close friend of mine, Mrs. Annabella Richards, has been swindled. She taught in the same school I do, but left a few years ago

to marry a wealthy man. He died not long ago, and Annabella is a rich widow. I won't give you any more details now, but I certainly hope you can visit me and help her. Bring your friends Bess and George if you like, and say hello to my brother for me.

Lots of love,
Aunt Eloise"

"Well, Dad, what do you think?" Nancy asked.

Mr. Drew laughed. "I think that you want to go and I see no reason why you shouldn't. The mystery sounds interesting. I'll be eager to hear more about it."

Nancy jumped up, kissed her father, and hurried to the telephone. First she called George Fayne, a slender, dark-haired girl who enjoyed her boyish name. Then she contacted George's cousin Bess Marvin, who was a slightly plump, pretty blond with dimples. Both girls loved to help Nancy on her mystery cases, and together they had solved many of them.

Bess and George were keen to join Nancy on her trip to New York. Their parents, after some persuasion, furnished the money. It was arranged that the young sleuths would leave River Heights the following day.

As Nancy packed her bag, the Drews' lovable housekeeper, Mrs. Hannah Gruen, came into the girl's bedroom. She had lived with Nancy and her father since Mrs. Drew's death, when Nancy was three years old, and had been like a mother to her. The two had shared many secrets and adventures.

"Nancy," Hannah said, "judging from past performances, you're likely to get into all sorts of ticklish situations. I beg you to be careful. You know you're an indispensable member of this household!"

Nancy chuckled. "I'm glad to find out I'm really needed here. But you know, when I'm working on a case, it's pretty hard to keep from running into danger."

"I know," Hannah agreed. "Your father and I will be wishing you the best of luck all the way."

The following afternoon Mr. Drew drove the girls to the airport. They boarded a plane that took them directly to La Guardia Airport in New York. After debarking, they were met in the terminal by Nancy's tall, attractive Aunt Eloise and her friend.

"Nancy, it's wonderful to see you!" Miss Drew exclaimed. "And Bess and George. I want all of you to meet Mrs. Annabella Richards."

After hugs, kisses, and excited welcomes, the group walked outside and awaited Mrs. Richards's chauffeur-driven car. Ten minutes passed, but it did not arrive.

The annoyed woman frowned. "Roscoe is always so prompt and reliable," she said. "I can't understand why he isn't here."

"Could you tell us something about your mystery while we're waiting?" Nancy asked.

Mrs. Richards nodded. But before she could begin, a strange man walked up to her. "Are you Mrs. Richards?" he asked.

"Yes."

"Your chauffeur, Roscoe, sent me to tell you your car won't start."

"Won't start!" the woman exclaimed. "He drove me here a little while ago and there was nothing wrong with the car. In fact, it was serviced recently."

"I don't know anything about that, ma'am," the stranger said. "Roscoe suggests you go home by taxi." With that, the man turned and walked off.

Mrs. Richards frowned. "I don't understand it," she remarked. "Well, I guess we'd better go."

She summoned a limousine and the five climbed inside. As the car pulled away, Mrs. Richards said, "I suppose Eloise has told you a little of my situation."

Nancy had a sudden hunch. It might be best if Mrs. Richards did not reveal her story for the taxi driver to hear.

She leaned over and whispered into the woman's ear, "Don't reveal any of your secrets now." Mrs. Richards nodded and changed the subject. The conversation became general until the group arrived at Aunt Eloise's attractive apartment.

Then Mrs. Richards went on with her story. "My husband was very kindhearted and charitable. He donated money to large and small organizations, and even to individuals. After his death I carried on this tradition, but the work became too much for me. I finally hired my husband's former secretary, who promised to take care of everything so I could go on vacation. About that time, a travel agent contacted me and offered a wonderful bargain world tour."

"Sounds fabulous," Bess said dreamily.

"It did," Mrs. Richards agreed. "The agent showed me enticing literature and I fell for it. A few days later he brought the plane tickets and hotel accommodations, and I paid him $3,000. It was too bad that I had not investigated the whole thing."

"Why, was something wrong?" George asked.

"Indeed it was. When I went to the airport, the airline named on the ticket had a counter, but no such flight."

"How dreadful!" Bess exclaimed. "And you paid all this money to a swindler?"

"Yes, I did," Mrs. Richards said sadly. She turned to Nancy. "Please help me find that man! I contacted the police, but nothing came of it. Maybe your friends Bess and George can help you. Your Aunt Eloise tells me you're wonderful young sleuths."

The girls smiled and accepted the challenge at once.

"What was the travel agent's name and where was he located?" Nancy asked.

"He gave his name as Henry Clark and his address as 14 Canalee Road in Queens. The police checked it and found both to be phony."

"What did he look like?"

"Oh, he was tall, handsome, and had a dark beard. He was a smooth talker and very pleasant."

"Did you pay him by check or in cash?"

"Cash. He said the airline would not take a personal check."

George spoke up. "He probably skipped town with your money."

"That's what the police think. They doubt they'll ever find him. Perhaps you girls can unravel this mystery for me."

"We'll do our best," Nancy promised. "Unfortunately we have very little to go on."

"I understand that," Mrs. Richards said. "And now I'd better get home." She turned to Miss Drew. "Eloise, may I call my apartment and see if Roscoe had the car fixed?"

"Of course."

Mrs. Richards dialed the number and spoke to her housekeeper, Trudie. Suddenly the girls saw her turn ashen white.

"That's terrible!" Mrs. Richards cried out. "I'll be right over. I hope nothing has happened to Roscoe!"

She put down the receiver. "Trudie told me a man called the apartment. He said I would never see my car again. Before she could ask about Roscoe, the stranger hung up. Oh, dear! I hope my chauffeur hasn't met with foul play!"

"So do I," Aunt Eloise said sympathetically. "I'll get a taxi for you. Let us know what happened, and if we can be of any help."

After the distressed woman had left, Aunt Eloise said she would start dinner. The girls followed her to the kitchen and helped prepare the meal.

While they were eating, Miss Drew announced, "With all this excitement, I almost forgot that I have four tickets to a magic show tonight. It's given by a group called the Hoaxters."

"That sounds interesting," Bess remarked.

Aunt Eloise nodded. "Annabella saw it and said it was fascinating. Incidentally, there is a big surprise in the show. She wouldn't tell me what it is."

The girls were eager to see the performance, which proved, indeed, to be most unusual. A dark-haired sleight of hand man with a perky mustache, listed on the program as Ronaldo Jensen, started with an amazing card trick. He asked people in the audience to name a card, then time after time he pulled the correct one out of his pack.

"How in the world does he do that?" Bess whispered to Nancy.

"I wish I knew," the girl replied.

Next, a young woman was brought onto the stage in a gilt chair with red plush upholstery. Her eyes were blindfolded. Another performer held a black cloth in front of her legs for a moment. When he pulled it away, her legs were gone!

The audience gasped, while the girl held her arms up high. The magician put the black cloth in front of them. Seconds later, the arms had disappeared!

"Oh, this is dreadful!" Bess cried out. "That poor girl!"

George grinned. "Don't be silly. You know it's only a trick!"

Her cousin settled back. "But it seems so real!"

Now the man held the cloth in front of the girl's body. When he removed it, the chair was empty!

"Oh!" Bess exclaimed.

Even Nancy was perplexed. She had seen many magic shows and knew how several of the tricks were done. But she could not figure out how this disappearing act was possible.

As the performer gradually restored the girl, section by section, Bess heaved a great, audible sigh of relief.

"Feel better now?" George teased her.

"Much."

Next, another member of the troupe stepped from the wings to the edge of the stage. He announced, "We are now inviting a few people from the audience to come forward and see how we do our tricks!"

At once Bess jumped out of her seat and started up the aisle, handbag swinging over her arm. She was one of the first to reach the stage.

The sleight of hand man accepted ten people, including Bess, then repeated his card trick. It was just as puzzling to the onlookers as it had been before, even though they were now standing very close to him.

Suddenly the magician pulled a watch out of a young man's ear. He compared it with his own watch. "Seems to be an hour ahead. Get it? A-head," he quipped, grinning.

As everyone laughed, the magician put the watch into his own pocket, telling the visitor he would return it later.

"See this!" he said, and produced a wallet from inside another man's collar.

"Hey, that was in my hip pocket which was buttoned!" the amazed fellow shouted. "How'd you do that?"

The magician chuckled. "We invited you to watch. You tell me! And don't worry about your wallet. It will be returned to you right after the show."

Bess was fascinated. Suddenly it occurred to her: Would these people really receive their property back?

She felt for her own handbag. It was gone! She stared intently at the sleight of hand man. He did not have the bag, and it was nowhere in sight!

2

Bess's Strange Caller

Bess startled everyone on stage by crying out, "Someone has taken my handbag!"

A woman standing near her exclaimed, "And my expense account notebook is gone!"

George jumped up and announced to Nancy that she was going on stage to help her cousin. Nancy held her friend's arm. "Please stay here. I'm sure all this is a hoax. Don't you remember that Mrs. Richards said there was a big surprise during the performance?"

George sat down again. "I guess you're right, Nancy."

By this time the magician was clapping his hands loudly to restore order on the stage. Over a microphone he announced, "This is all a hoax. Every missing article will be returned to its rightful owner at the end of the show. Please come back here afterward to get your property."

Members of the audience who had gathered around him acknowledged that they had come on stage out of curiosity and would wait to claim their property. They filed back to their seats.

"For a few minutes I was scared," Bess told Nancy, George, and Aunt Eloise. "Do you think they really mean what they say and will return our things?"

Nancy nodded. "I'm sure they will. If they hadn't been doing it in other shows, people would have notified the police."

Aunt Eloise added, "There has been no bad publicity or I would have heard about it."

Bess agreed, and her flushed face returned to the attractive pink and white it usually was.

When the show was over, George said to her, "Be sure to check your handbag and see that everything is still in it."

Bess caught her breath. "It's jammed with stuff. I hope I can remember what was there. Let me see: my wallet, credit cards, a little jewel bag with a bracelet and earrings. Perfume. My savings book. A letter from Dorothy Cross, the girl I met during my vacation in Maine. And, oh . . . yes."

"What?" George asked.

Bess lowered her eyes. "A picture of Dave."

Nancy smiled. "You wouldn't want to lose that for a million dollars, would you?"

"No, I wouldn't," Bess replied.

Dave Evans was a special friend of hers, and she knew that both Nancy and George carried photographs of their boyfriends, too. Nancy's purse contained a snapshot of Ned Nickerson in his football uniform, and George had Burt Eddleton's picture tucked in her wallet.

Bess hurried up to the stage with other members of the audience to claim her property. They were ushered into a back room. As people retrieved their possessions, they were asked to sign releases that read,

> I relieve the Hoaxters of any wrongdoing
> in playing a hoax on me.

"This is just a protection for us. We don't want to be accused later of not returning everything to you," the magician explained.

Bess found that the contents of her handbag were intact and signed the paper. Then she joined her friends and they left the theater with Aunt Eloise.

"That was quite an experience," Miss Drew remarked. "Annabella was right about a big surprise in the performance."

Nancy said nothing, but her mind was working fast. Why was it necessary for the Hoaxters to keep people's property for such a long time? They could have returned it at once. She began to feel suspicious about the troupe, but had nothing definite to go on.

As the girls prepared for bed, George yawned. "If the rest of the mystery is going to be filled with days like this one, we'll have plenty of excitement." The others agreed and said good night.

Directly after breakfast the following morning Bess received a phone call. A man who introduced himself as Howie Barker said, "I contacted your home in River Heights. Your mother told me where you were staying. I'd like very much to come and see you."

"I don't understand," Bess replied. "I've never met you."

"No, you haven't," Mr. Barker admitted. "But your mother felt that you might be interested in an offer I have for you. The company I represent is building a wonderful new seaside hotel. If you avail yourself of this opportunity, you will have perpetual low rates for yourself, your family and friends, and will get reservations anytime you choose to come."

"I don't know what to say," Bess told him. "My friends and I have plans for the day. Maybe some other time—"

Nancy and George stood close to Bess and had overheard the conversation. Nancy whispered, "Let him come!"

Bess looked surprised, but said to the stranger, "Well, all right. Can you make it right away?"

"I'll be there in half an hour," Mr. Barker said.

After Bess had hung up, she turned to Nancy. "Why did you want him to see us?"

Nancy told her that the scheme sounded like another swindle. "This Mr. Barker could be the man who sold Mrs. Richards the ticket for the fake world trip!"

"If that is so, then he might know we're on the case—" George began.

"And means to kidnap us?" Bess panicked.

"C'mon, Bess," Nancy said. "How could he possibly know of our connection with Mrs. Richards? I'd say he picked your name from some mailing list. You get more junk mail than anybody else I know. It's all coincidental, I'm sure."

George spoke up. "Why don't we ask Mrs. Richards to come over? If she can identify Barker as Henry Clark, we'll call the police and have him arrested!"

Aunt Eloise phoned her friend. The housekeeper answered and said Mrs. Richards was out and would not return until evening.

"That's too bad," Bess remarked.

Nancy said, "I have an idea how we might find out if Mr. Barker is the travel agent. Take his picture. Aunt Eloise, you have a camera, don't you?"

Miss Drew said, "Yes, and I happen to have fast film in it so we won't need a flash. Besides, the camera makes no noise when the shutter clicks. It'll be perfect for this purpose."

"Does it develop the picture instantly?" George asked.

"Yes. As soon as Annabella arrives home, you can show it to her."

As the time neared for Howie Barker's arrival, Bess became nervous. "I don't want to get mixed up in any kind of racket," she declared. "What am I supposed to tell him?"

"I'll stay in the room with you," George offered. "We'll figure out something."

It was decided that Nancy would hide and take the caller's picture while Bess and George kept him in animated conversation. Aunt Eloise could not wait for the stranger to arrive because she had classes at school. Before leaving, she warned the girls to be careful of any tricks the caller might play.

"I'm not going to let him hoax me!" Bess spoke up belligerently.

George added, "If you start to fall for any scheme, I'll take over."

Soon the house phone rang. Bess answered. The doorman announced that Mr. Howie Barker was there to see Miss Bess Marvin.

"Let him come up," Bess said, her voice betraying her slight nervousness.

Barker proved to be a good-looking, blond-haired man with gray at the temples, and a full blond-gray beard. The description was not like that of Henry Clark. The man was a glib talker. Bess ushered him into the living room, where Nancy was concealed behind a wall screen. She took several pictures when he walked in and others when he sat down on the couch.

"You girls will love this place," Howie Barker said, taking a large architect's drawing out of his briefcase. He spread it on the coffee table and with his pen pointed to the fine features of the place.

"Notice the little verandas off each bedroom. If you don't feel like going to the beach, you can sun yourself right there. If you don't want to go to the dining room, you can eat your meals out there, too."

George spoke up. "It's certainly a huge place. Where is it being built?"

Mr. Barker produced a brochure from his briefcase. It described the location as a secluded area of oceanfront in Maine.

"It has luxury as well as seclusion," he went on.

"I'm telling you, this is really an opportunity of a lifetime."

"Why did you pick my cousin for this offer?" George inquired.

"We have been approaching all the people who vacationed at the Silverline Hotel in Maine last season," Barker explained. "You see, the Silverline is owned by the same company, and we know their clientele would enjoy this kind of setup."

"What does it cost?" Bess asked.

"Only a thousand dollars. For that, you have guaranteed discount rates forever, much less than the regular price for a room."

"For a thousand dollars, you can spend a long time in a hotel," George pointed out.

"Not really," Barker objected. "Also, remember, your rates are guaranteed never to increase. Everything else goes up year after year. Right?"

Bess agreed. She was quite impressed with the proposal, but George thought of Nancy. Had she been able to take pictures of the man from every angle? Impatiently the girl looked at her wristwatch. Barker had been there twenty minutes, surely time enough to be photographed extensively.

Bess was about to say that she would try to get the money to avail herself of the offer, when she remembered Nancy's warning that this might be another swindle similar to Mrs. Richards's experience. She hesitated, then said, "The whole thing sounds wonderful. I'll tell you what I'll do. I'll contact a few people and let you know if I can borrow the money."

"Oh, that won't be necessary. Your mother told me you had your own savings account, and can spend the money as you wish."

"That's partly true, but I must think about your offer. Where can I find you?"

George fully expected the man not to give his address, but to her amazement he pulled a business card from his pocket and handed it to Bess.

"My phone number is on here," he said. "Be sure to let me know tomorrow." He stood up and shook hands with both girls, then they ushered him out of the apartment.

After George had closed the door, she smiled at her cousin. "Bess, I'm proud of you. For a moment I thought you'd fall for his scheme, but you handled it beautifully."

"It really sounds great," Bess countered as they entered the living room again. Nancy stepped from her hiding place, and the girls asked her if she had taken good pictures.

"Oh, yes, several," Nancy replied. "I'm sorry I didn't have a tape recorder to get the whole conversation. By the way, I don't think we should wait for Mrs. Richards to come home. Let's go to the police at once with these photographs and the card Mr. Barker gave Bess. We'll tell them our suspicions."

"How did the pictures come out?" George asked. Nancy showed them to her friends. They were excellent and the young detective felt sure that if the police had a record of the man, they could identify him easily.

The three sleuths quickly left the apartment and headed for the nearest police station. When they walked in, Nancy asked if it were possible to talk to the chief privately.

The desk sergeant asked the girls' names and the nature of their business. Nancy introduced her friends and herself and added, "I think we have a lead on a con man."

The sergeant looked at her in surprise, but made no further comment. He picked up his phone and dialed the chief's number.

After a short conversation, he said to Nancy, "Chief Raleigh will see you. Walk down the corridor and take the first turn to your left. Watch for the sign on the door."

In a few minutes the young detective and her friends were standing before the chief. He was a ruddy-faced man who reminded them of Police Chief McGinnis in River Heights.

"I understand you have some interesting information for me," the officer said, smiling.

Nancy nodded and took Barker's pictures from her handbag. Bess produced the man's business card.

"Have you any record of this person?" Nancy inquired.

The chief called in a deputy and asked him to look in the files. While waiting for an answer, Nancy told Chief Raleigh about the mysterious caller and the proposition he had offered Bess.

The officer frowned. "It certainly sounds like a swindle."

When the deputy returned, he said they had no picture of a suspect resembling the man in Nancy's photographs. The deputy had rubbed out the beard. Still the face did not resemble anyone in their file. Also, the name Howie Barker had not been reported in connection with any crime.

Nancy thanked the chief, who promised to investigate anyway. She left two of the photographs and the calling card with him as well as Aunt Eloise's address and phone number.

"We'll let you know if anything turns up," he promised.

On the way outside the building, Nancy said she hoped Mrs. Richards would return sooner than expected. She was eager to show her the photographs. "And there's something else I can't get out of my mind," she added.

"What is it?" Bess asked.

3

Poison!

Bess and George asked Nancy to tell them what was bothering her.

"How Howie Barker got your name and home address. I don't believe his story about having the list of guests of the Silverline Hotel. Bess, will you phone your mother and verify his story?"

When they reached Aunt Eloise's apartment, Bess called Mrs. Marvin.

"Oh, Bess, you didn't get into any trouble because I gave Miss Drew's address to Mr. Barker, did you?"

"No, but he tried to sell me a lifetime reservation in a new hotel. Did you tell him about my savings account?"

"No!" Mrs. Marvin exclaimed.

Bess cried out, "He claims you said I could spend it any way I wished!"

"That's not true."

"Nancy thinks he's a con man, and we've reported him to the police."

"Good."

When Bess repeated her mother's denial, Nancy bobbed her head. "I suspected that. I'll bet he was told about your savings book after the Hoaxters examined your handbag. And he knew about your vacation in Maine because they read Dorothy Cross's letter!"

The girls walked along the street silently for a while, then Nancy said, "I wish Mrs. Richards were home. I'd like to find out if Barker was her travel agent."

"Perhaps she returned earlier than her housekeeper expected," Bess suggested. "Why don't we call her?"

"Good idea," Nancy agreed and did so.

The girls were in luck. Mrs. Richards answered personally and invited them to come at once.

When they arrived, she ushered them into her living room. It was beautifully furnished in French Provincial decor with lovely statues and paintings.

"I'm delighted to see you," she said. "Do you have a clue yet in my case?"

"Perhaps," Nancy said. She told the woman about Bess's caller and showed her the photographs. "Is this the man who swindled you?"

Mrs. Richards studied the pictures intently. "No, I think not. Mr. Clark had a dark beard."

Nancy told her of Barker's offer to Bess, and Mrs. Richards frowned. "He certainly sounds like the man who came to see me. A glib talker and very personable."

Nancy nodded. "Have you heard anything more from him?"

"No," Mrs. Richards replied. "But lately I've had a ton of mail. It's mostly requests from charitable organizations, but there are two letters that might interest you. I'll get them."

She went into another room and returned a few moments later, handing Nancy two envelopes. One letter, neatly typed on very expensive stationery, was from a man who offered copies of rare paintings at ridiculous prices. He guaranteed that they were very special and a once-in-a-lifetime bargain. The letter read:

> Fool your friends. They couldn't tell the difference between the copy and the real thing!

George wrinkled her forehead. "That sounds like a con game!"

The others agreed. Nancy unfolded the second letter. It advertised a fine collection of old coins. The "bargains" were so cheap that the deal definitely sounded like a hoax.

"May I take the two ads with me?" Nancy requested.

"Certainly," Mrs. Richards replied. "I have no intention of following them up. I've been hurt once. That's enough."

Nancy put the letters into her handbag. "I'll try to find out more about these offers," she said.

"Mrs. Richards, you have a fascinating apartment," Bess commented. "Did you collect all the works of art in this room?"

"A great many of them, yes. Others were gifts to me. Would you like to see the rest of my home?"

"Oh, yes," the girls chorused.

As they were led from room to room, the young detectives realized that each was furnished in the style of a foreign country, including a Japanese room which Bess liked most.

"I don't care for it myself," George remarked under her breath. "I wouldn't want to kneel down every time I looked into the mirror of my dressing table!"

The others laughed.

"Japanese girls think nothing of it," Mrs. Richards said.

She slid aside a panel in the wall and pulled out a tufted silk comforter with gaily painted figures of dancing girls on it. She spread the puff on the floor and announced that this was a typical Japanese mattress.

"Personally I think that's why their women have such straight backs," she said.

"Don't they use a pillow?" Bess asked.

Their hostess answered by producing another item from the closet. It was cylinder-shaped, about six inches in diameter and covered with black material.

"This is very heavy because the pillow is filled with sand," Mrs. Richards explained.

"That's a pillow?" Bess asked in disbelief.

"Yes. However, many Japanese have adopted our Western ways and use beds, mattresses and somewhat softer pillows now."

Bess giggled. "They're smart."

"The reason Japanese women years ago needed to sleep on this type of pillow is rather interesting," Mrs. Richards went on. "Having their full-length hair professionally set was a long, costly process. To keep their hairdos intact between washings, the women slept with their necks against the hard pillows."

George grinned. "I'm glad I don't have to worry about that sort of thing," she said and shook her short, plainly combed hair.

Mrs. Richards led the girls through other rooms. Heavy silken drapes ornamented the windows and Oriental rugs lay on the floors.

The last room they came to was decorated in Florentine style. Everything was ornate, from the heavily carved furniture to the slatted, painted wooden blinds. In one corner stood a mannequin dressed in a Florentine soldier's uniform.

George remarked, "He looks pretty fancy for someone going into battle."

Mrs. Richards smiled. "I doubt that anyone wearing an outfit like this did much fighting. It probably belonged to a general."

Nancy walked closer to the figure and surveyed it from all angles. Suddenly she noticed a partially concealed pocket with a slight bulge. She put her hand inside and felt a small object.

"Something's in this pocket," she said to Mrs. Richards.

"Really?" the woman asked. "I didn't know that. Let's see what it is."

Nancy pulled out a small glass vial with a gold filigree covering. Mrs. Richards read an Italian inscription on the bottom. A startled look came over her face.

"Where in the world did this come from? I never saw it before!"

"Perhaps the vial was in the uniform for centu-

ries and no one ever noticed it," George suggested. "Does it contain anything?"

"A deadly poison!" Mrs. Richards replied.

Bess shivered. "Did the soldier carry it to use on an enemy?"

Mrs. Richards shook her head. "In the days when Florentine intrigue was at its height, nearly every member of the army carried a vial of poison in case he was captured. Rather than go to prison or be tortured, he would kill himself."

"Ugh!" Bess said. "That's terrible."

The others did not comment, but Nancy suggested they take the vial to a medical laboratory for testing. "We should find out if it's still potent," she said.

"There's a medical lab not far from here," Mrs. Richards said. "I've known the owner for years."

Since the lab was located nearby, she and the girls walked over. On the way, Nancy asked Mrs. Richards if she had had any news about Roscoe and her car.

"Oh, yes. He had a very trying adventure. He was parked not far from the terminal waiting for us, when suddenly two men jumped into the back seat. They ordered Roscoe to take them to a certain address. When he told them his car was not a taxi and they must get out, the men refused. One said Roscoe would be harmed if he did not follow their orders."

"Poor Roscoe!" Bess exclaimed.

Mrs. Richards went on. "There was nothing he could do, so he started for the place the men indicated. But they never got there."

"What happened?" George wanted to know.

"They told him suddenly to stop and get out of the car. Then one of the men jumped behind the wheel and drove away. Roscoe yelled at them but they paid no attention. The police never did locate my stolen car, and poor Roscoe was a wreck after he hiked back to town."

"That's a shame," Nancy said sympathetically.

"Roscoe blamed himself," Mrs. Richards went on. "But I told him it was not his fault. The insurance company is going to settle if my automobile is not found within a certain time period, and we're looking at a new car."

Nancy asked if Roscoe had heard the men say anything that might lead to their arrest.

"I don't know if there's any significance to this," the woman replied, "but one of them said, 'This is a good hoax on that rich widow.' Then the two of them laughed uproariously."

By this time the group had reached the medical laboratory. Mrs. Richards told Mr. Horner, the owner, that her young visitors had found the vial in an old costume and wondered if the poison were still effective.

Mr. Horner asked his assistant, whose name was

Enzo Scorpio, to take the vial into the lab and test it. Five minutes later the young man returned, confirming that it was potent.

"What kind of poison is it?" Mrs. Richards asked.

"It's extracted from poisonous mushrooms," the technician replied.

"In that case," Mr. Horner said, "the vial is more valuable than its contents. I believe it was made by an artisan in the fifteenth century. It's absolutely airtight. That's why the poison has not evaporated. As a matter of fact, if you would like to sell the vial, I'd be glad to buy it. I know a man who collects this kind of thing."

Mrs. Richards hesitated. Nancy felt sure that she was about to agree and grabbed the woman's hand, squeezing it tightly.

Mrs. Richards understood. "I don't want to sell it," she replied.

"I can't blame you," he said with a smile. "If you'd like to find out if it's genuine Florentine, I recommend you take it to a specialist on fifteenth-century artwork. The best man I know is at the Metro Museum in Washington, D.C."

Mrs. Richards's eyebrows shot up. "Oh? That's a good idea. I'm planning to visit a friend in Washington. . . . I'm flying out tomorrow morning on the shuttle. I'll certainly look up that man."

Mr. Horner wrote the specialist's name and address on a piece of paper, and handed it to Mrs. Richards. Then the group left the laboratory.

Nancy, Bess, and George returned to Aunt Eloise's apartment. Again they read the two advertisements that Nancy had brought from Mrs. Richards.

George said, "Would it be a good idea for you to contact these places and wire the money?"

"If we do that," Nancy said, "I'm afraid we'll never hear from them, and our money will be gone. But here's an idea. How about suggesting your scheme to the police to get evidence?"

"To do what?" George asked.

"Have a detective write from his home to the two companies and include checks that will bounce. When they're returned, the police can see where the con men tried to cash them. They can contact the companies' banks at once to find out more about the men and maybe get their addresses. One of the persons might be Howie Barker!"

George grinned. "Rubber checks! It's a terrific idea."

Nancy telephoned the chief who said the plan might work.

"Good thinking," he added. "Thank you."

When Aunt Eloise returned, she and the girls had

dinner. Then George said, "Let's see another Hoaxter magic show. This time *I'd* like to be a volunteer and go up on stage to watch their tricks."

"I hope you learn more than I did," Bess said.

When the moment arrived for people in the audience to join the artists on stage, George hurried forward and leaped up the steps. She was the first onlooker to arrive, but the sleight of hand man ignored her and selected ten other people.

"Sorry," he said to the rest. "That's all we can take."

"But I was here first!" George objected. "I should have—"

The magician looked at her stonily. "Young lady, I'm sorry. Please return to your seat."

George was tempted to argue further with the man, but he was already talking to someone else. Angrily she left the stage, wondering why he would not let her stay!

4

Airport Theft

When George returned to her seat, Nancy, Bess, and Aunt Eloise immediately asked her what had happened.

"The sleight of hand man wouldn't let me watch the performance," George replied.

"Why not?" Bess demanded.

George shrugged. "Maybe I'm not his type!"

Nancy frowned. "It's my guess the Hoaxters know we're amateur detectives and don't want any of us close enough to see their tricks."

"It's possible," George replied. "But I wonder how they found out who we are."

Next morning after breakfast Nancy called Mrs. Richards to ask if she had heard any more about the travel agent who had swindled her. Trudie, the housekeeper, answered and said that Mrs. Richards had already left for Washington.

"Do you know if she had any news from the police?" Nancy asked.

"No, she hasn't," Trudie replied. "However, a man phoned yesterday afternoon and asked for you."

"For me?" Nancy was surprised. "What was his name?"

"He didn't tell me. He said he had a gift to deliver to Nancy Drew and asked if you were living here. Also what kind of work you do."

"What did you tell him?" Nancy asked.

"The truth," Trudie replied. "I didn't see any reason not to. I said you and your friends were staying with your Aunt Eloise and that you were amateur detectives."

Nancy caught her breath. She was disappointed that Trudie had given out this information.

"I told the man if he wanted to leave the present here I would see that you received it," the housekeeper added.

Despite the fact that Nancy considered the matter most unfortunate, she remained calm. "Thank you very much," she said. "When the package arrives, let me know."

Nancy hung up and repeated the conversation

to her friends. "I'm sure there's no gift involved," she declared. "Somehow the caller found out that we know Mrs. Richards, and he used the present as an excuse to inquire who we are."

"Do you think he's the same man who fleeced Mrs. Richards?" Bess asked.

"It's possible," Nancy replied.

"So he's either a member of the Hoaxters or connected with them," George put in. "That's why they wouldn't let me stay on stage last night!"

"I don't believe he's a member of the troupe," Bess argued. "He's more likely a con man. We'd better watch our step."

George said, "What about Howie Barker?"

"None of the Hoaxters, according to the program, is called Barker," Nancy explained. "But it could be an assumed name. And the performers are so made up during the show, we wouldn't necessarily recognize him."

She was thoughtful for a few moments, then added, "Why don't we go to the matinee today and do some real sleuthing?"

"Good idea," George agreed.

Bess asked, "How can we? They'll remember us and most likely won't let *you* on stage either."

Nancy smiled. "I wouldn't walk up from the audience. I'd rather try to slip in backstage. Perhaps I'll find a clue there."

As soon the group had had lunch, they taxied to the theater. As the cab pulled up, all of them were amazed to find the building deserted.

Nancy said to the taxi driver, "Do you know whether the performance has been cancelled?"

"I heard," he replied, "that the show closed. The Hoaxters moved out bag and baggage."

"That's amazing," George remarked. "We were here last night and no announcement was made."

Nancy asked the man if he had any idea where the troupe had gone. He shook his head. "Do you want me to take you home again?"

Nancy decided to stay. She paid the driver and the girls got out.

"What's on your mind?" Bess asked Nancy.

"I'd like to find out where the magicians went. I suggest we question restaurant and store owners in the neighborhood."

The group divided. Bess and George began to inquire at shops, while Nancy checked the various eating places. When she walked into a luncheonette across the street, the hostess approached her and asked where she would like to be seated.

Nancy smiled. "Thank you, but I don't plan to stay. I was wondering if you could give me any information about the Hoaxters who left so suddenly last night. Have you any idea where they went?"

The hostess shook her head. "I'll ask the waitresses. Maybe one of them knows."

She went to the kitchen and returned a few minutes later with a pretty girl. "Susie, this young lady is trying to locate the Hoaxters. You say two of the magicians at dinner last night were talking about leaving."

Susie nodded and giggled. "One of them gave me an extra large tip and said, 'Here's something for you to remember me by.'"

The waitress said she had expressed regret at his leaving and asked where he was going. "He whispered in my ear, 'Don't tell anybody, but our next stop is Mexico City.'"

Nancy smiled. "I'm glad you *did* tell us, Susie."

The girl giggled again. "Oh, I'm sure he was only kidding about keeping it a secret, like I was kidding when I told him I'd miss him. I won't miss him, only his tips! He always gave me more than anyone else."

Nancy thanked Susie and the hostess and was about to leave when she noticed several luscious-looking cakes displayed on a glass counter near the door.

"Shall I take one?" Nancy asked herself. "Mm, I can't resist. They look delicious."

She bought a lemon layer cake, then walked out of the luncheonette. When she reached the theater where she was to meet Bess and George, the girls were not there. They arrived about ten minutes later.

Bess's eyes went immediately to the cake box in Nancy's hand. "Is there something rich and fattening inside?" She beamed.

"And it's not for you!" her cousin replied quickly.

"Why, George Fayne, as if I—"

"I've had terrific luck." Nancy interrupted the friendly squabble. "You'd never guess where the Hoaxters have gone."

"Where?" Bess asked eagerly.

"Mexico City!"

George lifted her eyebrows. "If they skipped town, they sure made a big jump!"

The others agreed. All felt that the troupe's sudden departure had not been planned.

"Do you suppose it was because of us?"

"I wonder," Nancy replied.

The group hailed another taxi and went back to the apartment. When they entered, the telephone was ringing. Nancy dashed to answer it.

"Oh, Nancy, I've been trying for hours to get you!" It was Mrs. Richards. She was hysterical.

"What's the matter?" Nancy asked.

"I'm beside myself! My vial of poison has been stolen!"

"When?"

"It must have happened at the airport in New York this morning. I had a long wait before my flight and dozed off in the lounge."

"Oh, dear," Nancy said. "Where are you now?"

"At my friend's apartment in Washington. Her name is Mrs. Marian Greening. Better take her phone number down in case you want to reach me." She gave the number, then said, "Oh, Nancy, what am I going to do? Not only is the vial valuable, but whoever stole it might not realize it contains poison and may harm himself or someone else!"

Mrs. Richards began to sob uncontrollably. Suddenly she gasped for breath.

"Mrs. Richards!" Nancy called out. "Mrs. Richards, are you all right?"

There was no reply, but Nancy heard a scraping noise. Then a man's voice sounded over the phone. "Don't worry," he said. "I'll take care of her."

The next moment the phone clicked. The man had hung up!

5

A Planned Accident

Nancy frowned. "That's strange," she muttered.

"What is?" Bess asked. She and George had rushed to their friend's side and wanted to know what had happened.

Nancy repeated her conversation with Mrs. Richards, saying the last thing she had heard from the woman was a gasp. "Then a man told me he would take care of her and hung up."

"Try calling back," George suggested. "He could have been her friend's husband."

Nancy dialed the number Mrs. Richards had given her. No one answered.

"Maybe the man took her to the doctor," Bess suggested.

"I don't know," Nancy said. "I'll ask the police to check on her."

She contacted the authorities in Washington and was connected with a captain. Quickly she explained the matter. "Could you send someone to Mrs. Greening's apartment to see that Mrs. Richards is all right?" she requested.

"Sure will," the officer said. "Please give me your name and number. I'll call you back."

A few minutes later the phone rang. Nancy answered. To her surprise, it was the Washington police.

"You've seen our friend already?" she asked, incredulous.

"No. I'm double-checking your story. We get so many prank calls, that whenever possible we confirm a complaint before sending someone out. An officer will drive to Mrs. Greening's apartment now. You'll hear from us soon."

Nancy and her friends paced about the living room restlessly, wondering what was happening in Washington. Finally the young sleuth could stand it no longer. She dialed Mrs. Greening's number. A policeman answered.

"This is Nancy Drew," she said. "I'm so glad you got there. Did you find Mrs. Richards?"

"Yes. She's right here. Apparently she fainted while speaking to you."

"But a man picked up the phone and said he would take care of her," Nancy pointed out. "Who was he?"

"A deliveryman who was putting food into the refrigerator while Mrs. Richards was talking to you."

"Oh? But I called back right after he hung up, and there was no answer."

"After Mrs. Richards fainted, he put her on the couch, then rushed down to Dr. Marsiono who has his practice on the first floor. Luckily the doctor was in and could come up. He revived Mrs. Richards. She's all right now."

"May I speak to her, please?" Nancy requested.

"One minute," the officer said and handed the receiver to the woman.

Mrs. Richards was still upset about the theft. "I suppose I got so worked up that I passed out while I was talking to you," she told Nancy.

"Will you be all right?" the girl asked, worried.

"Oh, sure. My friend will be home soon—as a matter of fact, here she comes now. What a surprise she'll have, finding the police here! Well, my dear, thank you for your help."

The following morning Chief Raleigh from the New York police asked the girls to come to headquarters. "We have news about the man Nancy Drew photographed," he said.

Nancy promised to go at once. Aunt Eloise had already left for school. Bess and George accompanied the young detective.

When the girls walked out of the apartment building, they noticed a car parked not far from the entrance. The driver appeared to be sleeping since his head was bent low over the steering wheel.

"Funny place to take a nap," Bess commented.

Just then a taxi drove up and the girls signaled for it to stop. They climbed in and Nancy gave the driver directions. He looked at her quizzically, but she volunteered no further information about their errand.

George noticed that the driver in the parked car had suddenly started his engine and was following the taxi. She wondered if this was on purpose.

Presently he drove up close behind them, then pulled out as if to pass. Instead, he deliberately sideswiped the taxi, whose right front wheel jumped the curb.

"Oh!" Bess cried out. She tumbled off the rear seat and hit her head.

Nancy, on the left side, got the full impact of the crash. Instinctively she braced herself on the backrest of the driver's seat and escaped injury. George managed to avoid getting hurt, but like Nancy, she was badly shaken.

With trembling hands they pulled Bess up to the seat. "Are you all right?" Nancy asked worriedly.

"I—I guess so. My head hurts where I bumped it, though."

"That man hit us on purpose!" Nancy declared angrily.

She looked out the window just in time to see their attacker rounding the next corner. Apparently there had not been enough damage to his car to disable it.

"Did you get his license number?" Bess asked hopefully.

"Yes," Nancy replied. "Luckily he was still close enough when I looked out."

George pointed to their driver, who was slumped over the steering wheel. He did not move and the engine was not running. Apparently it had stalled from the impact.

"He must be unconscious!" George exclaimed.

She jumped from the cab, opened the right front door, and slid across the seat. She tried to revive the driver but without success. Quickly she picked up the radiophone and called the taxi company. While waiting for a reply, she looked for the cab's license that was posted on the dashboard.

"Hello," she said after a man answered her call. "This is cab 52341. We were rammed deliberately by another car and Max Topping, the driver, is unconscious. Could you please notify the police and send an ambulance for him?"

The dispatcher promised to do so at once. A few minutes later the police arrived. Nancy gave them the license number of the car that sideswiped them and told the police what had happened.

Just then the ambulance pulled alongside the cab. Two men put the stricken driver on a stretcher, then carefully transferred him into their vehicle. Seconds later they were on their way to the hospital.

The police officers asked the girls where they were headed. When the men learned it was police headquarters, they offered to take them there.

In Chief Raleigh's office, a stenographer recorded Nancy's story. The young sleuth gave the details of the accident and signed the transcript. Shortly afterward a report came in saying the car which rammed the taxi had been stolen and was abandoned.

"That's unfortunate," the officer said. "We found only the owner's fingerprints on the steering wheel, so the thief must have worn gloves. Obviously the accident was planned because there was only minimal damage to the side of the car. The driver either had a grudge against the cabbie or you girls. Can you shed any light on the matter?"

"As I told you before, we suspect Howie Barker

to be a con man. But we haven't found any new clues."

The chief smiled. "We have, however. That's why I wanted you to come down. We received a new picture in the rogues' gallery that matches the photograph you've taken, Nancy. His full beard is one of his many disguises. The man is listed by the name of Ralph Rafferty. Originally he worked for the Francisco Insurance Company. He proved to be dishonest and went to prison for forgery."

"But now he's free?" Nancy asked.

"Yes. After being released from prison, Rafferty disappeared from the West Coast. He swindled someone out of a large sum of money in Chicago and is wanted again. Your clue will help us a great deal."

"Did you check the telephone number and address on his calling card?" Nancy asked.

"Yes. It was an apartment here in the city, but he moved out before we got there. We questioned the superintendent and other tenants, but no one knew anything about him. He was a resident only a short time. But we think he's still in this area."

"I'm not sure about that," Nancy said. "We suspect that he may be in cahoots with a group of performers called the Hoaxters. They left unexpectedly for Mexico City."

The officer's eyebrows shot up. "Oh? That's

interesting. I'll get in touch with the police there and ask them to be on the lookout for Rafferty, alias Barker."

"I certainly hope they catch him," Bess said. "He came near getting some money from me. He's a slick talker."

"And a very good-looking and likeable person," George added. "I guess it's easy for him to sell phony products."

"I'm afraid so," the chief agreed. "Thank you very much, girls."

He opened his desk drawer and handed Nancy the original snapshots she had taken. "We've made duplicates of these," he said.

When the girls left headquarters, Nancy suggested they go directly to Aunt Eloise's apartment and do no more sleuthing for the day.

"All I want to do is lie in a tub of hot water. I'm stiff all over," she confessed.

"And I'd like to go to sleep," George said. She still felt shaky from the accident.

Bess nodded. She had a terrible headache. Quickly Nancy hailed a cab and the girls climbed in. When they reached the apartment, she phoned the taxi company to find out how their driver was. The answer was a relief: he had suffered a slight concussion, but would be all right in a couple of days.

When Aunt Eloise returned from school later that afternoon, she was amazed by her visitors' story.

"You're lucky not to have been seriously injured," she said. "Did you get a good look at the man who ran into you?"

"Only a fleeting glimpse," George said. "Not enough to identify him."

They tried to figure out who the attacker could have been. Nancy said she had a strong hunch he was connected with the Hoaxters.

Aunt Eloise was inclined to agree. "But why did he want to harm you?" she asked.

There was silence for a few minutes, then Nancy said, "I think we should go to Mexico City and continue our sleuthing. We shouldn't let the Hoaxters get away from us!"

"You're right," Aunt Eloise said. "How I wish that I could go with you! But of course, that's impossible."

Bess and George felt Nancy's suggestion was a good one. George added with a sigh, however, "I'll have to phone home and try to get more money. Frankly, my detective allowance account is down to zero!"

6

Clue to a Suspect

Bess was the first to call her parents. While the other girls waited eagerly, she explained their plans and said she would like to join Nancy on her trip to Mexico. The Marvins readily agreed.

George phoned next, but she had a more difficult time getting permission. Mr. Fayne reminded his daughter that she had, indeed, used up her detective allowance.

"But Dad, this is *very* important!" George pleaded. "Would you lend me the money and after I get home, I'll earn some and pay you back?"

Mr. Fayne chuckled. "You're working hard now. How would it be if you got paid for being a detective?"

"No, Dad. If I accept money for my work, it would take me out of the amateur class. And I know Mr. Drew wouldn't like that. Besides, I couldn't work with Nancy and Bess any longer."

"Okay, you've convinced me," Mr. Fayne said fondly. He promised to raise her allowance to pay for the trip. "But be sure you solve the mystery!" he teased.

George laughed. "With Nancy carrying the ball we won't fail."

As soon as the girls had finished their calls, Nancy contacted her father and told him about the proposed trip to Mexico City. Then she phoned Mrs. Richards. Nancy was glad to learn that the woman was feeling fine, and revealed their plans. She asked Mrs. Richards, however, to keep their trip a secret.

"Of course I will," the woman promised. "But I think you should tell me where you're staying in case I need to reach you."

"At the Fortunato Hotel," Nancy replied. "We'll let you know what's happening."

She made reservations on a flight for early the next morning. After breakfast, they said good-by to Aunt Eloise.

"And thank you for your wonderful hospitality," Bess added.

The girls arrived in Mexico City during the

afternoon. While claiming their baggage, the three Americans heard nothing but Spanish spoken. Bess and George stared at each other. They did not understand a word!

"Nancy, I'm glad you speak Spanish," George said. "We'd have a hard time otherwise."

Nancy laughed. "You two should really learn the language. It isn't difficult."

The cousins made up their minds then and there that they would take lessons. Nancy was right. It was becoming more and more important for Americans to learn the language of their neighbors just across the Rio Grande River.

The girls took a cab to the Fortunato. When they walked up to the desk, Nancy said to the clerk, "We'd like a large room for the three of us."

"Your names, please?"

"Nancy Drew, Bess Marvin, and George Fayne."

"Nancy Drew?" The clerk stared at her. "Please wait a minute," he said. "The manager has a message for you." He turned and hurried into a back office.

Nancy looked at her friends. "I wonder what this is all about?" she said. "Not many people knew we'd be here and the ones who did promised to keep it a secret."

A good-looking Mexican in a white suit came from the rear room and addressed Nancy. "I will have to ask you to come into my office. There is something I must discuss with you."

The girls followed him and he motioned them to be seated in his small, paneled room. The girls were worried. Was bad news from home awaiting them?

The manager, who introduced himself as Señor Gonzales, said, "I am sorry to detain you, but the police telephoned and asked me to do so."

Nancy frowned. "How do the police know we are here?"

"They alerted every hotel in town," Señor Gonzales revealed. "We have your reservation."

The conversation had been in Spanish, and Nancy turned to translate for her friends. When Señor Gonzales realized Bess and George did not speak his language, he switched to English.

"The clerk told me you were here and I called Lieutenant Tara. He should be here any minute. Please be patient."

The girls looked at one another in dismay. Members of their families and Mrs. Richards were the only people who could have phoned! Just then the officer walked into the room. Fortunately he spoke English so that Bess and George could follow the conversation.

"I understand that you are detectives," Lieutenant Tara said.

Nancy replied, "I guess you might call us that. Why?"

"I have been told that you are practicing without a license."

"License!" Nancy protested. "We're strictly amateurs and never get paid for our work."

Lieutenant Tara's eyebrows shot up. "Can you prove it?"

The girls were stymied for a moment. They were in a foreign country! How could they possibly prove that they never charged for their detective services?

Finally Nancy said, "We have no proof with us. But if you phone my father in River Heights in the United States, he'll back up our statement. He's a lawyer. And you might phone Chief McGinnis of the River Heights police force. He has known me ever since I was a little girl."

The officer rubbed his chin. "Your father is an attorney?"

Bess answered, "Yes, and very well known!"

"We came to Mexico City to locate a con man who is wanted by the New York police," Nancy said.

"Amazing!" the manager said.

Lieutenant Tara picked up the phone and first called Mr. Drew, then Chief McGinnis. They confirmed the fact that the girls were strictly amateur detectives and Chief McGinnis said, "Nancy Drew is the daughter of a famous attorney and she is known for her talent in solving mysteries."

Lieutenant Tara thanked the chief and said good-by.

George spoke up. "Who gave you this false information about us?"

The officer hesitated. "I don't know. Our chief received the message. Why don't you ask him personally?"

Señor Gonzales offered to get the chief on the line. In a few moments Nancy was explaining to him the girls' mission in Mexico City.

He told her that the message had come from someone in the U.S. Department of Justice, but that he had not caught the man's name. He then asked Nancy if she and her friends had any more to tell.

"Indeed we have!" Nancy replied. "This is outrageous. We have never been investigated by the Department of Justice. Your anonymous caller gave you false information."

The chief cleared his throat, but did not comment. Instead, he asked to speak to Lieutenant Tara again. The chief told him that he saw no reason for detaining the girls and Tara should return to headquarters. When the officer finished, Tara smiled and relayed the message.

"Thank you," Nancy said. "That's a relief."

Bess grinned. "I feel a hundred pounds lighter!"

After Tara had left, Señor Gonzales apologized profusely to the girls. He told the desk clerk to give them a fine room with bath. "That may compensate for all the trouble we Mexicans have caused you." He smiled broadly.

The girls found the quarters delightful. While they were unpacking, the three friends talked about what had happened.

"I don't understand how the anonymous caller knew we were coming to Mexico City," Bess declared.

George said, "The Hoaxters left New York before we made our plans!"

"That's true," Nancy admitted. "Perhaps Howie Barker or another confederate stayed behind. He could have visited the luncheonette and learned from Susie the waitress that I had inquired where the Hoaxters had gone."

"I see what you mean," Bess said. "And after he found out we *knew* they went to Mexico City, he figured we would follow and warned the theatrical group."

"That's right. Then Barker called the police, pretending to work with the U.S. Department of Justice."

They had just finished unpacking when the telephone rang. Aunt Eloise Drew was calling. "I just heard from the New York police department," she told Nancy. "They have unearthed a clue to the thief who stole the vial of poison. His name is Enzo Scorpio."

"He's the assistant to Mr. Horner who owns the medical lab in New York!" Nancy exclaimed.

"That's correct," Aunt Eloise replied. "He's originally from Mexico City. The police think he may have returned there and advise you to keep your eyes open. You may be able to track him down."

"I wonder if he's trying to sell the vial," Nancy mused.

"It's likely that he'll approach a collector," Aunt Eloise said. "At least that's what Mr. Horner believes. He notified the police when Scorpio disappeared unexpectedly, taking all the cash in the lab with him."

After Nancy had hung up, Bess looked alarmed. "I hope that poison doesn't get into the hands of the con men. Can you imagine what would happen?"

Nancy nodded, then changed the subject. "What do you say we go see the Hoaxters?"

"Good idea," her friends agreed.

"I wonder if the show is the same here as it was in New York," George added.

The girls inquired at the desk where the magicians were scheduled to appear and learned that the theater was not far away. There was no matinee. The evening performance would start at eight o'clock.

Bess was worried that the girls would be recognized by the performers. "Why don't we disguise ourselves?" she suggested.

"How?" George asked.

"We could buy Mexican dresses, and shawls to wear on our heads. If anyone gets too close, we can just pull the shawls halfway up over our faces."

"Good idea," Nancy agreed, and the girls spent the rest of the afternoon shopping. They found an attractive boutique owned by Señora Clara.

"May I help you?" she asked in perfect English.

"What do you think of this one?" Nancy asked her companions. She was holding a pretty turquoise skirt in front of her.

"That is a beautiful choice," the proprietor remarked. "It matches your eyes so well."

"She's right, Nancy," Bess said. "If only I could find something to suit . . ."

"Your waist!" George laughed. "Señora, do you carry chubby sizes?"

Her cousin bristled. "Thanks a lot, George."

Señora Clara smiled. "You remind me so much of my favorite nieces in the States," she said. "I'm sure I can find something just right for all of you."

As promised, the young detectives were able to

select just what they wanted. When they arrived at the theater that evening in their attractive Mexican clothes and new hairdos, only a few minutes remained before curtain time.

The girls glanced at the program and noticed that the sleight of hand man was listed as Ronaldo Jensen, the same person they had seen previously.

Just before the performance started, a beautiful woman arrived and sat down in the aisle seat next to Nancy. She was expensively and tastefully dressed and carried a large beaded evening bag.

During intermission, she introduced herself to Nancy in Spanish as Señora Rosa Mendez, a lonely widow.

"My family lives in Oaxaca," she explained. "I have a darling little granddaughter named Dolores, but I don't see her very often because she lives too far away. I really miss her very much. I'll show you a picture of her."

The woman opened her purse and took out a snapshot of the little girl, who looked to be about nine years old.

"She's darling," said Nancy, gazing at the dark-haired, bright-eyed child. "I'm not surprised you'd like to see her more often. I'm sure the show will lighten your spirits," she added with a smile. "By the way, do you speak English?"

"Yes."

"Good," said Nancy. "My friends don't understand Spanish."

At the beginning of the second act, the Hoaxters performed a new trick. One of them raced down the center aisle, holding a flaming torch in his mouth. He crossed the rear of the theater and returned to the stage via a side aisle. Then he took the torch out of his mouth and extinguished the flames. The man opened his mouth wide to show that nothing inside had been burned.

"An amazing feat," Señora Mendez said to Nancy.

"Indeed it is," the girl agreed.

Just then the sleight of hand man appeared and invited members of the audience to come forward and watch how some of the tricks were done.

Señora Mendez said, "Oh, I'd love to see that!" Before Nancy could stop her, the woman left her seat and hurried down the aisle.

Bess whispered, "I hope she won't be approached by any of the con men later on. Señora Mendez looks as if she has plenty of money; just the kind of person they're after."

The show proceeded. Clever tricks were done by the magicians. The audience laughed and clapped. The people who had gone on stage had become so absorbed by the performance, none of them noticed that several of their watches, necklaces, wallets, and handbags had disappeared. The sleight of hand man assured them that all articles would be returned after the show.

"Please return to your seats," he requested.

Señora Mendez said to Nancy, "They took my handbag. Do you think they will really give it back to me?"

Nancy said she was sure they would, but added, "Did you have anything valuable in it?"

"Yes, I did," the woman replied. "My savings bankbook, some money, and several letters and papers that I would hate to have anyone else read."

"Do they contain something confidential?" Nancy asked, worried that the Hoaxters might take advantage of this.

"Yes," Señora Mendez answered. "There was important background information about my family that no outsider should know about!"

Nancy had a sudden hunch. She felt positive that such information could indeed be used to blackmail the woman!

7

Pyramid Chase

In a loud whisper, Nancy said to the distraught woman, "I'm sure you'll get your handbag back. My friends and I saw two Hoaxter shows in New York, and Bess's handbag was taken. But it was returned afterward."

"Oh, good," Señora Mendez said and settled back in her seat to enjoy the balance of the performance. As soon as the show was over, however, she dashed down the aisle and up the steps to the stage.

"Do you have property you wish to claim?" the sleight of hand man asked her.

"Yes, I do. I want my handbag at once!"

"Follow me," he said and led her into an office

backstage. She picked up her bag, opened it, and rifled through the contents eagerly.

"Is everything there?" the man asked.

"Eh, yes—yes."

He requested that she sign a paper releasing the Hoaxters from any liability. Señora Mendez did so, then hurried back to where the girls were waiting for her.

"Is everything all right?" Bess asked her.

"Fortunately yes."

Nancy hoped this was true. She felt, however, that she should warn Señora Mendez. "There is a possibility the Hoaxters looked at your property and found something pals of theirs could use to either swindle or blackmail you. Please call your bank and request them to hold any check they suspect is a forgery. Also, don't let any fast-talking salesmen con you into dishonest schemes, either by telephone or in person."

The woman promised to do so. "Now you have me a bit frightened," she said. "Shall I call the police when something happens?"

"Yes," Nancy replied, "and if you need our help, we'll be glad to do whatever we can. We're amateur detectives."

"Where are you staying?" Señora Mendez asked.

"At the Fortunato," Nancy replied and wrote

their names on a piece of paper. She handed it to the woman. Señora Mendez, in turn, gave Nancy her address and telephone number.

"Have you any plans for tomorrow?" she asked.

Nancy said no, and the friendly Mexican immediately invited the girls to visit the Pyramid of the Sun with her. Intrigued by the name of the ancient monument, the young sleuths accepted eagerly. Señora Mendez promised to pick them up at ten the following morning. When she arrived, Nancy and her friends were waiting in the lobby.

On the way Bess complimented Señora Mendez on her expert handling of the car. The traffic was fast and appeared dangerous.

"You're brave," Bess said. "I wouldn't like to drive here."

"We'll soon be out of the city," the woman replied with a smile. "The roads will be less busy then."

"How far is the pyramid?" George asked.

"About twenty-five miles," Señora Mendez said. Then she told the girls some stories of ancient Mexico.

"There's one legend which I have always liked," she said. "Native Indians were standing on the shore of the ocean when they saw a huge fish approaching. A white man was seated on its back. Since the Indians had never seen a white man, they were sure he must be a god. When he landed, they knelt before him and he became their ruler for many years."

"Where did he come from?" Nancy asked.

"Apparently from Europe. The legend does not say at what point he got astride the fish, which was probably a friendly dolphin. No doubt he was a crewman from a shipwrecked vessel and was rescued by the dolphin."

"Lucky fellow," Nancy said with a chuckle.

Señora Mendez smiled. "When the man became old, he longed to go back to his own land. The last time the Indians saw him, he was climbing onto a dolphin's back to leave Mexico."

"What a charming story!" Bess remarked.

George laughed. "And a pretty preposterous one."

Nancy did not have time to comment because Señora Mendez immediately launched into another tale.

"No one is sure when the first Indians settled around Mexico City. Archeologists, who have been digging here for many years, believe it was at least four thousand years ago. One group after another came to fight the inhabitants. If the new arrivals won the battle, they immediately imposed their own political, religious, and ethical ideas on the captured people. Our present-day ruins are all that is left of the Aztec and earlier civilizations."

"Did the Aztecs build the Pyramid of the Sun?" Nancy asked.

"Not according to some scholars who say it was part of a Toltec tribe's city that was a thousand years old when the Aztec people came to power."

"The Aztecs were a highly intelligent and cultured people," George put in.

"That's true," Señora Mendez said. "And now look up ahead. There's the Pyramid of the Sun."

The enormous, broad-based structure rose in steps straight up into the blue sky with only a few fluffy clouds to soften its stark lines.

"What are those other buildings?" Bess asked.

"There's the smaller Pyramid of the Moon," Señora Mendez pointed out, "and in the distance are a number of pyramids, temples and burial spots, including the well-known Temple of Quetzalcoatl. All these were built on both sides of an ancient road about four miles long, known as the Highway of the Dead."

Bess shivered. "Not a very inviting name."

Señora Mendez smiled as she parked the car in a lot some distance from the pyramid. "I assure you there is nothing scary about this place," she added as they headed toward the imposing structure.

Señora Mendez told them that the pyramid had been erected in honor of the Sun God whom the Indians worshipped.

"It certainly is huge," George remarked.

"Yes, two hundred and sixteen feet high," their Mexican friend explained, "and seven hundred and fifty feet around the square base."

On the side facing them shallow stone steps led to the top. Several people were ascending.

"Do you feel like climbing?" Señora Mendez asked.

"Oh, yes," the girls chorused.

"What's at the top?" Bess wanted to know.

"Nothing now," was the reply. "But a thousand years ago it was very different. Prisoners of war were marched up the steps and slain at the top by priests."

"Ugh!" Bess murmured. "I'm not sure I want to go up after all."

Señora Mendez said that there was nothing left to remind anyone of that cruel custom. "But there's a magnificent view which you shouldn't miss."

Bess finally consented to go. She was the last in line and after a while the rest of the group had advanced far ahead of her.

Suddenly a middle-aged woman a few feet above Bess cried out, "Oh, I'm falling! I feel faint! Save me! Save me!"

No one was near her except Bess, who saw the woman teeter, then begin to tumble down the steps.

"I must catch her before she hurts herself!" Bess

thought frantically. But she knew that if she remained in front of the stranger, she herself would be knocked down by the impact.

A quick thought flashed through Bess's mind. She had once read that in climbing or descending mountains or monuments, the Indians always zigzagged their way. They would take a dozen steps to the right, then to the left. This not only kept them from falling but helped conserve their breath.

Bess turned and braced herself. She caught the woman around her shoulders. Both teetered for a few seconds, then Bess regained her footing and started down sideways, dragging the woman with her.

By this time several tourists had hurried to the scene. Two husky men came up to meet Bess and her burden. They lifted the unconscious figure over their shoulders and carried her to the ground.

Bess was relieved. Thinking what might have happened, she was also nervous and upset. With shaking knees she sat down, trying to recuperate.

The woman who had fainted soon revived. When she learned of Bess's help, she called out in English, "Thank you very much for saving me! You're so brave you should have a medal!"

Bess was embarrassed by the praise. Quickly she rose, waved to the woman and hurried up the steps.

Her friends, who were close to the top, had heard the shouting. When Bess joined them, Nancy said, "That was a wonderful rescue!"

George patted her cousin on the shoulder. "Just great!" she added.

"Oh, forget it, everybody," Bess murmured. "Did you find any skeletons here?"

"No," Nancy replied. "But let's walk around a little while. Then I think we should go back to the hotel. Señora Mendez has been very kind, but we've taken enough of her time."

Bess agreed. "I'm rather weary myself."

The group descended and had reached the last step, when Nancy grabbed George by one arm.

"Look over there!" she exclaimed, and pointed to a man who was rounding a corner of the pyramid. Isn't that Enzo Scorpio, the poison thief?"

"He sure is," George answered.

She turned and ran in his direction. Nancy was close on her heels, and Bess followed. Señora Mendez stood still, staring after the girls in amazement.

Just then the suspect saw them. Quick as a wink he turned back and disappeared behind the great pyramid!

8

Startling News

The chase went on for some time. Nancy, Bess, and George took different routes to head off the fleeing suspect. They climbed up and down the steps of the Sun Pyramid, until the fugitive dashed away in a southerly direction. He ran toward the famous Temple of Quetzalcoatl. Even though Nancy concentrated hard on the chase, she could not help but admire the elaborate rows of carvings on the ancient structure depicting the fabled plumed serpent in whose honor the temple had been erected.

Suddenly Enzo Scorpio headed for the parking lot. Nancy had nearly caught up with the man when he jumped into a car, started the engine in a split second and roared away. His wheels churned

up a cloud of dust. Some of it hit Nancy full force as she came almost close enough to touch the vehicle's rear fender.

Coughing, she stopped short and bit her lips in frustration. Despite her anger, she managed to read the license number of the automobile. As soon as the dust had settled somewhat, she pulled a piece of paper out of her handbag and wrote the number down.

Bess caught up to her with George not far behind.

"What happened?" she asked.

"I almost had him, but he jumped into a car and took off!" Nancy replied.

"What terrible luck!" George exclaimed.

"Where's Señora Mendez?" Bess inquired.

The girls looked around and noticed the woman going toward her car. Quickly they followed.

As Nancy passed an athletic-looking young man, who was obviously from the United States, he said, "Want me to chase that guy with my car?"

"Thank you, no," Nancy replied.

The young man smirked. "If you're after a handsome fellow, how about me?"

The girls ignored his remarks and continued toward Señora Mendez. When they reached her, she asked why the girls had chased the stranger. Nancy explained and the woman was shocked.

"He stole a vial of dangerous poison?" she cried out. "He certainly should be put in prison for that!"

The girls agreed. Then Bess declared that she had had enough sightseeing and exercise for the day and would like to return to the Fortunato. Señora Mendez nodded and drove the girls to Mexico City.

When they reached their hotel room, Nancy at once phoned Lieutenant Tara.

"Before we left New York," she said, "a vial of poison was stolen from a friend of ours. We were told that the New York police suspect a man named Enzo Scorpio of the theft. We just saw him at the Pyramid of the Sun!"

"You know him?" Lieutenant Tara asked.

"Yes," Nancy replied and told the officer about their visit to Mr. Horner's medical laboratory. "We chased Enzo Scorpio, but he got away in a car," she added and gave the lieutenant the license number.

Tara thanked her and promised to track down the car. "I hope we can find out where Scorpio lives," he said.

Later in the afternoon he called back and told Nancy that the trail had led to a dead end. The car used by the poison thief had been rented but not by Enzo Scorpio. The man who had signed for the automobile had shown his license and given his address. When the police tried to contact him, they learned he had left town.

"We have no idea where he went or when he'll be back," the lieutenant told Nancy. "But if we manage to find out, we'll let you know."

Nancy was thoughtful for a moment, then said, "I think Scorpio will try to sell the vial to a collector. Do you know of any in Mexico City?"

"Hm," Lieutenant Tara said. "As a matter of fact, I do. He is a well-to-do man who has a large collection of ancient poison vials. His name is Fernando Pedroa. Ordinarily he would not be allowed to have them in his house, but we know he's trustworthy and gave him a special permit to keep the poisons. They are securely locked in a separate room."

Nancy said she and her friends would like to meet the man if possible. "Could you give us a letter of introduction?"

Lieutenant Tara chuckled. "I am sure that Señor Pedroa would love to see you and hear about the mystery. He's a very pleasant man. I will send a note of introduction to your hotel."

"Thank you," Nancy said.

A short time later a messenger brought the letter. "Let's call on the collector right away," Nancy proposed to Bess and George.

When they arrived at their destination in a taxi,

she asked the driver to wait until they found out if Señor Pedroa was at home.

Nancy rang the doorbell and a servant answered. He told her that Señor Pedroa was in the garden. She handed over the letter from Lieutenant Tara. While the servant went to deliver it, George paid the cabbie and dismissed him.

In a few minutes Señor Pedroa came to welcome the girls. He ushered them into his beautifully furnished living room. When the Mexican learned that Bess and George knew no Spanish, he spoke to them in fluent English.

Nancy quickly outlined their case about the poison, then asked if Enzo Scorpio had tried to sell him the ancient vial. The answer was no.

"We have seen this man in Mexico City," Nancy explained. "He worked for a medical laboratory in New York. Enzo Scorpio stole the vial from a friend of ours. The lab owner said the gold filigree poison container was made in the fifteenth century and is probably extremely valuable. The poison in it is still potent."

Señor Pedroa's eyes lighted up. "If it is a genuine piece it would be very valuable. I'd buy the vial if it were offered to me."

"We found it in a Florentine costume," Bess spoke up. "No one knows how long it was there."

Señor Pedroa smiled. "And you believe this

Enzo Scorpio stole the poison? What makes you so sure it was he?"

"The New York police told us. Enzo is a Mexican, so they suggested we look for him here."

George added, "When we went sightseeing at the Pyramid of the Sun this morning, we saw Scorpio. He noticed us and escaped in a car."

Señor Pedroa shook his head in amazement. "You girls are certainly wonderful detectives. I would like to help you solve your mystery. If I hear from Enzo Scorpio I'll contact you at once."

"And please notify the police." Nancy urged.

The man promised to do so, then asked if the girls would like to see his collection of antique poison containers.

"Oh, yes," they chorused.

He unlocked a heavy metal door. Behind it was a room lighted by fluorescent tubes. On the walls were bars so close together that no hand could reach through to the shelves behind them.

"I have to be sure that nothing will be stolen," Señor Pedroa explained. The glass-encased shelves were divided into compartments. In each stood a beautiful, handcrafted container.

"Many of them still have poison inside," the Mexican went on. "I try to trace the origin and find out what it is. But I'm not always successful. All these vials are old. They are genuine and valuable."

George pointed to a case filled with rings. "Are those the kind that hold poison?" she asked.

"You are correct," Señor Pedroa replied. "As you may know, poison rings date back to classical times. The great General Hannibal killed himself by drinking the fluid contained in the cap of such a ring."

Bess grimaced. "How awful!"

Señor Pedroa smiled. "You are right. It is not a subject we should dwell on. How about a cup of tea?"

"Thank you!" the girls accepted with alacrity.

He locked his collection room, then led the visitors onto a sunny patio, where the servant brought trays of luscious-looking petit fours and jam tarts. Bess had not thought about being hungry, but suddenly declared she was starved.

The servant poured tea for everyone and passed around the delicious cakes. By the time the girls stood up to leave, all of them were sure they would not need any dinner!

Nancy told Señor Pedroa, "We've had a delightful and informative visit. Thank you."

Their gracious host admitted he had enjoyed their company immensely and wished them luck in solving the mystery of the missing vial of poison.

When Nancy and her friends arrived at the Fortunato, they found a message for them at the desk.

Rosa Mendez had called and left her phone number.

"Please contact me at once," was written underneath the number.

The girls hurried to their room and Nancy put in the call. Señora Mendez recognized her voice and began to sob. She was barely able to speak and Nancy could hardly understand her.

"Please, Señora Mendez, say that again," she requested.

The woman cried out, "My granddaughter, Dolores, has been kidnapped!"

9

Stage Attack

"Kidnapped? When? How?" Nancy asked Rosa Mendez, utterly shocked.

Between sobs the woman explained that her nine-year-old granddaughter had been on her way home from school. When she did not arrive for hours after the expected time, her parents called the police.

"My daughter," Señora Mendez went on, "also phoned Dolores's teacher, who was amazed that the child had disappeared. Dolores had stayed late after class to help straighten the classroom, then started for home. The teacher got in touch with other students and asked if they knew where Dolores had gone."

"Did she have any success?" Nancy asked.

"Yes. Two girls saw Dolores get into a car. They had assumed that the driver and the woman in the back seat were friends or relatives. The girls were dreadfully upset to hear that their playmate had been kidnapped."

"I'm so sorry," Nancy said. "I'll do all I can to help you find her. Have you any clues?"

"There are none," the Mexican woman replied. "Oh, why did the kidnappers have to pick out *my* family?"

Nancy said, "I have suspected the Hoaxters of dishonesty for some time. They ask people to come on stage and by sleight of hand remove their possessions. They probably look among the articles to find out who of the owners are wealthy, influential, or famous. That's why I tried to hold you back when you went on stage. In your case, the men might have learned that you have a sizable bank account and also a darling granddaughter whom you adore."

"Oh, yes, I do," Señora Mendez cried out and began to sob again.

Nancy tried to calm her by saying, "I'm sure that either you or your daughter and her husband will receive a ransom note. Or you may get a phone message directly from Dolores."

"I hope we do. Then at least we would know that she is all right."

"I agree," Nancy said. "Please call me the instant you hear from the abductors. Meanwhile," she added, "I suggest you keep your phone line free in case the kidnappers or even the police want to get in touch with you."

"You are so wise," Señora Mendez said. "I will not talk any longer. But I'm very upset."

"You have good reason to be," Nancy told her. "Please try to calm down. Think only good thoughts for your granddaughter's return."

After saying good-by, Nancy told Bess and George what had happened. The girls were thunderstruck and agreed that Nancy's hunch about the Hoaxters was no doubt correct.

"I also think," Nancy told them, "that there is more to it than I have guessed so far. If the Hoaxters are successful in drawing capacity crowds, why should they need to be mixed up with con men and kidnappers?"

George nodded. "And why was it necessary for them to run away from New York?"

Bess was not listening. Instead she said, "I feel sorry for poor little Dolores. Oh, I hope she's not being mistreated! The poor child! She must be so frightened."

Nancy proposed that they go at once to the theater where the Hoaxters were performing and try to find out if her hunch really was correct.

Just then their telephone rang. Señora Mendez was calling again. She was very excited.

"We've had news!" she said. "My daughter and her husband received a hand-delivered note. But the person who brought it hurried away before they could ask him any questions. This is what the note said:

> "Your daughter will not be harmed, but she will be taken on a long journey."

"Is that all?" Nancy asked.

"Yes. And while we're relieved to know that Dolores is all right, we are extremely worried about this long journey. They might even take the child out of the country!"

Nancy conceded this was possible. The question was, why did the kidnapper plan to take their hostage away from Mexico City?

The young detective asked, "You're sure there was no demand for money?"

"Positive," Señora Mendez answered. "Well, Nancy, I won't talk any longer. But as soon as I have more information, I'll let you know."

The girls resumed their plan to attend the Hoaxters' performance. Nancy wanted to ask their leader point-blank why they kept people's possessions for at least half an hour.

She hailed a cab which let the girls off in front of the theater. No one was standing outside. Since it was an hour before show time, Nancy thought nothing of this. The front door was locked. George noticed a bell button and pushed it.

After a long wait, a maintenance man appeared. "What do you want?" he asked gruffly in Spanish.

Nancy told him that it was imperative the girls talk to the manager of the Hoaxters at once.

"He's not here. None of them are."

"When will they arrive?" Nancy asked in surprise.

"Maybe never."

"What do you mean?"

The man said the troupe had packed up suddenly and left. Nancy turned to Bess and George and quickly translated the information.

George said, "This is the second time they've skipped out of town!"

"And maybe they did it before that," Bess added.

Nancy addressed the maintenance man. "Is the manager of the theater in?"

The employee hesitated, then reluctantly opened the door. "I'll take you to his office," he said.

The maintenance man explained that the young ladies had come to talk with the manager, then went back to his work.

The gray-haired Mexican looked at them closely. "What's so important that you have to see me?" he asked.

Nancy noticed a sign on his desk with the name Señor Tomás on it. She explained that they had followed the Hoaxters from New York because certain people believed the troupe might not be honest.

"Do you know where they went?" she asked.

"No," Señor Tomás replied. "They left a note and enough money to cover the theater rental for the period they had reserved. I believe they departed last night."

"No one saw them go?" Nancy asked.

Señor Tomás explained that after the evening's performance which ended close to midnight, no one else had been in the building. Apparently a car or truck had been driven to the rear of the theater and loaded with the Hoaxters' props.

"When we arrived this morning, we discovered that all their possessions were gone," he added.

"Thank you very much," Nancy said. "Do you mind if we girls look around a bit to see if we can pick up a clue as to where the Hoaxters went?"

The manager glanced at them, puzzled. Finally he said, "Are you detectives?"

Nancy smiled. "Just amateurs. We're trying to help a friend."

Señor Tomás gave his permission and the group walked into the theater. No one was there. The girls went down a stairway to the dressing rooms. They noticed the maintenance man cleaning the floor.

He stared at them. "What are you doing here?" he demanded in Spanish.

Nancy replied, "We're just looking around."

The man became belligerent. "Looking around, eh? You're spying on me! Well, get out of here and fast!"

Although Bess and George could not understand him, they knew he was angry about something.

Bess said, "Nancy, we'd better go."

The cleaning man pointed to the door and motioned for the girls to leave. Fortunately Señor Tomás arrived just at that moment. When he heard about the altercation, he told his employee that the girls had his permission to survey the premises. They could stay as long as they wished. He added that the young detectives were trying to find clues to where the Hoaxters had gone.

"Do you know?" the manager asked him.

"No, I don't," the man replied. "And if I did, I wouldn't tell anyone. When a fellow wants to keep something secret, other folks have no right to pry."

"That's enough from you!" the manager reprimanded him. "And leave the girls alone!"

The cleaning man looked sullen and continued to mop the floor. Nancy thanked Señor Tomás, who left with a nod. Together, the girls went through the various dressing rooms but found nothing to indicate the whereabouts of the Hoaxters.

"This place is big!" George remarked. "Why don't we split up? That way we can cover more space."

"Good idea," Nancy agreed and the girls separated.

In a few minutes Nancy found herself on the stage. In the dim light it was difficult for her to spot anything the Hoaxters might have left. As she stood still, thinking about the mystery, something heavy suddenly crashed over her head. It almost knocked her to the floor!

Dizzily she struggled to extricate herself from the object and finally succeeded. Before her lay an oil painting that she had seen hanging on the wall during one of the Hoaxters's routines.

As she thought of it around her neck like a hoop, Nancy chuckled. Then her face became grim. "That painting didn't fall on me by accident!" she thought. "Someone deliberately jammed it down over my head!"

She looked in all directions but saw no one. "I'll bet it was that disgruntled cleaning man," she reasoned.

Just then a pretty Indian woman with a mop and bucket walked onto the stage. She stared at Nancy in amazement. Noticing her rumpled hair and disheveled blouse, she asked in Spanish what had happened.

Nancy explained and the Indian shook her head in sympathy. "That is very bad!" she declared. "I am glad you were not hurt."

The woman introduced herself as Sara. Then the girl detective asked her if she had seen anyone on stage a few moments before.

"Yes," Sara replied, "the maintenance man."

"I thought it was he," Nancy said.

She now questioned the woman about the Hoaxters's sudden departure.

Sara said she had not heard why the troupe had disappeared. "I did not like them," she added. "I think they were up to no good!"

"Have you any idea where they went?" Nancy asked.

Sara suddenly looked frightened. "I know, but they threatened to harm me if I told anyone!"

"Oh!" Nancy exclaimed. Here was a wonderful clue, the young sleuth thought, but how could she persuade Sara to tell her what it was?

10

A Setback Reversed

The cleaning woman began to mop the floor. Nancy was afraid that she would not reveal where the Hoaxters had gone. While the young detective tried to figure out how to persuade Sara, she picked up a dust cloth and wiped off the stage furniture.

Sara looked at her and smiled. Nancy smiled back. "Sara, if the Hoaxters have left, how can they harm you?"

The woman hesitated, then replied, "You are right. I overheard the men say they were going to Los Angeles. They realized I was standing close enough to hear their conversation, and accused me of eavesdropping. But I had no such intention.

That was when they threatened to harm me if I told anyone."

"I'm glad you *did* tell me," Nancy said. "Los Angeles is a long way from here. I wouldn't worry if I were you."

Sara was relieved. She told Nancy that ever since seeing the men take wallets and handbags she had not trusted the performers. "I think they ran away because something happened," she said. "But I have no idea what it was."

Nancy wondered about the information. Suddenly she had an idea: No doubt one of the patrons complained to the police about having to give up his wallet until the end of the show. The police in turn must have asked the Hoaxters to come to headquarters and explain. Since they want nothing to do with the authorities, they left. The same thing probably happened in New York!

"Sara," she said to the woman, "the maintenance man wasn't very nice to us when we came in. Is he always so grumpy?"

Sara glanced up from the mop she was using.

"I do not like him. He does as little work as he can get away with and is forever looking for tips. The Hoaxters gave him big ones. I know because he used to brag about it."

"Did he receive large tips because he did special favors for the magicians?"

Sara shrugged. "I do not know, but it is possible. Or perhaps he found out some secret of theirs and they paid him to keep quiet."

Nancy changed the subject. "Did anyone not connected with the show ever come here to see the Hoaxters?"

"Oh, yes. Two fellows came twice. One was called Howie, the other Lefty. They arrived after the performance and talked to the Hoaxters in a dressing room with the door locked. No one else could hear what they were saying."

At this moment George and Bess arrived on stage. Nancy introduced them to Sara and said the woman had given her some good clues.

"Did you girls learn anything?" Nancy asked.

"Nothing," Bess replied.

George added, "At one point the cleaning man followed me though the theater, but I managed to avoid him. I didn't come across anything to help solve the mystery, however."

Sara had nothing else to contribute either, so the girls said good-by to her, walked off the stage and out the back door.

"Sara mentioned Howie and Lefty visiting the Hoaxters," Nancy told Bess and George excitedly. "I'm sure that was Howie Barker. I wonder who Lefty is."

"Maybe he's another con man," Bess offered.

While the three girls were waiting for a taxi in

front of the theater, Nancy brought her friends up to date on her conversation with Sara.

"Well, where do we go from here?" Bess asked.

"To Los Angeles!" Nancy replied promptly.

As soon as they reached the Fortunato Hotel, she called the airport to make reservations. As Nancy hung up, she frowned.

"No flights?" George asked.

"An air strike just started and may last for a month!" Nancy responded. "What'll we do now?"

"Drive," Bess suggested.

"Do you realize how far it is?" Nancy asked.

"Over twenty-five hundred miles!" George answered.

"Right. It'll take us five days if we drive ten hours a day!"

"That's better than staying here for a month," George declared.

"I suppose so," Nancy said unenthusiastically.

Bess sighed. "I'm not looking forward to that long haul either. But we can take turns driving and perhaps even make it in four days."

Nancy nodded. "Okay. Let's rent a car tomorrow."

The next day directly after breakfast their telephone rang. Señora Mendez was calling. She sounded hysterical.

"Oh, Nancy, come here at once. Please!" the woman sobbed.

"What happened?"

Señora Mendez said she could not tell her over the phone, but she had something very important to show the three sleuths.

"We'll take a taxi and be over as soon as possible," Nancy promised.

When the girls arrived at her residence, the Mexican woman showed them a letter that she said had been left on the front doorstep.

"My maid heard a knock and went to answer it. When she opened the door, no one was there but the letter lay on the mat. She brought it to me and I almost fainted. Please read it."

Nancy unfolded the note that was flat but originally had been folded like a fan. It was on a long, narrow sheet of paper and the words that ran from top to bottom were composed of letters or words cut from a newspaper. The message was:

Get
ready
to
deliver
$100,000
ransom
in
unmarked
bills
in
a
small
light-

weight
sack
in
hundred
dollar
denominations
to
assure
release
of
Dolores
8
hours
later
totally
unharmed
by
her
poor
needy
abductors.
X
directions
will
follow

"Have you called your daughter?" Nancy asked.

"Yes. She has heard nothing. I told her I would gladly pay the money, but she is afraid Dolores may not be returned even though the ransom is paid. That's why I'm so upset. I don't know what to do and I can't ask anybody to help me!"

"Why not?" Nancy countered. "We girls will continue to work on the mystery for you."

The woman pointed out there was another part to the note that they had not read yet.

"Turn it over," she directed.

The remainder of the message warned Señora Mendez that harm would come to Dolores and her family if anyone contacted police or detectives.

The Mexican woman walked up and down the living room in great agitation. "So you see," she said, "I'll have to ask you girls to forget the case!"

Nancy, Bess, and George were stunned. They appreciated the grandmother's concern about the safety of her family, but the young sleuths did not want to give up trying to find the child.

Nancy went to the distraught woman and put an arm around her shoulders. "We are not part of the police and we are not professional detectives," she said soothingly. "We are only amateurs and the note does not include us. Please let us continue to work on your case."

Señora Mendez hugged Nancy and kissed her, then consented to let the girls proceed in their hunt.

"But what can you possibly do?" she asked. "You have no idea where the kidnappers have taken my Dolores!"

"We suspect," Nancy replied, "that the Hoaxters are involved in this, as I told you before." She paused.

"Yes, yes, go on," the woman urged.

"We found out," Nancy continued, "that they have gone to Los Angeles. Possibly they took Dolores with them. The whole troupe left here abruptly without giving the theater manager any advance notice."

"Oh, if you could only find Dolores!" Señora Mendez said, gazing at the three girls in admiration.

Nancy examined the ransom note more carefully, reading the words over and over. "I believe there's a code message hidden in the wording."

"It's hidden all right," Bess commented.

"A message for whom?" George asked.

Nancy replied, "My guess would be that it was intended for someone connected with the kidnappers."

"But why would it be folded again and again before being sent to Señora Mendez?" Bess questioned.

Nancy was thoughtful. "Perhaps this folded note was not meant for her. It could have been delivered to Señora Mendez by mistake. Suppose there were two identical notes," Nancy went on. "One was folded, the other not even creased. The plain one may have been the ransom note for Señora Mendez, the folded one a copy for a confederate."

"I still don't get it," Bess admitted.

"The clue to a hidden message for the confederate must be in the folds!" Nancy declared.

"But there's a fold under every word," Bess said.

"That's the strangest kind of code I ever heard of."

"Maybe the fan is the identification of the group." Nancy said.

"You know," George spoke up, "this reminds me of a game we used to play as children. A sheet of paper and a pencil were passed around a group. Each player would write one line, then fold the paper over and give it to the next person. When all the players had written on it, someone would open it and read the story. Usually it was a silly one about somebody in the group. Once the paper said I was a mad elephant who liked to dance!"

Nancy was not paying strict attention. She was already working to decipher the ransom note. First she read every second fold, next every third, then the fourth.

Suddenly she cried out, "I have it! The code is in every fifth word!"

"Well, Sherlock Holmes, what does it say?" Bess urged.

Nancy smiled and replied, "It says, '$100,000 in sack to 8 by X.'"

"Hm," said Bess. "To me that makes no sense at all. If that's a code, how are you ever going to break it?"

"Yes, how?" George challenged her.

Nancy replied, "I don't know, but I'm not giving up. We must solve this! It's too good a clue not to follow!"

11

An Odd Invention

"I think the 8 and the X are the solution to the puzzle," Nancy said. "The 8 could stand for the eighth letter of the alphabet, namely H for Howie. But 'by X'?"

"The twenty-fourth letter of the alphabet," George said. "Or perhaps it signifies the twenty-fourth day of the month."

"Or it could mean a signature," Bess volunteered. "People who cannot write sign their name by making an X."

George sighed. "It's hard to be a detective. You have to be clairvoyant!"

Nancy laughed. "There are more possibilities."

"Oh, no!" Bess shook her head in desperation.

"Perhaps the message was not meant for a confederate of the kidnappers at all, but for us!" Nancy suggested.

"I don't understand."

"Maybe the crooks want to lure us to a certain spot on a certain day where they can set up a trap!"

"Oh, don't say such a thing," Bess begged. "You make chills go up and down my spine."

"Calm down, my dear cousin," George said with a chuckle. "I'm sure if our enemies want to trap us they would have left more specific directions!"

Nancy asked Señora Mendez if any of the girls' guesses gave her a clue to the solution of the puzzle.

The woman shook her head. "Nothing occurs to me," she replied. "Do you think it could refer to something in Los Angeles?"

"We'll try to find out when we get there," Nancy replied.

After making an exact copy of the ransom note, the girls said good-by to their Mexican friend and left. On the way back to the hotel they stopped at a car rental agency. Nancy told the owner where the girls wanted to go.

He smiled and said, "My partner flew to New York last week and now has to go to Los Angeles for a month or so. He wants someone to bring his car to him. We'll be glad to give it to you as a rental and you can leave it in Los Angeles. Usually we require our cars to be returned to this country."

"Great!" Nancy said. "I suppose we came just at the right time."

The manager nodded. "The car will be ready for you to pick up by seven o'clock tomorrow morning."

The girls were happy with the arrangement and left the agency.

"We'll have some free time this afternoon," Bess said. "Why don't we go back to Señora Clara's dress shop and see if we can find another Mexican outfit?"

George smiled. "I haven't any money to spend, but I wouldn't mind looking."

When the girls arrived at Señora Clara's, no customers were in the shop. The friendly woman greeted them with a smile. "Hello again. Look around all you wish," she said. "I'll be busy for a while because a man is coming to offer me some wonderful new stock."

"What kind of stock?" Nancy asked, intrigued at once.

"In a company that has developed a fabulous fabric," Señora Clara explained. "It sounded very interesting."

To Nancy it sounded like a scheme the con men would invent, and she was suspicious at once. "Did you by any chance see a performance of the Hoaxters when they were in town?" she asked the dress shop owner.

"Yes, indeed," Señora Clara replied. "Weren't they fantastic?"

"They were," Nancy admitted. "Did you go up on stage?"

"Yes."

"I must tell you something we found out regarding the group that might concern you." Nancy explained the girls' suspicions and the various things that had happened to people who had attended the show.

Señora Clara was alarmed. "You mean the man who is coming here might try to swindle me?"

"It's quite possible," Nancy replied.

"But what shall I do? I have already made the appointment."

"Don't buy anything," George advised.

Señora Clara agreed. "Perhaps you would like to stay with me and see if you recognize the caller."

"We'd be glad to," Nancy said. "If he's Howie Barker, he would recognize us, so may we hide somewhere? Perhaps in a spot where we can get a good look at him?"

"Of course. One of the dressing rooms has a perfect view of my desk," Señora Clara declared. "And since I have no private office, this is where I'll sit when I talk to the man."

"Good idea," Nancy said and the girls crowded into the small cubicle. Its louvered door had slats through which the young detectives could look.

"This will be perfect," Nancy said.

Señora Clara smiled. "Just don't sneeze!"

Bess giggled. "We'll do our best not to."

A few minutes later two men entered the shop. They were well-dressed, good-looking, and very polite. When the taller one came closer and addressed Señora Clara, the girls stiffened. He was Barker, the man who had tried to swindle Bess!

"My name is Barker," he said. "I spoke to you on the telephone a little while ago. This is my colleague, Mr. Cadwell. We would like to tell you about a new firm that has developed a most fantastic fabric."

"Please be seated," Señora Clara said and pointed to two chairs next to her desk.

Mr. Cadwell pulled a brochure out of his briefcase and handed it to Señora Clara. It showed a little girl wearing the same attire in different settings. One picture depicted spring, with the child sitting in a field of crocuses; the next one summer, where she was perched at the side of a pool. In the third picture the girl was climbing a tree with bright yellow and reddish leaves, and the fourth showed her seated on a sled surrounded by snow.

"You see," Mr. Cadwell said, "this material can be worn at any time of year. It has a natural, built-in thermostat which adjusts itself to the wearer's body temperature. It works for everyone in all climates!"

"That's amazing!" Señora Clara said. "You mean this fabric can be worn comfortably 365 days a year in all climates?"

"That is correct."

"Do you have a sample with you?"

"Certainly."

The man produced several pieces of cloth from his briefcase. They were of different colors and textures, but each felt like a lightweight wool.

Señora Clara examined the samples but said nothing.

"This fabulous new invention," Mr. Cadwell went on, "is called Silk-O-Sheen. It is not mass-produced yet, but the inventor is setting up his first plant. We offer stock in this venture to people in the clothing business for a mere ten dollars a share. Now, how much can I sign you up for, Señora Clara?"

Nancy, who had observed the scene closely from the girls' hiding place, bit her lips. Would Señora Clara fall for the swindle?

But the businesswoman had a ready answer. "I'd like to think about it first," she said. "Besides, I have to consult my accountant to see if I have any extra cash to invest."

"Surely you have money in your cash register right now?" Mr. Barker urged. "You can give us a down payment of 20 percent and pay for the rest later."

"I never make hasty decisions," Señora Clara said coolly. "If you will leave me your card, I'll be glad to let you know in a day or two."

The men, who had been extremely affable until now, stopped smiling. Cadwell put the samples and the brochure back into his briefcase and snapped it shut angrily.

The visitors got up and bowed curtly. "You are making a big mistake!" Mr. Cadwell said. "And I'm telling you . . ."

Just then his companion glanced at a nearby chair. On it lay a small cloth wallet with the name Bess embroidered on it. "Who else is here?" he asked.

Señora Clara did not answer but she got up to retrieve the wallet. Bess Marvin's heart began to pound. It was hers!

Barker hurried to the chair and picked up the wallet. Señora Clara plunged toward him, crying out, "Leave that alone! Give it to me!"

Quick as a flash Howie Barker opened the wallet and read Bess's full name on her driver's license. The next second the store owner grabbed the wallet, while the man dashed to the louvered door and yanked it open.

"So!" he cried out angrily. "You girls deliberately spied on us! You'll be sorry for this!"

With that, he and Mr. Cadwell sped furiously out of the shop.

12

Smugglers

George and Nancy ran after the men but soon stopped. Barker and Cadwell had jumped into a chauffered car and were out of sight in the heavy traffic a few seconds later.

"I couldn't see the license plate," Nancy said in disappointment.

As she and George returned to the shop, Bess asked worriedly, "What did Barker mean by that threat?"

"I don't know," Nancy replied, "but he'll think up something to harass us."

Señora Clara looked at the girls, puzzled. Then she said, "You'd better watch your step. I think those men could be very mean, even dangerous!"

"I think so, too," Bess said, sighing. Then she

added, "Now that we've averted a disaster, I'd like to look at dresses."

Nancy laughed. "Go ahead. "I'll phone the police, meanwhile, and tell them what happened."

"Please do," Señora Clara said. "You can sit at my desk. And you know, Cadwell did not leave me a business card. That makes it even more obvious to me that they are swindlers."

Nancy reported the incident to the authorities while Bess bought a lovely summer dress. Then they said good-by to Señora Clara, who wished them luck.

Early the next morning Nancy went to the car rental garage to pick up the automobile for the girls' trip. As she entered the large parking area, she glimpsed a man hurrying out a side door.

"He looked like Howie Barker!" she thought and started to run after him.

Suddenly she stopped short, telling herself it was a good thing the man had not seen her. Otherwise he would guess that the girls were leaving Mexico City!

"If I caught him, I'd have no evidence anyway," she decided and went to her rented automobile.

When Nancy arrived at the hotel, the girls packed their belongings in the trunk of the car, then rode off. Because of their early start, they had not had breakfast. An hour later Bess declared that she could not go much longer without food.

"We're far away from the city already," she said. "I wonder where we could find something to eat."

George asked, "Would you like some Mexican food?"

Bess confessed that at this point she was starved and would eat any kind of food.

"How about an enchilada sundae?" George teased.

"With hot fudge and whipped cream? Yick!" Bess frowned.

George winked at Nancy. "I saw a sign with an arrow back at the last side road. I couldn't read it, but the sign had pictures of tortillas and enchiladas on it."

Nancy turned the car around immediately, then took the side road. About a mile ahead they came to an Indian settlement. Women were seated on the ground cooking over low stone fireplaces. When the girls stopped, the natives looked up and smiled. Several children ran to the Americans, followed by barking dogs. Nancy and her friends jumped out of the car and approached the women.

Bess asked, "Do you serve breakfast?"

The woman closest to her glanced at the others in her group. They all shrugged.

George said, "I guess they don't speak English."

Nancy tried the same question in Spanish, but the only word the women seemed to understand was *comer*, which meant "to eat." They bobbed their heads.

One of the women pointed to the food being prepared. There were different varieties of tortillas and enchiladas, eggs scrambled with hot peppers, strong cocoa, ripe pineapples, and small bananas.

"Why do they have to put hot peppers with the eggs?" Bess complained.

Nancy replied, "In Mexico peppers are used as a health food. One time, when there was a great polio epidemic all over the United States, doctors found that there was not a single case of the disease in Mexico. Upon inquiry they learned that this was due to the daily use of peppers in the native diet."

Bess said she would like to fix her own scrambled eggs. "Nancy, ask the lady if I may," she urged.

Although Nancy felt sure the women would not understand, she complied with Bess's request.

The Indians held a conference, then suddenly a young, pretty girl chattered something excitedly. She raced off, but soon returned holding a live hen that squawked and tried to wiggle out of the girl's arms. She held onto it tightly and talked in her Indian dialect. To the amazement of the Americans, the hen laid an egg in the girl's palm!

Nancy and her friends laughed. Apparently the

Indians had thought that Bess wanted a newly laid egg!

The girl handed it to Bess, who picked up an empty pan. She took some cooking fat from a crock and melted it. Then she broke the egg on the edge of the pan and quickly scrambled it with a wooden spoon. The natives smiled and shrugged.

Nancy and George decided to brave the already prepared scrambled eggs seasoned with hot peppers. Unlike Nancy, who laid the peppers aside, George bit into one. Her eyes bulged as the spicy vegetable stung her mouth. She swallowed it quickly and gulped down a piece of cooling pineapple.

"When it comes to food," Bess smirked, "I guess I am the only sensible one—besides Nancy, of course!"

George grimaced, then broke into a mischievous smile. "I guess I deserve that for teasing you so much about your forty-inch waist!"

"My waist isn't forty inches!" Bess declared, causing George to giggle.

"You two!" Nancy remarked, shaking her head.

After paying for the meal, the girls drove off. They joked for several miles.

George continued to tease Bess. "Alongside those really stout Indian women you looked pretty good."

Nancy remarked that the younger ones were very

attractive. "I guess the older people have wrinkled skin and squinting eyes from the harsh sunlight."

The girls took turns driving and went as far as they could each day. They stopped at motels only when they were too tired to go on. It was an exhausting and uneventful trip. Bess regretted many times that she had suggested they take a car instead of waiting for the air strike to end.

After lunch on the fourth day the young travelers reached the border. Here they were stopped by a customs official in a snappy-looking uniform.

"We have nothing to declare," Nancy told him.

He requested to see driver's license and looked at it closely. "Nancy Drew!" he asked. "You mean you are not going to declare certain property you are concealing."

"I don't know what you're talking about."

"I'll tell you. Hidden in your car is a valuable jade figurine that you stole from a museum in Mexico City!"

"What!" all three girls exclaimed, stunned.

"You must have us confused with someone else," Nancy declared. "We are not thieves and you will find nothing in this car except our personal belongings."

The official paid no attention to her remark. Instead, he asked for the key and opened the trunk. He pushed aside the girls' baggage and looked in back of the spare tire. Presently he pulled out a box that the young detectives had never seen before. Inside lay an exquisite piece of jade carved in the form of a boat with a woman in it surrounded by water lilies.

"How beautiful!" Bess cried out. "Officer, we never saw this before."

The man stared at her disdainfully. "You are all good actresses, but you have been caught. You are smugglers!"

Nancy firmly denied the charge. Disturbing thoughts raced through her mind. What would happen to her? Would she receive a heavy fine? Even be sent to jail if she could not pay?

She looked at the man. "Where did you get the tip that we were carrying this jade piece?"

The officer refused to answer.

Bess was frightened. She stared into the distance and saw a handsome young man who was also apparently a customs officer. While Nancy continued to argue with the official, Bess smiled coquettishly.

He smiled back at the pretty girl. "Is there anything I can do for you? You're much too cute to be in trouble."

Bess blurted out her story and even let her eyes become moist. This was too much for the young man. He took her by the arm and led the tearful girl back to the group. Then he addressed the official who had searched the car.

"Why don't we check with the police in Mexico City, Mr. Rivera? This young lady tells me Lieutenant Tara knows them and can confirm that they are amateur detectives working on a case. After all, the tip could have come from one of their enemies."

The older man bobbed his head. "You watch the girls while I go inside and call. But don't let them get away until I come back!"

He went into his office, and Bess thanked the young officer for his help. Soon Mr. Rivera returned. For the first time he smiled.

"All right, young ladies, I believe we can let you continue your journey. Lieutenant Tara told us he would vouch for you personally. And I will see to it that the jade piece is returned to the museum."

"Thank you," Bess said with a sigh of relief. "I could see all of us in jail for the next twenty years!"

After the girls had driven a distance into the United States, Nancy said to Bess, "Thanks for your help. That was clever of you to play on that handsome guy's sympathy."

George laughed. "It's a good thing your friend Dave Evans wasn't there. He'd have been green with jealousy!"

As dusk was settling, the girls reached Los Angeles. Since they had made no reservations, Nancy stopped at the first hotel they came to. George went inside to inquire about a room. When she returned to the car, her face had a worried look.

"What's the matter?" Bess asked.

"There's a big convention in town. Hundreds of detectives from all over the United States are meeting here, and no hotel or motel has any rooms left."

"What are we going to do?" Bess asked.

No one spoke for a few minutes, then suddenly George remembered something. "Former neighbors of ours moved out here last year," she announced. "They invited my family and friends to visit them any time. Suppose I phone them."

"Wonderful!" Bess said. "Do it right now."

George went into the hotel again and looked up her former neighbors' name in the phone book. Mrs. Vetter was delighted to hear from her.

"Where are you?" she asked.

When she was told about the girls' predicament, she said, "This is great! All of you come right over. We'd love to have you stay as long as you wish."

"Oh, thanks so much," George said. "You're a lifesaver."

When she walked out of the phone booth, her eyes were twinkling. Nancy and Bess, who had followed her into the lobby, were eager to hear what she had learned.

"Everything is okay," George reported. "The Vetters would love to have us visit."

Elated, the trio went outside again. They headed for their car which was parked a short distance from the hotel. It was not in sight!

Nancy was puzzled. "I'm sure we left it right here!"

The girls walked farther down the street. By the time they reached the next intersection, they knew that their car had been stolen!

"Oh, no!" Bess wailed. "Do you realize all our luggage is gone, too?"

13

The Invisible Hand

George was angry. she stomped her foot on the sidewalk and exclaimed, "Can you imagine our car being stolen right in front of a hotel full of detectives?"

Bess was more upset over the loss of their baggage. "What are we going to wear?" she asked. "I don't have enough money with me to buy a new wardrobe."

Nancy tried not to show her agitation. "Why don't we do some sleuthing and see if we can find a clue to the thief?" she suggested.

The girls walked back to the spot where they had parked the automobile. A light truck stood in its place now, but Nancy noted a large, rumpled piece of paper underneath. She pulled it out.

"What's that?" George asked, curious.

Nancy spread it out. "A poster advertising the Hoaxters!" she exclaimed.

The cousins leaned forward to read it. The poster gave the name of the theater and the performance schedule.

"We're in luck!" Nancy said. "I have a hunch that one of the Hoaxters took our car. Let's go over to the theater immediately and find out!"

"But how did they know we were in Los Angeles?" Bess asked. "And what car we were driving?"

"They knew about the car because they planted the jade figurine in it," Nancy declared. "I thought I saw Howie Barker leaving the garage when I picked the car up. But I can't see how they could have possibly followed us all the way here."

"Perhaps they had one of their partners waiting at the border," George suggested. "When he realized that we were not being detained, he followed us."

"You're probably right," Nancy admitted. "When we arrived and went into the hotel, he took our car!"

Soon the girls reached the theater. A man stood at the front door. He was made up, with a gray wig, mustache, and beard. The girls did not recognize him.

Nancy decided not to speak to him. Instead, she led the way through an alley that opened into a fenced-in parking lot. It was bordered by the street behind the theater and was almost filled to capacity with cars belonging to patrons of the evening performance.

"Do you think ours might be here?" Bess asked tensely.

"I hope so," Nancy replied. "Let's separate and check them all."

Each girl took a section of the parking lot and walked up and down the rows. Suddenly Nancy spotted their rented car parked near the fence! She hurried up to it, took the keys from her handbag, and opened the trunk. To her relief, the girls' baggage was still there!

As she slammed the trunk lid shut again, Bess and George joined her. From a distance they had seen her stop and open the luggage compartment.

"Is everything safe?" Bess asked worriedly.

Nancy smiled at her friend. "All your clothes are intact. And now we'd better get out of here as quickly as possible."

The girls piled into the car. It took some maneuvering on Nancy's part to get away from the fence. When she finally drove through the gate into the street behind the theater, the gray-bearded man they had noticed earlier ran toward them.

He yelled at the top of his lungs, "Stop thief! Stop thief!"

George leaned out the window. "We didn't steal this car!" she shouted. But they were already too far away for the man to hear her.

Fortunately, there was little traffic on the back street and Nancy proceeded quickly. After a few blocks she noticed a policeman and stopped. She told him what had happened.

The officer promised to inform headquarters about the incident. "You will be required to come in and sign a report," he said. "Where are you staying?"

"At the Vetters' on Dale Drive," Nancy said. "Can you tell us how to get there?"

"Sure."

The policeman gave her directions, and twenty minutes later the girls pulled into the Vetters' driveway. A gray-haired couple came out to greet them.

"George, how are you!" Mrs. Vetter exclaimed, hugging her former neighbor. "And I remember your cousin Bess. She was at your house several times when I stopped by to see your mother."

George introduced Nancy, who was warmly welcomed by the friendly couple.

"We've heard so much about your mystery solving," Mr. Vetter said, "that I'm delighted to meet you at last. Now, if you girls will let me have the car key, I'll take your luggage inside."

Mrs. Vetter showed the visitors to an attractive guest room and soon they were unpacking their clothes.

"I think we should call home and tell everybody where we are," Bess said.

George yawned. "Do you realize what time it is? Eleven o'clock here. That means it's two in the morning in River Heights. We'll have to wait until tomorrow."

Mrs. Vetter had prepared a midnight snack. When the girls had finished unpacking they all sat around the dining room table to eat ham salad sandwiches and dainty chicken sandwiches. For dessert they had hot chocolate and tarts filled with plum jam.

"Oh, this is good," Bess declared. "We were so eager to get here that we skipped dinner."

George nodded. "I wasn't even hungry until I saw the food. And now I'd like to go to bed. I'm exhausted."

"Go right ahead," Mrs. Vetter said. "You can tell us all the news tomorrow."

Even though the girls were extremely tired, they awoke early the next morning. When they came downstairs, all of them realized that their hosts were not up yet.

"This is a good time to call home," Nancy declared. "I'll start with my father."

Mr. Drew had not left for his office, and she told him what had happened since she had last spoken to him. She also gave him the Vetters' address and phone number.

"And what news do you have?" she asked. "Is everything all right at home?"

"Fine," Mr. Drew said. "I've heard from Señor Pedroa in Mexico City. He said the police tracked down Enzo Scorpio, the poison thief, but the man disappeared before they could arrest him."

"That's too bad," Nancy said.

"Yes. And now Hannah would like to say hello to you," her father added and handed the phone to the housekeeper.

Hannah Gruen told Nancy she had received a call from the girls' friends, Ned, Burt, and Dave. "They want to come to the West Coast and join you," she reported.

"Wonderful!" Nancy exclaimed. "Hold the line while I speak to Bess and George."

She quickly discussed the request with her friends, and both were eager to see the boys. Just then Mrs. Vetter walked into the room. George asked her if she would mind having three more guests, and the woman smiled.

"Of course not! The more the merrier!"

"Thank you so much," Nancy said, then relayed the invitation to Hannah.

Later in the morning, the young detective called Señora Mendez in Mexico City. "What is the latest word on the kidnapping?" she asked.

"It is not good," the woman answered, her voice trembling. "I received another ransom note, telling me to put the money into a sack and deposit it in a certain trash container attached to a big eucalyptus tree outside of town."

"And you followed the instructions?" Nancy asked.

"Yes, I did. The kidnappers warned me not to tell the police, but I asked that two of their detectives watch the place secretly, and grab whoever came to take the ransom money."

"Were they successful?" Nancy asked eagerly.

"No. But the money is gone!"

"You mean the ransom disappeared but the police failed to catch the man?"

"Exactly. It seemed as if an invisible hand reached into the trash can and removed the sack. There was no trace of anyone coming or going."

Nancy was amazed to hear this. "Was the tree tall," she asked, "or a low one with lots of branches and leaves?"

"It was not too tall and spread out a good bit," Mrs. Mendez replied. "It was bushy and full. Why do you ask?"

"I think I know what happened," Nancy said. 'The thief might have hidden in the treetop before the police detectives took up their positions. When it was dark, he shinnied down, took the sack, and retreated into the branches again until the following day. After he saw the police check the trash can and drive away, he probably felt it was safe to come down."

"Oh, Nancy, I'm sure you're right."

"Have you heard anything about Dolores?" the young detective asked.

Señora Mendez began to cry. "No, we have not. There was to be a phone call after the money had been picked up to tell us where we could find Dolores. But neither I nor my daughter and her husband have been contacted. We're frantic with worry!"

"That's dreadful and very unfair," Nancy remarked. "As you know, Señora Mendez, I believe that Dolores was taken to Los Angeles. I will hunt for her here. Please don't worry too much. Hold hopeful thoughts."

"I'll try," the woman replied, her voice still shaky. She begged the young sleuth to start work immediately. "And keep me informed about any clues you pick up. I will pray that you succeed."

When Bess, George, and the Vetters heard the report, they were aghast. All of them agreed that the kidnapper was a totally heartless person.

Later in the morning, Nancy was summoned to

police headquarters to make a formal charge against the thief who had stolen her rented car. When she returned to the Vetters, after dropping off the car at the designated address, George said, "Are they checking out the man who raced into the parking lot, yelling 'Stop thief!'?"

"Yes, they are," Nancy replied. "But even though I described him as best I could, he was so made up that it will be hard to identify him. Too bad we didn't recognize him by his voice."

Bess spoke up. "Well, I'm glad we didn't. I don't want to have anything to do with any kind of thief . . . carnapper, childnapper or dognapper, you name it!"

Nancy and George laughed. The subject was dropped for the time being, because the Vetters had invited some friends to their house to meet the girls. The party was scheduled for four o'clock and no one left until after nine. By then, the young sleuths had been so distracted by the conversation that they had almost forgotten why they had come to Los Angeles.

"But first thing tomorrow morning," Nancy said, "we must do some detective work."

That night everyone went to bed early. They had been asleep several hours, when suddenly all were awakened by the smoke alarm. It was beeping at a tremendous rate!

The girls jumped out of bed, put on bathrobes and slippers, then dashed into the hall. Their hosts had already hurried downstairs, and the young detectives followed. The house was full of smoke, so they rushed outdoors.

"Where's the fire?" Bess asked. "I don't see any flames."

"In the laundry room in the wing," Mr. Vetter answered.

He went to call the fire department, then picked up the garden hose. He played it through the windows of the laundry room, trying to extinguish the flames.

"My husband thinks someone set the fire deliberately," Mrs. Vetter declared.

The girls looked at her, shocked. Was the perpetrator one of their enemies?

14

More Tricks

It was impossible for the Vetters and their guests to go into the laundry room. The smoke was too thick and acrid. Firemen soon arrived and quickly extinguished the blaze. Luckily not much damage had been done to the washer and dryer, but the walls were covered with soot and the floor was full of foamy water.

"This place is a mess," George remarked. "Mr. and Mrs. Vetter, I'm terribly sorry. There is a good chance that this fire was set by enemies of Nancy, Bess, and me."

"What do you mean?" one of the firemen asked, amazed.

George looked toward Nancy, as if requesting

her to carry on. The young sleuth nodded and gave the firemen a brief sketch of the case on which they were working.

"Hm," one of them said. "It does look as if you have a point, miss. Men, let's see what we can find."

After looking around carefully, they came upon a scorched can of inflammable fluid that had been hidden behind a hamper.

"Here's what was used to set the blaze," a fireman, who said his name was Scotty, told the Vetters and their guests. "I'll report all you've told me to the chief. Would you care to give me the names of the people you suspect?"

Mrs. Vetter interrupted. "Oh, Nancy, don't do that! You may be harmed if those wicked men find out you've reported them."

Nancy conceded that the woman had a point. Furthermore, she did not have a single bit of evidence to prove her accusation.

She said to Scotty, "I suppose I'd better not reveal any more at this time. I have no proof, only suspicions."

After the men had left, Mr. Vetter said he thought all of them should go back to bed. "We'll talk more about it in the morning."

As he closed the outside door to the laundry room, he asked his wife if she had left the door unlocked on purpose.

Mrs. Vetter shook her head. "I'm always very careful to lock it."

"Then whoever set the fire must have had a master key," her husband remarked. "There is no evidence here that the lock was forced."

Nobody slept very soundly for the rest of the night. Everyone wondered if the smoke alarm would go off again, or if something else might happen to the house. By morning Nancy said she was convinced that the girls' enemies had somehow tracked them down. But how?

"In any case," she said to Bess and George, "I think we should leave. It's not fair of us to put the Vetters through any more frightening experiences."

"I agree," Bess added.

George said, "Let me talk to them. After all, they're doing a good deed by giving us a place to stay while we're trying to find the con men and their associates."

Before Nancy or Bess could comment, George had hurried out of the room. To their surprise she returned in a few minutes.

"The Vetters won't hear of our leaving," she reported. "Both of them said they are enjoying this mystery, and besides," George chuckled, "they're looking forward to the boys' visit."

"Then that settles it," Bess said, giggling.

When the young detectives arrived at the breakfast table, Nancy thanked their hosts for such a generous attitude. "You're really good sports," she said. "And I think the fire proves we girls are on the right track of little Dolores's kidnappers."

Bess added, "We must be getting so close to them that they're trying to drive us out of Los Angeles."

"Well, they're not going to succeed!" George announced vehemently.

"I'd like to phone Dad," Nancy put in. "Maybe he's had news about the Maine hotel and the company that supposedly produces the Silk-O-Sheen fabric."

Mr. Drew reported that he had not been able to unearth anything. "The firms are probably fictitious, and any literature about them is phony, too," he declared. "But I need more time to prove it."

Nancy brought him up to date on what had happened since she had last talked to him. "It seems to me you're in great danger, Nancy," he said in concern. "Perhaps you had better come home."

"Oh, Dad, you don't mean that!" Nancy protested. "Besides, we'll get help soon. Ned, Burt, and Dave are coming out here."

"I know. Mrs. Marvin told me. Dave phoned her to get your address."

"What!" Nancy exclaimed. "When?"

"Yesterday morning."

"But I gave the boys our address myself. Dave didn't have to call Mrs. Marvin—and you know, I'm beginning to wonder if he did!"

"You mean it was an impostor who called?" Mr. Drew asked.

"Yes. Maybe the same man who started the fire in the Vetters' laundry room last night."

"But how would he know about Dave?"

"When the Hoaxters took Bess's handbag during the performance in New York, they probably found her picture of Dave with his name and address on it."

"Why don't you phone Dave and find out if he spoke to Mrs. Marvin?" Mr. Drew suggested.

"I'll do that right now. And thanks for the info, Dad."

Nancy hung up and dialed Dave's number. He answered promptly. When Nancy asked him if he had inquired about their address, he was amazed.

"Of course I didn't," he said. "Why should I? I already knew where you're staying."

"That's what I figured," Nancy replied. "But someone called Mrs. Marvin and soon afterwards a fire was set in the Vetters' laundry room."

Dave gasped. "I think we boys had better get to Los Angeles in a hurry. You need our protection!"

Nancy chuckled. "You may be right."

When the rest of the group heard about her conversation with Dave, they were convinced that the call to Mrs. Marvin had, indeed, been a ploy of the arsonist.

Nancy then got in touch with Señora Mendez. The woman told her that a third ransom note had been mailed to her from Mexico City.

"It told me to leave more money on a bench at an intersection near my home and promised Dolores would be set free after the ransom was paid."

"Did you comply with the request?"

"Yes. This time I hired a private detective, who carried a walkie-talkie so he could communicate with me. He dropped the package at the designated spot and walked away. He hid and kept watch from a distance."

"What happened?" Nancy asked eagerly.

"Nothing," Señora Mendez replied sadly. "No one picked up the money, and Dolores was not brought home. Oh, Nancy, what am I going to do?"

The girl took a deep breath. "Don't lose faith," she said. "I have a strong hunch that everything will turn out all right. Perhaps the kidnappers suspected that you had hired a detective and for that reason did not go through with the exchange. But I'm sure Dolores is fine."

"I hope you're right," Señora Mendez replied.

"I'm trying to keep calm, but my poor daughter is ill with worry."

Then the Mexican woman changed the subject. "I have a message for you, Nancy. I had a phone call from Señor Pedroa. He is the one you went to see about his collection of poisons, isn't he?"

"That's right."

"He said he couldn't reach your dad, so he left a message with me. A man named Ozne has contacted him about selling the rare vial of poison from the fifteenth century."

"Did Señor Pedroa say anything else?" Nancy asked.

"No. But I believe he made an appointment with Señor Ozne, who is to visit him soon."

"Thank you very much for the message," Nancy said. "I'll follow it up, and I'll let you know how we progress."

After she finished talking, Nancy thought about the person who wanted to see Señor Pedroa. Suddenly an idea came to her. She jumped up and hurried to Bess and George.

"Listen to this!" she said. "A man named Ozne has contacted Señor Pedroa about a rare fifteenth-century vial of poison!"

"Ozne?" George asked, raising her eyebrows.

"You know what that means?" Nancy said excitedly.

"No, of course not."

"It's Enzo spelled backwards!"

Bess was startled. "You think he's Enzo Scorpio?"

"I'm sure of it," Nancy replied. "I'll call Señor Pedroa immediately and suggest that when Ozne arrives, he have the police arrest him."

15

The Watermark

Señor Pedroa was amazed by Nancy's theory. "No doubt you are right," he said. "I will do as you suggest and ask the police to be here when Señor Ozne comes with the poison. I am sure that with your description I will recognize him as well as the beautiful gold filigree covering on the vial."

He said good-by but called Nancy back in half an hour. "Everything went as planned," he reported. "Señor Ozne came to me and was apprehended by the police. The vial he was trying to sell me was not the one you described. It was a cheap one, not authentic and had no value!"

Nancy was surprised to hear this. "Are the police holding the man anyway?" she asked.

"Yes. He refuses to talk and they suspect that he is, indeed, Enzo Scorpio who is wanted by the New York authorities. They will investigate. But no one knows what he did with the genuine vial that was stolen from your friend."

When Nancy repeated the conversation to her friends, the three speculated on where the valuable vial was.

"Maybe he lost it," George suggested.

"Or he could have sold it to someone else," Bess added.

"Too bad he won't talk," Nancy said. "But I'm glad he was caught anyway."

"Right," George said. "Now all we have to do is find Dolores and catch the Hoaxters!"

"Speaking of the Hoaxters," Bess said, "I'd like to know why they bother with con games when they're making a hit in the theater."

"It could be greed," Nancy said. "According to Dad there are people who are never satisfied with their money or position. They always want to be richer or greater. Often they'll resort to illegal means to gain their ends."

Bess giggled. "And that, my dear friends, is the lesson of the morning."

The other two laughed and George asked what was next on the detectives' agenda. Nancy told her that she wanted to study their copy of the first ransom note very carefully. She spread it out on a table and the girls went over it again and again.

Nancy always came back to the same conclusion. "The message has to be '$100,000 in sack to 8 by X,'" she said.

"We assumed that 8 stands for the letter H and means Howie," George spoke up. "Could it be that H and X are street names and refer to a certain intersection in Los Angeles?"

"Possibly," Nancy said. "Let me ask Mrs. Vetter if she has a map of the city."

She returned a few minutes later with a map. It was old and torn but usable. Nancy spread it out on the table and the girls looked at the street index.

"Oh, no!" Bess frowned. "Everything from O on is missing, so we can't determine whether there are any street names starting with X."

"Yes, we can," George said. "We'll have to scrutinize every inch of the map, that's all."

Each girl concentrated on part of the map. After a while Bess said, "I'm getting cross-eyed. I really feel sorry for the printer who put this together."

"And we've come up with a blank," George added. "There's no such intersection."

"Wait a minute," Nancy spoke up. "You just gave me an idea, Bess, when you mentioned the word printer. I'm going to call Señora Mendez and ask her to look for a watermark on the original ransom note."

She hurried to the phone and was soon talking to their Mexican friend. "Please hold the paper to a strong light and see if you can make out a name or design," Nancy requested.

"All right. I'll be back in a minute."

Señora Mendez was gone so long, however, that Nancy was afraid the woman had forgotten her. Finally she came back on the line.

"It was difficult to distinguish the watermark on the paper," she said, "but I believe it's a fern leaf."

"Thank you," Nancy said. "This might be a good clue. Let's hope it leads somewhere."

Señora Mendez's voice, which had been strong up to now, wavered. "Nancy," she said, "you are such a dear, and I'm putting a great deal of faith in you."

"I'll try to live up to it," Nancy assured her.

The young sleuth said good-by, then looked through the advertising pages of the telephone book. There was a long list of stationers. She copied it and asked Bess and George to accompany her on a search for the fern marked paper.

The first shopkeeper they interviewed was very obliging. He had never heard of such a watermark but looked in his order catalog. No such design was listed.

"It may have been used some time ago and is no longer being made," he said.

The girls thanked him and left. During the rest of the afternoon they visited one stationery store after another without learning anything. It was not until they inquired at the last one on their list that they had any luck.

The gray-haired manager looked thoughtful, then said, "Yes, I recall one company that used a fern design. But I don't remember the name of it. I'm sorry. Would another type of paper suit your needs?"

"I'm sure it would," Nancy replied, not wishing to reveal the reason for their inquiry. She selected a box of pale blue paper with matching envelopes, and the girls left.

"What are you going to do now?" Bess asked.

"What I always do when I get stuck on a case," Nancy replied. "Call my dad."

The girls returned to the Vetters' and Nancy phoned Mr. Drew.

"More trouble?" he asked.

"Not really," she said. "Before I ask a favor of you, did you find out anything about the Maine hotel and Silk-O-Sheen?"

"Yes, I did," Mr. Drew replied. "The hotel is legitimate. A large stack of prospectuses disappeared, however, as well as orders for stock certificates. Apparently they were stolen."

"I'm convinced of it," Nancy said. "Barker and

his pals got hold of the documents and are trying to peddle them illegally!"

"Right," her father agreed. "The other story about a Silk-O-Sheen fabric is fictitious. There is no such thing."

"So it exists only in the minds of Cadwell and Barker!" Nancy exclaimed.

"That is true. As a matter of fact, you might say it was a complete fabrication."

Nancy laughed. "Dad, did you mean to make that pun?"

"What do you think?"

"I think you fabricated the fabric-ation on purpose!"

Mr. Drew chuckled. "What's the favor you wanted to ask me?"

"I'm trying to find a company that makes paper with a fern watermark. So far I haven't had any luck."

"I'll work on it," her father promised, "and start immediately."

At dinner Mrs. Vetter suggested that the girls take some time off from their case and go to a comedy movie with her and her husband.

"I think that's a great idea," Bess said. "My brain's whirling like the blades of a helicopter."

"Yours could never go that fast," George teased her cousin, and the others laughed.

As soon as the meal was finished, the group set off in Mr. Vetter's big car. Five minutes later Nancy noticed that another automobile was following close behind them. She asked their host if he would mind taking a circuitous route to the theater in case they were being trailed for some sinister reason.

"I'll be glad to," he said. "Is this going to be another detective chase?"

"I hope not," Nancy replied. "But we'll soon find out if the intentions of that other driver are good or bad."

Mr. Vetter turned left, then right a few times. For several blocks the pursuer did not leave them and Nancy was convinced that her enemies were on their trail.

Finally a break came. Mr. Vetter managed to scoot through an intersection just as the light turned red. The car behind them had to stop. By the time it was able to cross the street, Mr. Vetter had turned another corner and was out of sight.

"Oh, I'm so glad to be rid of him!" Bess exclaimed in relief.

"So am I," George added. "I couldn't have kept my mind on the movie, thinking our enemies were after us again, maybe to harm us!"

Mr. Vetter parked in the lot of the large motion picture theater and the group went inside. For two hours their minds focused on the delightful comedy that unraveled on the huge screen. When the show was over, they walked into the lobby, smiles on their faces.

"Didn't you love the detective clown who always consulted his big, long necktie when he picked up a clue?" Bess asked.

The others laughed and George said, "I think he stole the show."

Suddenly Nancy stopped short. Waiting in the long line for the next show were Cadwell and Barker!

"Look over there!" she whispered to her friends. "We must . . . ."

Just then the two con men realized that they had been spotted. Nimbly they stepped out of the line and rushed through the open front door!

16

Hijackers

The girls pushed through the crowd in the lobby, trying to reach the two con men.

"Hey, take it easy, girlie," an annoyed man called out.

"Sorry," Nancy replied and hurried on, brushing past another man.

"What's going on?" he asked. "A fire?"

"Excuse us," said Bess, who was right behind Nancy.

George was elbowing her way through the crowd ahead of the other two. When she reached the door, a guard grabbed her by the arm.

"Look, miss, you're making a nuisance of yourself!" he scolded her.

"We just saw two con men the police are looking for," George replied. "Please let me go! We want to stop them!"

"Who are you?" the guard demanded. "Plain-clothes detectives?"

"In a way," George said, as Nancy and Bess caught up to her. By the time the girls convinced the guard that they were telling the truth and he agreed to let them go, it was too late. Barker and Cadwell were out of sight!

The girls separated and ran down the street a short distance, but it was no use. The con men had vanished. Disappointed, the young detectives met Mr. and Mrs. Vetter in the parking lot and explained why they had hurried away.

"Too bad you lost your suspects," Mr. Vetter remarked. "Perhaps you should report the incident to the police."

Nancy agreed. He drove to headquarters, where the girls gave a full account of what had happened.

"Even though the two con men got away," George added, "we know for sure that they're in Los Angeles."

"Do you think they were the same people who followed you to the movies?" the sergeant on duty asked.

"Probably," Nancy answered. "After they lost us, they might have stopped for dinner and then decided to see the show."

"We'll keep an eye out for them," the sergeant promised.

When the group arrived home, the telephone was ringing. Nancy dashed to answer it and learned Ned Nickerson was calling.

"I've been trying for the past three hours to get you," he said. "Burt, Dave, and I are leaving here tomorrow morning at nine on Continental Flight 388. Will you meet us at the airport in Los Angeles?"

"We sure will," Nancy promised. "It will be wonderful to see you."

Ten minutes before the plane was scheduled to land, the girls arrived at the airport. They found a large group of people near the Continental counter. Everyone seemed to be extremely agitated and worried. Nancy asked what the trouble was.

"Flight 388 has been hijacked!" a woman blurted out.

"Hijacked!" the three girls chorused. "Where? When?"

They were told that very little was known about the holdup at this time. The hijackers, who would not reveal their names, had not given any reason for taking over the plane.

Nancy, Bess, and George were too stunned to talk for a moment. They visualized all sorts of dreadful things happening to their friends.

Suddenly Bess spotted a familiar face among the

crowd. She whispered to the others, "I see one of the Hoaxters—the sleight of hand performer. He's over there!"

Nancy and George were startled. Why was he at the airport? Was he waiting for someone?

Bess had an idea. "Nancy, you were never on stage. Why don't you find out what you can from him?"

"Like what?" Nancy asked.

"Like whom he's expecting on this flight."

Nancy hesitated. "Remember, he recognized George *before* she went on stage. I'm sure he'd recognize me. I'll have to change my appearance a little if I want to talk to him. Bess, may I borrow your scarf?"

"Sure."

Nancy took the scarf and disappeared into a rest room. When she came out, the girl detective had hidden her hair and put on a good deal of makeup, which changed her appearance considerably.

"This is terrific for an instant disguise!" George praised her.

"Let's hope so," Nancy said with a smile.

Casually she walked over to the magician, pretending to be nervous and in need of someone to talk to.

"I'm so worried about a friend who's on board," she said. "I hope he's safe. Do you, too, have a friend or relative on the hijacked plane?"

"Yes, my wife," the man replied. "She was coming here to help me with my work."

Just then a voice sounded over the loudspeaker. "Attention, please! I have good news for people expecting passengers on Continental Flight 388. The hijackers have been overpowered and no one was hurt."

A great cheer went up from the crowd and a voice called out, "Tell us more!"

The announcer, who stood at the airline counter, said that the plane would land in El Paso, Texas, where the hijackers would be turned over to the police.

"It will then refuel and continue nonstop to Los Angeles," he concluded.

The sleight of hand man, like everyone else, looked relieved. He said to Nancy, "The plane won't be here for a while. I'm going to leave and come back later." He hurried away.

To pass the time, the girls walked around the airport, looking at shops and stopping to buy flowers for the Vetters. At last the flight was announced.

"Thank goodness!" said several of the people who had gathered to welcome passengers.

Ten minutes later Bess exclaimed, "I see them! I see the boys!"

The young sleuths rushed forward to greet their friends.

"We're so glad you're safe!" Nancy cried out. "What a frightful experience you must have had!"

Burt said, "It was hair-trigger going for a while. As far as we could learn, the hijackers wanted a free ride to South America. But we never did find out why."

Ned took Nancy's arm. "Now put us to work," he said, grinning.

She laughed. "Oh, there's plenty for you to do." Quickly the girl detective outlined their case and mentioned the sleight of hand man as one of the suspects.

"His wife was aboard your flight," she added.

"Wait a minute," Ned said. "I bet I know who she is. When the hijacking was announced, she acted like a spoiled child. She made all kinds of demands, which, of course, nobody could meet, and insisted that it was extremely important for her to get to Los Angeles and help her actor husband on stage."

"Oh, that's how you found out who she is," Nancy said.

Ned went on, "She became very agitated. No one could quiet her, not even the hijackers, who threatened her."

Dave spoke up. "See that woman with the enormous blond hairdo?"

"Hm-mm, where?" George replied.

"Down there at the last ticket counter."

George strained her neck over the milling crowd. "Oh, yes, now I see her," she said after a moment.

"Well, that's the one!"

"I'll be right back," George declared and darted after the woman. "Are you the wife of one of the Hoaxters?" she blurted out when she caught up to the stranger.

"Yes. Where is he?" the woman asked gruffly.

"He told me that he would be back later. He was here for a long time, then left."

The woman stared at George. "Are you a special friend of his?" she demanded crisply.

George stepped back. "I—"

The woman gave her no chance for a reply. "You must be, or he wouldn't have told you his plans."

"You're wrong," George said quietly.

Her calmness nettled the blond woman. She began to shriek insults at George, gesticulating wildly.

George was so stunned that for a moment she was speechless. Suddenly the woman raised her hand and slapped George hard on one cheek. Before the girl could recover her wits, the stranger hit her again. George did not know what to do. Should she fight back or run away and avoid further embarrassment?

17

A Hoax Exposed

Adroitly George dodged the blows of the irate stranger. The athletic girl had taken lessons in judo and wondered if she should use her skills now. This proved to be unnecessary, however.

"I saw the whole thing!" a guard called out as he rushed up to stop the fight. "Do you wish to bring charges against this woman?"

"I think not," George replied.

"Well, I'll have to report the incident anyway, so if you change your mind later, you can." He turned to the woman. "Your name, please."

"Mrs. Horace Browne," the woman sputtered. "My husband is a magician. He works for a famous group called the Hoaxters!"

"Lady, I don't care whom your husband works

for. It doesn't give you the right to attack people in this airport!"

Mrs. Browne stared at him in suppressed anger. Then she gave George a scorching glance, turned on her heels and walked away.

"Are you all right, miss?" the guard asked George.

"Fine."

"Okay. Then I'll go back to my post."

Nancy, Bess, and the boys had caught up to George and were aghast when they saw her reddened face.

"What happened?" Burt asked.

Quickly George explained, adding, "If that guard hadn't arrived, I would have tried one of my judo tricks on that crazy Mrs. Horace Browne . . . that's her name. So the sleight of hand man's real name is Horace Browne. You were right, Nancy, Ronaldo Jensen is only his stage name."

"That's a good clue for us," Nancy remarked.

"I'm going to have a word with that woman one of these days!" Burt muttered.

"Why did she hit you, George?" Bess asked.

"Because she thought I was her husband's girlfriend!" George replied, making a face. The others laughed.

"What a silly idea!" Bess said in disgust.

After the group had arrived at the Vetters' and were comfortably seated in the living room with little cakes and cups of steaming chocolate, Nancy told the boys about the mystery on which the girls had been working. When Ned, Burt, and Dave heard about the swindle with the temperature-controlled clothing material, they roared with laughter.

Ned remarked, "It's a wonderful idea. Anybody who could invent something like that would become a millionaire."

Nancy looked at him. "How about you? You're majoring in science. Such an invention should be easy for you!"

"Sure," Dave added. "You wouldn't mind making a million, would you?"

"And taking us all on a great trip!" George said. "How many say *aye* to that?"

"*Aye!*" the others shouted at the top of their lungs.

Ned grinned. "Okay," he said. "If I ever make a million on clothing or anything else, I'll take you all to the moon!"

When the hilarity died down, Nancy said, "I have something else to tell you." She briefed the boys on the fern-watermarked stationery.

"If you'll excuse me for a moment, I'll call Dad to see if he has any word for me yet," she added and went to the telephone. Unfortunately, Mr. Drew had not been able to track down the manufacturer. "But I'll keep trying," he promised.

"Fern watermark?" Dave said after she had hung up. "Maybe I can help you. An uncle of mine is in the printing business. He produces bank notes, fine stationery, and all kinds of high-quality paper. Shall I call him and ask if he ever heard of the design?"

"Please do!" Nancy urged.

Dave was on the telephone for some time. When he returned, the young man was smiling. The others were sure he had learned something important.

"I have an answer for you, Nancy," he said. "The Fern Printing Company is a small outfit located in Philadelphia."

"Great!" Nancy exclaimed. "I'll see if I can get the number from Information."

After several unsuccessful attempts, she was told that the firm had no listed number. Disappointed, Nancy gave up.

"Why does a legitimate business firm have an unlisted number?" she asked herself and returned to her friends. They discussed the matter. Finally she said, "I'll call the police and tell them what we know. Perhaps they can find out Fern's private number for us."

It took the Los Angeles police department a while to supply the information, but finally Nancy was told that the firm had problems with their bills and were temporarily using the direct line of the president.

"Thank you," Nancy said, writing down the number. "I'll let you know if I learn anything important."

She hung up, then dialed the number. A woman answered. "Fern Printing Company. May I help you?"

"Yes, I'm interested in a certain type of paper—"

"I'll connect you," the receptionist interrupted. "Just a minute, please."

Nancy's heart was pounding. Was she about to make a great discovery?

A few moments passed, then a man said, "Harrison speaking. Who is this?"

Nancy evaded the question. "I understand that you manufacture fern-watermarked stationery. I haven't been able to find it in the stores here in Los Angeles. Is there someone who could show me a sample sheet of the fern pattern?"

Mr. Harrison paused briefly. "I'm afraid we don't have any in stock right now but I can give you the name of someone who buys from us."

"Oh, that would be wonderful," Nancy replied.

"It's Mr. Horace Browne who lives in Los Angeles."

Nancy's heart began to pound. What an incredible revelation!

"He should be listed in the phone book," Mr. Harrison went on. "But here's his address anyway."

Nancy wrote it down quickly. "Thank you very much," she said. "I'll send you an order as soon as I've seen Mr. Browne's paper."

"Fine. It will be available soon."

Nancy rejoined her friends. "Guess what!" she said. "I found out that Horace Browne is using the fern watermark!"

"That proves the ransom note was written by him!" George exclaimed. "Nancy, what terrific evidence!"

Ned added, "Now all we do is find out his address and confront him with the proof."

"I have the address, too," Nancy said. "All we have to do is look up his number."

George went to get the phone book. But to their dismay, the young people found that Horace Browne was not listed.

"That doesn't surprise me," Ned remarked. "If he's a crook, he'd keep under cover."

"Right," George said. "It wouldn't be wise for us to call and let him know we're coming. He'd be sure to suspect something."

Nancy agreed. "Tomorrow we'll see him personally. It's too late now. Meanwhile, I have another idea. Why don't we go to the Hoaxters' show?" She turned to Ned, her eyes twinkling. "How would you like to do a little detective work at the theater?"

18

Ned's Disguise

Ned smiled at Nancy. "Do you want me to go up on the Hoaxters's stage and pull a few tricks of my own?"

"In a way, yes. When they take your wallet, there'll be a piece of paper in it torn from a small notebook. In the corner will be the Vetters' phone number."

Ned's eyebrows shot up. "What for?"

"As bait. I want to get the fingerprints of the man who rifles through wallets. Afterwards, I'll dust the paper with magnetic powder so the prints will become visible."

Ned whistled, "Smart move! How to get evidence without really trying."

"That's right. Just make sure that the paper is still in your wallet when it's returned to you after the show. It will prove that the Hoaxters are the first link in the criminal chain."

Ned pretended to be puffed up with his assignment. He stuck his fingers into the armholes of his sleeveless sweater and paraded around the room. The others laughed and wished him luck.

George said, "There's only one catch. If Mrs. Browne is on stage, she may recognize you."

Nancy suggested that when they arrived at the performance the boys go in by themselves and find seats on the left of the auditorium, while the girls would sit on the right.

Ned and his fraternity brothers agreed to the plan, and Burt added, "This way we won't be connected with Nancy Drew, the well-known girl detective!"

Nancy smiled but did not reply. She decided that she must telephone Señora Mendez and find out if there had been any further word from the kidnappers. When she heard the phone ringing in the Mendez residence, Nancy had a few seconds of hope that the child might have been returned. But as soon as her Mexican friend answered, the young sleuth knew she was wrong.

"The dear child has not come back to us," Señora Mendez told her, "and we still have no idea where she is."

"Have you or Dolores's parents received any other ransom notes?" Nancy asked.

"Yes, two. But both were fakes."

"What do you mean?" Nancy asked.

Señora Mendez said that money had been requested in both of them. It had been delivered to the specified places, but was never picked up.

"Oh, Nancy, I'm so worried that Dolores may be held for another reason besides money," the child's grandmother wailed. "I was told that certain people steal children and sell them to couples who want to adopt them."

The thought horrified Nancy, but she said calmly, "I doubt that anyone would do this with a girl as old as Dolores. She would be bound to reveal her name and where she came from and would be returned to you."

Señora Mendez said this thought made her feel better. "My private detective picked up one clue that makes it seem almost certain that Dolores is in Los Angeles," she added. "He was so sure of it that he personally called the Los Angeles police and told them his suspicions."

"What was the clue?" Nancy asked eagerly.

"One of the recent ransom notes had been made up from words cut from a newspaper just as before. My detective, who lived in Los Angeles for years, remembers that one of the papers in that city uses a special type of print in its entertainment section that he has never seen anywhere else. He's positive the words were taken from that paper."

"Have you heard from the police?" Nancy inquired.

"No. But I'm worried that the kidnappers may have found out I have a detective working on the case and that he has been in touch with the police. Perhaps that is the reason they haven't returned the child. But why are they sending me fake notes?"

"Maybe they're trying to tell you that they won't play for real as long as you have the detective involved," Nancy replied. "But I suggest that you not let him go just yet. What you told me about the newspaper clue only reinforces my suspicion that Dolores is here in Los Angeles. I'd like to hunt for her a little longer."

"All right, Nancy. But please call me tomorrow and let me know if you've had any success."

After Nancy had reported her findings to the Vetters and her friends, she said, "Tomorrow we'll call on Mr. Browne who buys the fern stationery. Mr. Vetter, where is his home located?"

"It's in an area of very expensive houses with large grounds. Many of them are fenced in. You might have a hard time trying to enter."

"I'll take a chance," Nancy replied with a determined set to her chin.

After dinner that evening the six young people set off to see the Hoaxters' show. The boys walked to the corner and took a bus, while Mr. Vetter lent his car to the girls. When they arrived at the theater, it was filling rapidly. The three detectives did not see their friends.

"We'd better not look for them too hard," George advised. "If there are any spies watching us, they may catch on to our little scheme."

The girls sat down and studied their programs. They were surprised to see that a new act had been added to the performance.

"This is the one where the sleight of hand man works with his wife," Bess whispered.

Soon the show started. The girls had seen it so many times that they were not particularly interested in it until Mr. Browne, alias Ronaldo Jensen, invited members of the audience to come on stage.

George said, "I hope Mrs. Browne doesn't recognize Ned."

He himself had had the same idea. When Ned reached the stage, the girls had a hard time to keep from laughing. He was wearing a mustache and beard!

"Ned must have rented or bought them on the way to the theater," Bess said in a low tone.

Apparently Ned's disguise worked. The woman gave no sign that she had ever seen the young man before. He was relieved of his wallet by the sleight of hand man without his noticing. Then it was held up for those in the audience to see, along with handbags, watches, and jewelry.

As in previous shows the articles were taken away, and their owners told to return after the performance. Later they filed into the back room behind the stage to claim their property.

The girls, meanwhile, had gone to the Vetters' car and were already on their way home. "I hope Ned got his wallet back with the piece of paper intact," Bess said.

"We'll soon find out," Nancy told her.

After the girls arrived at the Vetters', they paced up and down the living room impatiently, waiting for the boys. Finally they walked in.

"I have it!" Ned said jubilantly. "Nancy, bring your magnetic powder!"

Nancy had already brought the small fingerprint kit she carried in her suitcase. Gingerly she removed the paper from Ned's wallet and dusted it. Everyone held his breath. Would fingerprints show up?

19

The Young Prisoner

"The fingerprints are showing up!" George exclaimed.

The young people watched in fascination as the blank white paper revealed the ends of fingers on two hands.

"Are they the left and right hands of the same person?" Bess asked.

No one was sure. This was one thing the police would have to decide.

"Let's go now!" George urged.

"It's too late. We'll have to wait until morning," Nancy said.

After breakfast the following day it was decided that only Nancy and Ned would go to headquar-

ters while the rest of the group helped the Vetters with various chores.

When Nancy showed the fingerprints to the chief in his office, he was impressed. "Excellent work," he complimented her. "I'll have these traced at once. Please wait outside in the lobby. I'll let you know the result as soon as I can."

Almost an hour passed before the couple were summoned back into the chief's office. He smiled at them. "These prints belong to a wanted criminal named Sam Gambro. I'd like you to look at photographs of him and see if you can identify the man."

An enormous book lay open on a side table. The chief explained that it contained mug shots of various people who either were or had been prisoners.

"Gambro is on this page. Can you identify him?"

Nancy gazed for several seconds at the picture under which was the name Sam Gambro. He was heavyset, dark-haired, and jowly.

Finally she shook her head. "As far as I know, I have never seen this man before. So I guess he's not part of the Hoaxters's group. But he could be one of the con men who work with them."

"Possibly," the officer replied. "In order to find out, this is what we'll do. I'll send a couple of detectives to the Hoaxters who, I know, are rehearsing at the theater this morning, and have my men take their fingerprints. The detectives will pose as 'The Committee for the Protection of Entertainment in Los Angeles.'"

Nancy and Ned laughed, then went home. They told the waiting group what the chief was planning to do. All of them listened eagerly for the telephone to ring. Finally it did. Nancy answered.

"Miss Drew? This is the chief calling. The fingerprints our men brought back that belong to the sleight of hand man of the Hoaxters match those of Sam Gambro. This means he and Horace Browne are the same person."

"But Browne doesn't look anything like the man I saw in the photograph!" Nancy exclaimed.

"He must have had plastic surgery and lost a lot of weight," the chief said.

"Will Browne be apprehended?" Nancy asked.

"Yes, indeed. My men are already on their way back to the theater."

When Nancy hung up, George said she was eager to watch the sleight of hand man being arrested. "Let's go to the theater, too," she suggested.

The young detectives crowded into the Vetters' car and drove off. When they arrived at the theater, they met three policemen coming out of the building.

"Where is your prisoner?" Nancy asked them.

With a chagrined look one of the officers replied, "The Hoaxters have skipped out!"

"Again!" George exclaimed.

"Yes. Not only are the performers gone, but so are all their costumes and props. They must have become suspicious when we fingerprinted them under the pretense of being 'The Committee for the Protection of Entertainment in Los Angeles.'"

The other officer spoke up. "We've already alerted all squad cars in the area. I'm sure someone will sight them. They couldn't have gone far yet."

After the officers had driven away, Dave said, "Nancy, what's next on the sleuthing program?"

"We're going to Horace Browne's house," she replied. "Remember, I got his address from the Fern Printing Company."

"Do you think he'll be there?" George asked.

Nancy shrugged. "If he's not, perhaps we can pick up a clue to where he went."

She drove to the part of town in which Browne lived. As Mr. Vetter had told them, it was a residential area with large, attractive homes. Browne's had a high picket fence around it, and the house could barely be seen from the outside. There was an entrance gate, but it was locked. Ned pushed the bell button, but no one answered.

Bess sighed. "What'll we do now?"

"Let's split up and walk around the property," Nancy suggested. "Ned and I will go to the right. The rest of you take the left. Perhaps we can find out if someone's home."

Quickly the young people hurried off. Just inside the fence were high hedges, and it was impossible to look over them. After Nancy had walked around the corner and partway down one side, she said, "Ned, I want to look into the garden. Would you let me climb onto your shoulders so I can peer over the fence?"

Ned bent down. "Go ahead," he said, holding out his interlocked hands for her to step into.

Nancy climbed to his shoulders and balanced herself on the side of the fence. She managed to look over the top and beyond the bushes and had a good view of the garden. On a patio she spotted a man reclining in a lawn chair. He was sound asleep.

Excitedly Nancy leaned down to Ned and whispered, "Sam Gambro, alias Horace Browne, alias Ronaldo Jensen, is sleeping not far away. We must capture him!"

"But how?" Ned asked.

"We'll have to get over the fence. If I jump to the other side, can you make it on your own?"

"Sure. No problem. Go ahead. I'll follow."

Nancy realized that she would have to clear the bushes in order not to scratch herself badly. With determination she stepped to the top of the fence, then pushed off as far as she could. With a soft thud the girl detective landed on the lawn, unhurt.

She looked over her shoulder and saw Ned take

off from the top. He jumped gracefully and in an instant came down next to her.

"Great!" she whispered.

On tiptoes they approached Horace Browne. They were about a hundred feet away, when he suddenly awakened. Turning, he spotted the couple. The next second Browne jumped from his reclining chair and sped toward the house. He vanished through a door and they heard it slam shut and lock.

The couple looked at each other. They had been so near success!

Nancy, however, was not ready to give up. She noticed another door and hurried toward it. Fortunately this one was not locked. She dashed inside with Ned at her heels.

They found themselves at the foot of a stairway. From somewhere above, they heard faint cries for help in Spanish.

"That could be Dolores!" Nancy whispered. "Come on!"

She and Ned rushed up the stairs, but halfway to the second floor, they met Mrs. Browne coming down.

"Get out of here!" she shouted. "You have no right to be in my house. I'll call the police!"

Nancy ignored the demand. She said, "Where's Dolores?"

The woman seemed taken aback. She did not reply. The cries of the child continued. "Let me out! Let me out!"

Ned pushed Mrs. Browne firmly aside, so that Nancy could continue up the stairs. Then he followed. The couple scooted upward faster than the woman could climb. They crossed the second floor hallway and followed the cries for help to the third floor.

"Help! I want to see my mommy!" came another pleading cry.

Ned glanced back to see what Mrs. Browne was doing. She seemed undecided for a moment, then started up after the couple.

At the top of the stairway, there was a narrow hallway with a door opposite the stairs. Quickly Nancy pulled on the knob, and they looked inside.

She and Ned stood appalled at what they saw. A beautiful, dark-haired little girl of nine sat on the edge of a bed, her left ankle chained to one of its front legs!

"Dolores!" Nancy cried out and rushed to the child's side. "We're friends. We came to rescue you. We'll have you out of here in a minute!"

As she hugged the little girl, and Ned sped over to help unclamp the chain, the door was slammed shut and locked. Something heavy was pushed against it.

Ned turned back and tried to open the door. It would not budge. Now not only Dolores but he and Nancy were prisoners also!

Little Dolores became hysterical. Her few moments of joy at having been rescued were gone. She was a prisoner again!

Nancy tried to soothe her and even sang a little Spanish lullaby she knew. Ned, meanwhile, was working at the locked door. Unable to budge it, he rammed his body against the wood, hoping to splinter one of the panels. His efforts were in vain!

Finally he walked over to Nancy and they conferred on what to do. There was a tiny window high up on the wall that opened on hinges. They both knew that though one of them might crawl through it, there was no way to reach the ground safely.

"I wonder what became of Bess, George, Burt, and Dave," Nancy said. "I hope they'll find a way to rescue us!"

Dolores had become quiet now. She sat on Nancy's lap and clung to her. The young detective said, "Suppose you tell me how you got here."

"I stayed in school late to help my teacher," the little girl replied. "When I came out, all my friends had gone. A strange woman walked up to me and said, 'Are you Dolores?' When I said yes, she told me that my mother was ill and had asked her to bring me home in her car."

"So you climbed in?" Nancy asked.

"Yes, in the back seat with the woman. A man was driving. I did not know who these people were. Later I found out they were Mr. and Mrs. Browne. Mrs. Browne offered me a piece of candy."

"Did you eat it?"

Dolores nodded. "Afterwards I became very sleepy. I did not wake up until I found myself lying on the bed in this room." The little girl shivered. "And chained to the foot of it. I heard Mr. Browne say we all flew from Mexico City to Los Angeles."

"That was a dreadful experience," Nancy said. "How were you treated after you got here?"

Dolores said that Mrs. Browne and another woman had taken turns looking after her. "They brought me meals and helped me take a bath. They even washed my clothes. I kept asking them when I was going home. One day Mrs. Browne got mad at me and said, 'You're not going anywhere until your rich grandmother pays us a lot of money!'"

Nancy translated what she had learned into English for Ned, who understood some Spanish, but not as much as Nancy did.

He remarked, "That candy must have contained something to put the child to sleep."

Nancy agreed. "This way they could bring her to Los Angeles without any trouble."

As she and Ned were trying to figure out how to escape, their four friends were on the way to help them. While looking over the fence and bushes, they had seen the couple approach the sleeping man in the lawn chair and had witnessed his dash into the house.

They realized that Nancy and Ned were following him, so they, too, climbed over the fence. Just before they reached the mansion, Mr. and Mrs. Browne ran out the front door carrying suitcases.

"They're escaping!" Dave exclaimed.

When Nancy and Ned did not appear, the young people became worried about them. Were they prisoners in the house?

20

Escape!

"Hold it!" Dave commanded as the young detectives surrounded the fleeing couple.

"Get out of our way!" Mr. Browne hissed, lashing out violently.

Fists were flying for a few moments but soon the magician and his wife were subdued and led into the house again. Bess went to phone the police. Meanwhile, in the hallway, Horace Browne managed to tear himself loose and began to fight with renewed vigor. The boys realized he had some knowledge of judo. George's skills, however, matched his. She and the boys, who were steeled by years of football practice, soon had the belligerent couple under control again.

In the rear of the hall George noticed a closet with a key in the lock and suggested they secure their prisoners inside until the police arrived. Angrily the Brownes yelled and banged on the door. After a while, however, their cries subsided and they became quiet, resigning themselves to their fate.

"I hope that magician won't use any of his tricks and get out," Bess remarked.

Nancy and Ned had heard the commotion downstairs and started to pound loudly on the door of their attic prison.

"Listen!" George said. "Someone's up there. Probably Nancy and Ned!"

She and her companions were about to hurry to the third floor when a police car drove up to the house. Three officers rushed through the open door. They were the same men who had tried to arrest the Hoaxters at the theater, only to learn they had moved out.

Quickly the young people told them about their prisoners. "One is Sam Gambro, alias Horace Browne, alias Ronaldo Jensen, the magician. The other is his wife who works with him," George explained.

"Good work!" one of the officers, named Young, said admiringly. "We caught Browne's colleagues on their way out of town, but they wouldn't tell us where he was. I'm glad you found him!"

Again there was banging from the third floor as Nancy and Ned tried to make themselves heard.

"What's going on?" Officer Young asked, alarmed. "Who else is here?"

"I believe Nancy and Ned are locked up somewhere," George said. "We saw them follow Mr. Gambro into the house before we caught him."

The four amateur detectives dashed up the stairs with Officer Young and one of his partners. They found that a large chest had been pushed in front of the attic door. Quickly they shoved it aside, then raised the bolt.

Bess opened the door and everyone stopped short in utter amazement, staring at Nancy, Ned, and the little girl.

"Meet Dolores," Nancy said with a smile of relief on her face.

As the others exchanged stories, Bess cried out, "Oh, you poor child!" She knelt and hugged the little girl, who up to now had been clinging to Nancy.

In Spanish, Nancy explained to Dolores that the newcomers were their friends.

"You mean now I can go home to my mommy?" the little girl cried out.

"Yes," Nancy replied. "The police will arrest the bad people who brought you here."

Dolores was ecstatic. "Please, may I call my mommy and daddy on the telephone?"

"Indeed you may," Nancy replied.

The group hurried downstairs and in a few minutes Dolores's parents were on the line. Their daughter talked and threw kisses into the phone, promising she would be home soon.

Then she turned to Nancy. "And now I want to speak to my grandmother." Nancy put in the call, and there was a happy, excited conversation in Spanish between Dolores and Señora Mendez.

Meanwhile, Officer Young had unlocked the closet on the first floor, let out the two prisoners, and snapped handcuffs on them.

"Before you take the Gambros away, may I ask them a few questions?" Nancy requested.

At this the couple winced and the magician said, "You know?"

"Yes," the young detective replied.

"Ask them all you want to," Officer Young said, "but let me read them their rights first."

When he finished, Nancy looked straight at the sleight of hand man. "Was it one of your con men who swindled our friend Mrs. Annabella Richards out of $3000 for a phony world trip?"

Gambro scowled. "I'm telling you nothing!"

"I think you should," his wife spoke up. "Officer, won't it be better for us if we cooperate?"

"I can't promise you anything, but I'll put in a good word for you if you make our investigation easier," Young replied.

Gambro hung his head. He realized that the game was up and shrugged. "It was Howie Barker. He pretended to be a travel agent named Henry Clark."

"And who waylaid Roscoe and stole Mrs. Richards's limousine?" Bess inquired.

"Howie and Lefty Cadwell. I told them that was a stupid thing to do. They had trouble getting rid of the car and finally put it in my garage," Gambro replied.

George asked, "When I came on stage at your show in New York, why wouldn't you let me stay?"

"After Howie tried to sell your friend space in the Maine hotel, he told me you were staying with Miss Eloise Drew. I'd read about Nancy Drew and became suspicious. Somehow Howie found out you knew Mrs. Richards. I called her housekeeper and she confirmed that you girls were detectives."

"Who rammed our taxi in New York when we left my aunt's apartment?" Nancy questioned.

"One of my co-workers," the sleight of hand man admitted. "He was supposed to keep an eye on the place and scare you enough so you'd go back home. Unfortunately, he didn't do a good job."

"You also had people watch us in Los Angeles at the Vetter home!" George accused Gambro. "Once a car followed us but we outmaneuvered it. And one of your men set a fire in the Vetters' laundry wing!"

Gambro nodded. "Too bad I had such inefficient associates," he grumbled. "Their attempts to frighten you off the case always failed!"

Bess spoke up. "Why didn't you return Dolores after the first ransom was paid?"

The prisoner scowled. "That was my wife's idea. She thought we could get more money out of Señora Mendez. Instead, we got into heaps of trouble!" He sent his wife a searing glance.

She retorted, "We wouldn't have if your man in Mexico City had collected the second ransom so we could leave Los Angeles as planned!"

"How could he? Señora Mendez had the cops on him!"

"I know there was a hidden message in the ransom note," Nancy spoke up. "'$100,000 in sack to 8 by X.' What did it mean and whom was it for?"

"It was for our Mexican contact who collected the money. He was to deliver the sack to Howie Barker on the 24th of this month."

"That was yesterday," George pointed out. "Did Barker get the ransom money?"

Gambro suddenly realized that besides going to

prison he would also lose his share of the ransom. He became sulky.

"Why should I tell you any more?" he growled. "I've confessed too much already."

Further questioning netted no more information, so two of the police officers took their prisoners to headquarters. Officer Young remained behind.

Nancy asked him, "Would it be possible for us to search the house? Perhaps the $100,000 is hidden here."

Young smiled. "You're in luck. When we found out that the Hoaxters had left the theater, we obtained a warrant to look for clues in any suspicious places. We haven't used it yet."

"Terrific!" Nancy said. "Let's split up and search every inch of this house."

The young people and the police officer examined each room and scrutinized all the furniture. At one point George cried out, "Come here, everybody! I've found the stolen vial of poison!"

The others stared at it in amazement. Bess exclaimed, "This is definitely the one Enzo Scorpio stole from Mrs. Richards!"

"You're right," Nancy agreed. "I recognize the filigree."

George added, "Enzo must have sold it to Sam Gambro, then tried to palm off a cheap imitation on Señor Pedroa! Well, I'm glad Enzo is in prison, and Mrs. Richards will be happy to get her vial back."

The search went on with renewed interest. Ned found a letter indicating that the two con men, Howie Barker, alias Ralph Rafferty, alias Henry Clark, and Lefty Cadwell were staying at a hotel in San Francisco. The letter also revealed that the name of the ransom collector in Mexico City was Alfredo Scorpio. He was the father of Enzo and a cousin of Gambro.

"Now I get it!" George cried out. "Enzo got in touch with Gambro and sold him the poison!"

The officer agreed. "I'll relay this information to headquarters at once!"

While he was busy, the young people completed their search. Nothing more turned up, and the hiding place of the ransom money remained a mystery.

Nancy suggested that they leave and take Dolores to the Vetters. On their way out, she had an idea.

"Let's take a look at Mrs. Richards's limousine which is supposedly in Gambro's garage," she suggested.

Officer Young locked the front door and everyone went to the garage. Mrs. Richards's car was there, with the keys under the floor mat. The group searched it quickly and Nancy asked Ned to open the trunk. There was nothing inside except the spare tire. Ned lifted it out. A sack lay underneath!

Excitedly Nancy pulled the drawstring. Bundles of money fell out!

"The ransom!" she exclaimed. "Dolores, we've found your grandmother's money!"

The little girl clapped her hands and Nancy scooped Dolores up in her arms. Everyone was overjoyed to have recovered the $100,000, which was quickly counted. All of it was there.

Officer Young asked, "Will you give me a ride to headquarters? I'm sure the chief will be surprised when I walk in with all this money!"

When Nancy and her friends arrived at the Vetters' house, the couple, who spoke Spanish, immediately made little Dolores feel welcome. Everyone played games with her and much to the child's delight a meal was served consisting partly of Mexican dishes.

While they were eating, Dave asked, "Nancy, have you thought of a name for this mystery?"

The girl detective was silent for a few moments, then replied, "Yes. I'll call it *The Triple Hoax*. The first one that the Hoaxters pulled was to defraud Mrs. Richards. The second one was to kidnap Dolores."

"And the third?" Ned asked, puzzled.

Nancy grinned. "You perpetrated the third hoax when you went up on stage at the show and permitted your wallet to be taken. From the paper inside we obtained the fingerprints of the sleight of hand man which wound up the case."

Secretly Nancy wondered if she would ever have another case to work on. But a new one, called *The Flying Saucer Mystery*, was soon to come her way.

That evening, Nancy received a surprise telephone call from the chairman of the convention of U.S. detectives.

"We understand that you and your friends are amateur sleuths," he said. "We would like you to attend our banquet tomorrow evening."

The young people were delighted with the invitation. "We have a little girl with us," Nancy said. "Will it be all right to bring her along?"

"Indeed it will," the chairman replied. "We'll expect you all at seven o'clock."

The next day Nancy, George, and Bess bought Dolores a complete new party outfit. At six thirty the group took a limousine taxi to the banquet hall.

The headwaiter checked the visitors' names at the door, then led them through a maze of tables. Finally he pointed to where Nancy and her friends were to sit. They stopped short in amazement.

A large group was gathered at the table, including Mr. Drew, Hannah Gruen, Aunt Eloise, Mrs. Richards, the Vetters, Señora Mendez, and a couple who were introduced as Dolores's parents. "Surprise!" they cried as the little girl rushed to her family.

Nancy's face wore a broad grin. "How wonderful!" she said. "Who arranged this get-together?"

Her father said the chairman had learned from the police that Nancy and her friends had done a fine job solving the mystery, and the detectives wanted to show their admiration.

During dinner, everyone chatted gaily. Mr. Drew said that the two checks sent to the suspicious mail order houses had bounced as expected.

"Those companies were phony and their officers have been arrested. They were part of the widespread Hoaxter outfit."

When the meal was over, the chairman stood up and gave a speech that made Nancy blush. He described the young sleuths' work in uncovering the illegal schemes of the Hoaxters and the con men, all of whom had been apprehended. Then he mentioned the missing vial of poison that had been recovered and the arrest of Enzo Scorpio and his father, Alfredo.

Finally he asked Dolores to stand up. He told the audience how she had been kidnapped and that

Nancy Drew, with the help of Bess, George, and their friends from Emerson College, had found the child and restored Dolores to her family.

"Nancy, we detectives want you to have something to show not only our admiration but our thanks for such a wonderful job," he declared and reached down alongside his chair. He pulled up a framed award stating exactly what the girl detective had done.

"How marvelous! Thank you!" she exclaimed.

As he presented it to her, there was loud applause, a standing ovation, and wild cheering from Nancy's many admirers.

THE FLYING SAUCER MYSTERY

The Flying Saucer Mystery was first published
in the UK in a single volume in 1981 by
William Collins Sons & Co. Ltd.

1

A Spooked Horse

"Good-bye! Good luck! And be careful, Nancy. This new mystery you want to solve sounds dangerous!"

The words of farewell were spoken by Mrs. Hannah Gruen, the Drews' housekeeper. She kissed the eighteen-year-old, titian-blond girl and hugged her affectionately.

"I'll be *very* careful," Nancy promised, adding lightly, "Has anyone got the best of your favorite detective yet?"

"No, but there's always a first time!" Hannah replied as Nancy jumped into her father's car.

Without further discussion, Carson Drew, a distinguished lawyer, headed for the River Heights airport. As they pulled up to the terminal, two girls stepped out of a sedan.

"Bess and George!" Nancy exclaimed.

Bess Marvin and George Fayne were cousins and were Nancy's closest friends. The three girls, who were going on a camping trip in the Shawniegunk Forest, now set their large backpacks and sleeping bags on the sidewalk in front of the terminal entrance. Mr. Drew and Mrs. Fayne said they would park their cars and come back to see the girls off.

"I had to leave so much at home!" complained Bess. She was Nancy's age and pretty—but slightly plump.

"Well, I brought lots of rain gear and not much else." George giggled. She was an attractive slim brunette. "If it doesn't rain, I'll be out of luck!"

"If it does"—Bess frowned—"I'll be wetter than a guppy."

"You mean a whale!" George laughed.

"Thanks a lot, George!" her cousin replied, narrowing her eyes.

That was Nancy's signal to lead the way to the ticket counter where the girls' camping equipment was weighed and checked in. They each picked up a ticket and seat assignment, and walked to the departure gate.

Mrs. Fayne and Mr. Drew arrived just a few minutes before takeoff. As the boarding announcement was made, Mr. Drew kissed Nancy. "I hope you solve the mystery, honey," he said as a twinkle came into his eyes. "But be on the lookout for strange creatures in the forest!"

Bess shuddered. "What do you mean, Mr. Drew?"

Nancy's father refused to explain further. "You'd better hurry, or you'll miss your plane."

The girls scooted quickly through the check-in area and soon were seated side by side in the plane.

"I had no idea this trip would be dangerous," Bess said. "I thought it was going to be fun."

"It should be," Nancy replied. "After all, I did promise you a mystery, and isn't solving mysteries fun? I'll tell you more about this one when we join the boys."

The trip had been arranged by Mr. Drew. At his suggestion, the girls had asked their boyfriends to meet them in a little town at the foot of the wooded Shawniegunk Mountain where the small plane would land. Jan and Hal Drake, their guides, were to be there also.

During the two-hour flight, the three teenagers hardly spoke to one another. Each was wondering what lay ahead. Bess and George knew there was bound to be danger—as well as a thrilling adventure—on a trip with Nancy.

By the time the plane landed, the boys were already there. Tall, athletic Ned Nickerson was

Nancy's boyfriend. Burt Eddleton, a short, husky blond, was George's friend, and Bess's special companion was blond, green-eyed Dave Evans.

The boys introduced the Drakes, an attractive couple who had lived in the area since their marriage a few years before.

"I'm sure all of you are going to have as much fun here as we do," said Jan, a vivacious blond with streaks of gray in her hair. "We love to camp out and ride through this magnificent forest."

"Sounds wonderful," Nancy replied. "Is everything set for go?"

Hal smiled. "At your service. Follow me."

The young people picked up their backpacks and sleeping bags and followed Jan and Hal to a long shed where several horses were tied up.

"Here's your means of transportation," said Hal. He was a tall, slender man with a ruddy complexion and a firm jaw. His mouth turned up at the corners in an engaging grin.

"Oh, how marvelous!" George exclaimed, dropping her things in a heap and admiring the line of horses. She patted and spoke to each one while Hal and the others conferred over which animals they ought to use.

"What's the name of my horse?" Nancy asked, as she mounted easily.

"Susan B," Hal told her as she leaned forward to hug the beautiful, young bay mare.

"You and I are going to solve a big mystery!" she whispered to Susan B.

Ned mounted his horse and rode alongside Nancy, saying, "This is Goalpost. Appropriate?"

"Appropriate, but I don't believe it." Nancy smiled. "Somebody must've known the captain of Emerson College's football team was coming. Even so, I'm sure you're not going to find any goalposts in the forest."

"But I can run for a touchdown!" Ned quipped. "The solution to the mystery may be right there."

Within minutes the string of riders and horses started off. It was not long before they came to the forest and followed Jan up a steep trail.

They had ridden about an hour when the stony path led them to a pleasant spot by a mountain brook.

"Oh, doesn't it smell wonderful here?" Bess said, breathing in the pine scent. "And look at all the wild flowers."

Sweet-smelling woodbine was entwined around stately trees and white flowers peeked through ground shrubbery.

Jan signaled for the procession to halt. The riders dismounted, allowing the horses to rest while Jan unloaded a sack of picnic food from one of the two packhorses.

Before letting the horses graze, Hal and the boys led them to the brook for a refreshing drink. After tethering two of the horses, everyone sat down on the ground to enjoy a variety of sandwiches, as well as tomato juice and nutcake.

"Now, Nancy, let's hear about the mystery we're going to solve," Ned suggested, after tasting a ham sandwich.

Nancy leaned forward and spoke softly. "Dad received word—secretly of course—that several people in the vicinity of Shawniegunk Mountain had seen a UFO come down and disappear. Some of them even hunted for it."

"Was it from outer space?" Bess quivered.

"Everyone thought so," Nancy said, causing her friend's look of alarm to change to fright.

"Didn't they notify the authorities?" Burt asked.

Nancy shook her head. "Apparently not. They were afraid of being laughed at. Anyway, they failed to find the UFO. Nevertheless, they were sure it had landed. There was a similar rumor about ten years ago, but nothing came of it."

"And we're supposed to find this flying saucer?" George inquired.

"Yes, we are," Nancy replied. "Not only find it but try to learn something about the craft and where it came from."

Dave grunted. "That sounds like a big order."

"But a real challenge," Ned added.

The words were scarcely out of his mouth when

Bess screamed loudly and jumped to her feet.

"What's the matter?" George asked her cousin.

Too frightened to answer, Bess merely pointed. A snake was wriggling away from her!

Hal ran to see if the snake was poisonous. He called back, "It won't hurt us."

Bess was still shaking. "It cr-crawled r-right across my b-boot!" she stammered. "I thought snakes didn't like people. I thought they stayed away from them!"

"That's usually true," Hal agreed. "But even snakes have an appetite for good home cooking."

"So you scared off your soul mate!" George teased.

Ignoring the remark, Bess declared that from now on she was going to eat standing up. "And I plan to walk around a lot, too."

Her friends laughed.

As Bess spoke, her eyes fastened on the slithering reptile. It was crawling toward the horses.

"The snake's going for my horse!" George gasped. "I must stop it!"

Before she could, however, the snake paused in back of the animal, then slowly wriggled up her rear leg. Instantly it spooked the horse, causing him to throw off the snake and run off at breakneck speed into the dense forest.

"Oh!" George exclaimed. "Burt, come quickly!"

Together they raced after the galloping horse but could not catch it. Meanwhile, the rest of the riders were trying to calm the other agitated animals and keep them from bolting, too. Ned and Dave offered to take their horses and go after the runaway.

Nancy clung to her horse's bridle and talked gently to the mare. She was having trouble with Susan B, who appeared to be terrified. Finally the horse settled down.

Burt was shamefaced. "It was so stupid of me not to tie the runaway horse when she finished drinking in the stream."

"She's so gentle and obedient," George remarked quietly, almost unaware of Burt's arm around her shoulder. "I hope she comes back."

Jan and Hal tried to comfort the distraught girl, too. "Horses hate snakes," Hal said, "and with a scare like that, yours would have pulled free anyway."

"What would you do if a snake crawled up your leg?" Jan added.

This made George and the others smile. "I think we'd all run!" she said.

While the campers waited for the two boys to return, they packed up, ready to move on. In twenty minutes Ned and Dave reappeared, leading George's mount. Excitedly, the girl ran to her horse and got astride.

Once more the group was on the move. Jan led them higher and higher up the mountain.

At one point Bess remarked, "I'll bet the view from here would be gorgeous if we could see through the trees."

Jan agreed and said that before dark they would reach an area where they could see for miles. "Hal and I think someone camped at the spot for quite some time, even cleared a little section of the forest and grew a vegetable garden. In any case, it will be a good place for us to camp."

When the riders arrived at their destination, Jan suggested, "Why doesn't everyone unpack for the night? I'll start cooking supper."

"May I help?" Bess asked eagerly.

"If you like," Jan said, removing a sack from one of the packhorses.

A few minutes later she cried out, "Oh, we left our cooking utensils at the picnic spot! How could I have been so forgetful and left one of the sacks on the ground?"

Nancy offered to go back.

"Not alone," Jan answered quickly. "I'll tell you what: we'll draw lots. I'll get four sticks and mark one, then we'll choose by couples. Whoever gets the marked stick will go."

Nancy was delighted when she and Ned drew the lucky stick. Instantly she mounted Susan B and Ned mounted Goalpost, and they set off down the narrow trail. The trip, Jan and Hal figured, would take at least an hour.

When two hours had gone by and it was dark, the riders still had not returned. Everyone was worried.

"Nancy and Ned are good horsemen," Bess said, "but lots of things could have happened."

A little while later Jan lay down and put her ear to the ground. "I hear horses coming," she called out.

As she stood up, the campers were startled by eerie screams in the distance.

2

The Wildcat

The campers froze with fear when they heard the screams in the quiet forest.

Bess cried out frantically, "Nancy and Ned must have been attacked by a wild animal! Oh, what'll we do?"

"We must find them!" George shouted.

"I'm sure," said Hal, "those screams were coming from the north."

"I'd say just the opposite," George countered. "What do you think, Burt?"

"West," he answered, "and Dave thinks east."

Everyone felt helpless. Finally Jan spoke up. "I believe those screams were from a wildcat. I've heard similar ones before."

Bess was even more terrified. "Oh, Nancy and Ned may have been clawed to pieces!" she exclaimed.

George looked severely at her cousin. "Don't say such things!" she flashed back. "Let's hope Nancy and Ned are nowhere near a wildcat."

As a matter of fact the couple was not far from the menacing cat. They had found the missing bag of kitchen utensils, fastened it to Ned's saddle, and started back to camp. Unfortunately, they had taken the wrong branch of a trail which led them away from their destination. Unaware of their mistake at first, they kept riding. Finally, however, the sun set and as darkness came on, the two riders stopped and looked at each other.

"Are you thinking the same thing I am?" Nancy asked. "We're lost!"

"I'm afraid you're right," Ned conceded. "We'd better turn around and head for the other trail."

Susan B and Goalpost started off in the opposite direction. A few feet before they reached the fork, Nancy caught sight of two glowing eyes and the shadowy outline of an animal on a branch of a pine tree.

"Ned!" she called. "Look up there! Some creature is watching us!"

As the boy gazed upward, the animal hissed, then broke the stillness with an unearthly scream. Chills went up and down the riders' spines. The frightened horses reared and whinnied.

"We'd better run for it," Ned suggested, urging Goalpost to go fast. "It's a wildcat!"

The gleaming eyes in the tree fascinated Nancy. As she rode past the cat, she wondered if the beast would spring at her and Susan B. Nancy's heart pounded.

Suddenly she and Ned were startled by the sound of a sharp whistle followed by the soothing voice of a man.

"Now, Kitty, behave yourself!" he said coaxingly. "Stop trying to scare folks!"

At once the glowing eyes sank back. Evidently the animal had jumped out of the tree and disappeared into the dark forest.

"Who's there?" Ned called, as he and Nancy stopped.

"Old Joe," came the reply.

A light was shone in the riders' direction. A couple of minutes later a tall, slender man of about seventy appeared. His hair was gray and he had a beard that was as unkempt as his clothes. Was he one of the "strange creatures" her father had warned her about? Nancy wondered.

The man's friendly smile, however, and his kindly blue eyes made her dismiss the idea.

"Howdy!" he greeted the couple. "What are you

folks doing riding around in the dark? You're strangers here, aren't you?"

Quickly Nancy explained, then introduced herself and Ned. "We're camping with a group of friends a little way up the trail."

Ned added, "You called yourself Old Joe. Will you tell us what your full name is? And do you live around here?"

"My full name is Joseph Austin. Folks in the village gave me the nickname of Old Joe. I kind of liked it, so I kept it. I rarely use my last name."

"By the way, many thanks for scaring off that hissing creature," Nancy said. "What was it? A wildcat?"

"Yes."

"We were sure he was going to attack us."

"Oh, Kitty, as I call her, wouldn't attack unless something bothered her."

"Well, she sure wasn't friendly to us," Nancy grumbled.

Old Joe laughed. "Oh, it had nothing to do with you directly. I have a dog, Trixie. She was teasing Kitty. I suspected that, and came up here to see what was going on. Then I heard Kitty scream, and hurried. I must say it was a surprise to meet you folks."

"You mentioned a dog," Ned said.

"Oh, Trixie is too smart to let Kitty get the jump on

her," Old Joe replied. "She likes to tease Kitty but when the wildcat gets enough of it, she hisses and spits at the dog, even screams sometimes. Kitty and I have known each other for a long time. In fact she was just a kitten when we first became acquainted. Her mother must have abandoned her and she kind of brought herself up. I leave food out for her up near my cabin. It's some distance from here. You must come and visit me there."

Old Joe explained that he was a naturalist by preference. "I was in business once in the city but I didn't like it. As soon as I made enough money to retire I came up here where I used to spend my summers as a boy.

"Now all I do is study the behavior of wild animals toward man. Most won't attack unless they're extremely hungry, or are protecting their young, or are frightened or threatened by a human being or another animal.

"Of course, this doesn't apply to tigers," the naturalist added. "They'll attack for no reason at all."

Nancy remarked, "Wildcats and tigers are related, though, aren't they?"

"They're distant cousins. I'm glad there aren't any tigers in the United States. You know," he went on, "so far as is known, man is not the natural source of food supply for any other creature. I believe that man's worst enemy is man himself."

Nancy and Ned liked the elderly gentleman more

and more. He was not only a naturalist but a philosopher as well.

"We're heading for our camp," Nancy said. "Wouldn't you like to ride along and meet our friends?"

Old Joe chuckled. "I'd like that very much, but to tell you the truth, I prefer walking."

He and the riders followed the trail which Nancy and Ned had missed, and shortly they arrived at the camp.

"Oh, thank goodness, you're all right!" Bess said, hugging Nancy.

Everyone was overjoyed to see that she and Ned and the horses were safe. They also were delighted to meet Old Joe, who captured their hearts immediately with his quiet sense of humor and evident love of nature.

The campers had built a fire and now they all sat around it, listening to the comforting crackle, while supper was served to the latecomers.

"I don't buy much food from the store," Old Joe said. "I get practically everything I eat from in the woods."

Bess's eyes opened wide. "You mean you might eat wildcat meat?"

The man's eyes twinkled. "No, but I do catch rabbits and groundhogs. One of the best dishes you'd ever want to eat is groundhog stew."

That did not sound appealing to Bess, but she kept

silent. Old Joe said there was good fishing in the mountain streams and all sorts of delicious berries and plants.

"One of my favorite dishes is stewed wild rose leaves."

Although Bess knew she was being teased, the plumpish girl decided that if she ate some of this natural food, the scale might reflect the benefits. She was always making promises to herself to modify her eating habits, but never actually followed through.

The rest of the campers were more interested in hearing about Old Joe's adventures in the forest. He entertained them with wildlife stories including one about his rescue of a bear cub.

"Got himself caught in somebody's makeshift trap. I set him free but you know what? He followed me home! Craziest bear I ever met. Well, I figured he was hungry so I fed him and told him to scat. But next morning he was scratching at the door just like a puppy."

"Does he still live with you?" Bess asked in amazement.

"Oh, no. He only stayed with me until he was old enough to go out into the forest and forage for himself. Never did see that bear again, so I imagine he survived on his own."

Now the elderly man stood up and said he must

get back to his cabin. "I expect all of you to come over and visit me. My little cabin and everything in it is handmade," he remarked. "I'm rather proud of my accomplishments and I'd like you to see them. You've shared your food with me, so now it's my turn to feed you."

The campers thanked Old Joe for the invitation, then said good night. Suddenly George stopped him and asked, "Have you ever seen a flying saucer around here?"

The campers waited breathlessly for an answer.

3

Mountain Mishap

Old Joe looked at the group, startled. "You've heard about the flying saucer?" he asked in surprise. "I thought only a few natives knew about that."

Nancy told the naturalist that a client of her father's had contacted him and divulged the secret. "Dad is a lawyer. He said people around here who knew about the flying saucer were afraid to report it for fear of being laughed at."

Old Joe smiled. "I think that's partially true. As for myself, I never could be sure whether it was a real unidentified flying object from outer space or some government experimental aircraft."

"Then you've seen it?" Ned asked.

The naturalist said indeed he had. "The saucer usually appears at night and has very bright lights. I've seen only white lights, but some folks say at times they're red, other times green, and even yellow.

"One man reported seeing the whole saucer turn bright red. It looked as if it were ready to burn up, but the thing flew away and disappeared."

Old Joe's listeners were intrigued by the strange story. All of them hoped that the mysterious flying saucer would return soon so they, too, might see it.

Dave asked, "Do the people who have seen it think there are human beings aboard?"

The naturalist smiled and shrugged. "Nobody's ever seen anyone come out. But I'd say one thing. If humans are aboard, they must be the best pilots in the whole universe."

Burt added with a chuckle, "And they're flying a super craft."

Old Joe said he really had to leave. Again he invited the group to come to his log cabin. "I'll show you some crude drawings I made of the flying saucer."

"That's great!" George remarked. "It's too bad you didn't take any photographs of it."

The naturalist said that some of the local people had tried to, but their high-speed cameras had been unable to capture anything but a blur.

"That's strange," Nancy remarked under her breath.

"I'll give you directions to my place," Old Joe said. He asked for paper and pencil, and drew a map of trails to his cabin. When he finished the zigzagging line, he looked squarely at Nancy. "I have a mystery of my own that I'd like you to solve," he said. "I'll tell you about it when you come to see me."

Intrigued by the prospect of another mystery, Nancy wondered what it might be, but Old Joe gave no hints. The campers decided they would call on him the next morning, and the naturalist was delighted.

After he had gone, Nancy thought excitedly, maybe Old Joe's mystery concerns his cabin. He did make a point of telling us that everything in it is handmade.

The following morning the campers packed up their belongings. Jan made sure this time that nothing was left behind.

"All set!" she called at last.

Everyone mounted a horse. Hal rode in front, carrying Old Joe's map. It led them onto a narrow side trail which apparently was a dry brook that became a torrent of water when there were cloudbursts or melting snow. Now the path was filled with small stones.

The riders had not gone far when Ned, who was following Nancy, suddenly cried out, "Goalpost has gone lame!"

At once, Nancy reined in Susan B and dismounted quickly to examine Goalpost's hooves.

"There's a stone wedged in this one," Nancy said, as she carefully lifted Goalpost's right foreleg.

She hurried back to her horse, opened the saddlebag, and took out a hoof pick. With Ned's assistance, she managed to dislodge the stone.

She patted the horse's nose and gave him a little hug, saying, "Now do you feel better, you nice old thing?"

Ned smiled. "Thanks for your help, Nancy." He, too, patted the animal.

By this time their friends were out of sight. When Nancy and Ned caught up with them, the group had stopped to discuss what they should do next.

"The forest is becoming more and more impenetrable," Hal announced. "It's impossible for the packhorses to get through because the trees are so close together. I suggest we tie them here and go on to Old Joe's without them. I'll check our walkie-talkies in case we get split up."

He examined the compact radiotelephones that were being carried in his and Jan's saddlebags. "They're okay," Hal said a few minutes later. "Let's go on. If any place is too narrow to pass through, pull your legs, saddlebags, and stirrups to the back of your horse."

Bess called out from the rear of the line, "Where are we going? I don't see the trail anymore."

"That's true," Hal replied somberly. "From here on it seems to be just a series of deer tracks. Let's hope they'll lead us right to Old Joe's cabin."

Ten minutes later George, who was riding directly behind Hal, pointed ahead. "Now what do we do?" she inquired.

As the others drew near, they could see an enormous fallen tree trunk blocking their path. Its diameter was higher than the backs of their horses.

"What a monster!" Dave exclaimed. "I wonder how tall the tree was."

The group dismounted, tied the horses, and spread out along the giant trunk.

Ned remarked, "My guess is that this oak must be over fifty feet long."

Bess stood back to admire it, saying, "What a gorgeous tree it must have been when it stood. How old do you think it is?"

"Anybody know how to read tree rings?" Ned asked.

Jan made her way to the end of the trunk where it had broken off. Unfortunately the tree had splintered apart and the rings could not be read accurately.

"Sorry," she said. "Probably Old Joe can tell us because it looks as though the tree trunk has been lying here a long time."

"One thing is certain," Hal added. "It wasn't sawed down. The tree fell either because it was diseased or because it was struck by lightning."

Burt had walked to the other end of the tree and announced that it would be impossible to get through the limbs and branches without a lot of hacking.

"We must have taken a wrong turn," the boy said. "If Jan's right, then I doubt Old Joe would have sent us this way."

Jan consulted the hand-drawn map. "Let's climb over and go the rest of the way on foot," she suggested.

"Yes, let's," Bess agreed. "We've been riding for hours and I'm starved. I bet Old Joe will have a good lunch for us."

Her cousin George teased, "I hope you'll like the menu. Remember, he lives on goodies from the forest. You'll probably have a broiled bullfrog, tasty worm salad, and for dessert, persimmons to pucker your tongue."

Everyone except Bess laughed. She made a face. Now the campers scrambled up the trunk and sat astride it the best they could.

To their dismay the group discovered they were

at the precarious edge of a steep decline at the foot of which there was a rushing stream filled with rocks, some of them large and treacherous.

Jan asked, "What do you say, everybody? Do we go ahead or turn back?"

For several uneasy seconds no one answered. Then Nancy said, "I think we should try it. Old Joe is expecting us and remember, he wants to tell us about his personal mystery. I'm dying to learn what it is so I can try to solve it. Besides, I want to see his sketches of the UFO; don't you?"

Ned concurred. "Isn't that the purpose of this trip?"

The others agreed. Jan suggested they go in pairs. "Take it slow and easy on the descent. Remember the saying, 'Haste makes waste,'" she cautioned. "Let's hope we can walk along the stream, which I think is the one on Old Joe's map."

Ned jumped down first and caught Nancy's hand as her feet touched the ground. The Drakes went next, followed by George and Burt. None of them had mishaps.

"Our turn," Dave told Bess. "There's nothing to worry about. I'll go first and catch you. Okay, partner?" Before he jumped, Dave paused for an answer.

Suddenly Bess said, "Wait! I—I'm so dizzy."

Instantly she lost her balance and rolled off the

trunk down the mountainside. There were fewer trees and bushes on the slope, evidently because of logging operations. Bess began to tumble faster.

"Oh, no!" Dave cried out, jumping off the trunk.

He dashed after her and caught his foot in a trailing vine that almost caused him to plunge headfirst. By now, Bess was far ahead of him and rolling rapidly toward the turbulent rock-filled water!

4

Trixie, Lifesaver

Quickly Dave regained his balance. He dug both heels into the mountainside as he ran to rescue Bess. She was only a few feet away from the dangerous stream!

Too far away to assist the helpless girl, the other campers watched in horror. Would Dave reach Bess before she fell among the jagged rocks and injured herself badly? She might even drown!

Without any warning, a large retriever bounded from among the trees. With lightning-fast leaps, the dog got to Bess. She grabbed the girl's belt in her teeth, braced herself against the hillside, and stopped Bess's descent in the nick of time.

"Oh, thank goodness!" George murmured.

Within seconds Dave was bending over the girl. She was unconscious and badly scratched.

"Bess! Bess!" he cried out, patting her cool, clammy cheeks.

The dog now stood alongside her, whining and looking at Dave for orders.

By then, Nancy, Ned, and the other campers had hurried back along the stream. Jan, who said she was a nurse, examined the unconscious girl for broken bones and concluded there were none.

Meanwhile, Nancy and George took wads of tissues from their backpacks, dipped them in the cold water, and applied them to Bess's forehead and the back of her neck. Ned and Burt daubed more cold water on her scratched face and arms. Presently Bess opened her eyes but said nothing.

Nancy whispered to her, "I'm so glad you aren't badly hurt, Bess. Why don't you lie right here until you feel better?"

For nearly ten minutes, Bess rested, then opened her eyes again. Finally, with Dave's help, she sat up.

"I don't think I'd better walk any farther. You all go along without me," she said quietly. Just then she noticed the retriever. "Where did you come from?" she asked the dog, who was wagging her tail.

"She saved your life," Dave told Bess, and explained what the animal had done. "I don't know where she came from."

Bess hugged the beautiful dog and thanked her. In reply, the lovely animal leaped out of her grasp, then ran back and forth along the stream, barking.

"Why is she doing that?" Bess asked.

Nancy guessed that the retriever wanted them to follow her. "Are you Trixie? Are you Old Joe's dog?" the girl detective asked.

The animal wagged her tail briskly and gave a number of short barks.

Nancy laughed. "I think this is Trixie and she wants to take us to her master's cabin." She patted the animal. "Okay, Trixie. Wait until we get the horses and then you lead us to Old Joe."

Jan said she would stay with Bess until the others returned. "I suggest that you leave one of the walkie-talkies with us so we can communicate with you if necessary."

Burt reminded, "It's going to be tough getting the horses down here. They can't climb over that tree trunk. We'll have to bypass it somehow."

"Right," Dave agreed. "We don't want any broken legs."

It took some doing to bring the horses down the mountainside. When they all arrived, one of the walkie-talkies was unpacked and left with Bess and Jan.

The other campers mounted and followed Trixie.

She stayed close to the bank of the stream. The going was rough but uneventful.

As a crudely built log cabin came into view, Trixie hurried on alone, barking wildly. Old Joe came outside immediately and welcomed the group with a big smile.

After counting the number of visitors, he asked, "Where are the other two?"

Nancy explained and added that Trixie was indeed a heroine.

The naturalist praised his pet. "I sent her to find you folks," he said. "I was afraid you might get lost. Evidently she met you at the right moment."

He invited the group to tie up their horses and come into the cabin. As he had told them, it was very unusual. It consisted of a single room with everything he needed in it.

In one corner stood a hand-carved wooden bed. The coverlet had been made from wild goat hide. Several bearskin rugs lay on the floor. The walls were covered with deer heads, and stuffed chipmunks and mounted birds adorned the windows. There was a huge stone fireplace next to which stacks of wood were piled high.

A large wooden dresser stood along one wall of the room. On top was a small wooden barrel holding a beautiful bouquet of wild flowers.

"This is lovely," Nancy remarked, leaning over to smell them.

Old Joe opened the top drawer to display the wooden forks, knives, and spoons he had made. Some of them were short and others very long. The latter, he explained, were used for holding meat over an open fire.

Were the blunt-looking knives sharp enough to cut meat? the onlookers wondered. The naturalist read their thoughts and suggested that the boys try them out. Ned picked up one and examined the edge. He almost cut his finger!

"It's sharp all right," he commented.

Old Joe laughed, then said, "I guess we'd better get some lunch ready." He called to Trixie. "Go fetch us some fish from the stream," he ordered, explaining to his guests, "She is an expert at catching trout in her teeth. When she brings them up here, how about you boys preparing them for cooking? Do you have hunting knives with you?"

"Yes," they chorused.

"Good. Then you girls can set up a three-legged spit to hang the fish on," Old Joe suggested, "while the boys gather some dry wood from the forest to make the outdoor fire for cooking it."

"All right," Nancy said, "but first I want to check on Bess."

She soon made contact with her walkie-talkie. Bess said she was better. "But I got really scared when we saw a giant staring at us from among some trees."

"A what?" Nancy asked in disbelief.

"A giant. He's a real tall Indian with his hair pulled over half his face. He had on some kind of suit made of leaves."

"Sounds strange," Nancy commented. "Did he talk to you?"

"Sort of," Bess said, "but we couldn't understand him." Nancy suggested that perhaps the man was speaking in his native Indian language.

"Probably," Bess replied, adding, "He didn't hurt us. In fact he gave us some lunch. He threw a handful of delicious nuts to us, then disappeared into the forest."

When the conversation finished, Nancy asked Old Joe if he knew who the giant Indian was.

"I'm not sure," her host answered, "but if he's who I think he is, the Indian is harmless. Evidently he has lived in the forest all his life. I remember hearing about him when I was a young man. The authorities tried to capture him but never could. Since he was harmless, they finally gave up."

George asked, "Did you ever catch a glimpse of him?"

"Not for many years," the elderly man replied.

George next asked the naturalist if any other Indians lived in the area. Old Joe shook his head.

George giggled. "Then maybe he doesn't belong here. Perhaps the spaceship dropped him off!"

Ned grinned. "So now we have a new kind of spaceman. An Unidentified Flying Indian!"

As the others laughed, Trixie bounded up to them with a large trout in her mouth.

"Good dog," Old Joe praised her. "I think there's enough food here for all of us. You won't have to get any more."

Ned took the fish. He cut off the head and tail and threw them away, then expertly slit the fish open and removed all the bones, then cut the rest of the trout into small pieces.

Soon the spit was put up and the fire started underneath it. Old Joe hooked the chunks of fish onto the spurs of the three-legged rig. The welcome aroma of cooking fish filled the air.

Up to now there had been a gentle breeze, but suddenly the wind blew hard, toppling over the spit and the fish. The burning wood scattered. Nancy quickly grabbed a nearby bucket of water and doused the remaining flames.

"Are we going to have a cyclone?" George asked, gazing at the darkened sky.

Old Joe looked worried. "I don't know," he answered, "but this is exactly what happened once before when the flying saucer appeared."

5

The Spying Stranger

The sky became more overcast and the wind blew stronger by the moment, whipping leaves off the trees. Everything that was not stationary was thrown helter-skelter.

Old Joe cried out, "Watch for a brilliant light in the sky!"

Every few seconds the campers gazed upward as they scurried around, trying to save what they could. The tripod had collapsed and scattered. The pieces of fish had sailed through the air and disappeared.

"The fire is spreading!" Dave exclaimed.

Quickly he and Burt stamped out bits of burning wood that had blown from the embers, while

Nancy and George rescued several handmade bird feeders from various trees.

In the meantime, Ned had gone to quiet the nervous horses, who were whinnying and stamping excitedly, trying desperately to break loose.

"Whoa there, Goalpost!" he commanded firmly.

The animal obeyed. This had a calming effect on the others until suddenly Nancy gasped.

"The light!" she exclaimed and pointed to the sky. "Here comes the flying saucer!"

The whirling object hurtled through the sky, its two headlights flashing brilliant beams across the treetops. Almost instantly the UFO disappeared from view, and the wind stopped blowing.

"Where did the ship go?" Nancy asked Old Joe.

"I reckon it landed in Dismal Swamp," he replied. "That's where the saucer went last time it came."

"Where's that?" the young detective questioned him.

The naturalist pointed. "The swamp is between this mountain and the next—way down in the valley." The other mountain, he noted, was called Teepeeskunk. "A long time ago a tribe of Indians lived over there. They used to catch skunks and sell the fur in town, so the natives gave the mountain that name."

The campers laughed.

"And I suppose Dismal Swamp is pretty dismal." George grinned.

"*Very* dismal," the elderly man replied. "No one ever goes near the place. It smells mighty bad. If you're planning to take a look at the mysterious flying saucer, you'd better wear a gas mask!"

Nancy held her nose and giggled. "I don't care what it smells like," she said. "I must go there and investigate. Otherwise, how will we know if the spacecraft really came from outer space?"

George said she wondered how Bess and Jan had gotten through the windstorm. "I think we should call them right now on the walkie-talkie."

Ned pulled it out of his backpack and tried to signal Bess and Jan. He pushed the buzzer button again and again, but there was no response.

"Maybe something happened to them," George remarked in a worried voice.

Nancy, too, was very concerned. "We must find them right away!" she said and turned to Old Joe. "I'm sorry to leave in such a hurry. I promise to come back soon to hear about your mystery and help you solve it."

"Thank you. There's no rush. The mystery has been waiting a long time."

Hal, a capable woodsman, offered to lead the search for his wife and Bess. "I can make excellent time alone. Just follow my trail," he directed. "I'll leave blue chalk marks on trees."

Old Joe said he certainly hoped the missing campers were all right. "Perhaps they found shelter from the wind inside a cave or among some trees," he suggested hopefully. "I'm sorry about lunch. But wait a minute. I'll give you all something to eat on the way."

He scooted into his cabin and returned in a few minutes, carrying handfuls of something wrapped in huge grape leaves. "I think you'll enjoy eating this pheasant meat I cured. I bagged the little fellow right here in front of the cabin."

The campers thanked him, then Hal trotted off on his horse. Before the others could catch up to him, he was out of sight. Apparently Hal had chosen a shortcut back to where Jan and Bess had been left.

The riders found themselves jumping over small fallen trees and splashing through rivulets. Although Hal's path was fairly visible, the group realized it was hard on the horses and stopped to rest.

Admitting she was as tired as her horse, George sighed. "I thought I was pretty tough," she said, "but this forest almost has me beat."

Burt laughed, tweaking her chin affectionately. "Coming from you that's quite an admission."

For a few moments no one had much to say. Finally, Ned stood up. "Everybody set?"

He led the way, stopping frequently to identify

Hal's trail. The blue chalk marks seemed rather faint and far apart as underbrush trampled by Hal's horse had begun to spring back.

When all of them were at last convinced that they were lost, Nancy noticed a small gouge on a tree. "This is new," she observed. "Maybe Hal ran out of chalk and made this nick as a marker."

Following the direction it indicated, the riders finally reached the spot above the river where they had left Bess and Jan. Hal was there, talking with them.

Nancy and George dismounted at once and ran up the short slope. Both girls cried out, "Bess, are you all right? The windstorm didn't injure you and Jan?"

Bess smiled weakly. "I wouldn't say I'm all right, but I feel better."

Hal suggested they leave their horses on some level ground he had found beyond the slope. While the boys took the animals there, Jan explained to Nancy and George that the strong wind and overcast sky had frightened both of them. "We were fearful we might be blown into that rocky stream so we decided to climb a little higher up the mountain. We found shelter in an overhang."

She said their horses were nervous but were all right.

"I'm so relieved," George said.

When the boys returned, Ned asked, "Is your walkie-talkie broken? We couldn't reach you."

Bess said they had not heard it. "I guess the wind made too much noise, or maybe the sound didn't carry into the overhang."

Ned explained that they hadn't tried until the wind died down. He examined the set and found a loose wire that he immediately reattached. He asked Nancy to try calling him. Now the buzzer worked perfectly.

Bess told the others that the Indian with the long black hair had spied on them again.

"This time he wasn't wearing the suit of leaves. He had on a short deerskin jacket and long pants made of the same material. I've decided he's rather nice-looking after all. I just wish he could speak English."

Dave pretended to be jealous. "I'm very glad the Indian doesn't," he muttered, causing a blush to creep over Bess's face.

"Oh, Dave," she said shyly.

Burt cleared his throat, equally embarrassed. "I wonder where the Indian comes from and where he hides out."

Hal replied, "Possibly he's a descendant of the Indians who used to live around here."

"You mean," Dave spoke up, "that the tribe lives

somewhere else now, but he has returned here to see where his forebears lived?"

Hal nodded.

"Maybe the guy's a hermit," Dave suggested. "You can't tell whether or not he understands English just because he won't speak it."

Burt concurred, adding, "He could be deaf and dumb."

"Could be," Bess agreed.

Jan had picked some delicious wild strawberries. As the campers sat on the ground to eat them, the conversation turned to the flying saucer. Nancy told Jan and Bess about their visit with Old Joe and his story of the spaceship landing in Dismal Swamp between the mountains.

George added quickly, "According to Old Joe the swamp smells horrible. Maybe it has gas in it."

"Then I'm going to keep away," Bess announced.

"Well, I'm not," Nancy said, "and the sooner I go, the sooner I can solve the mystery of the flying saucer."

"Where is Dismal Swamp?" Jan asked. "I never heard of it and I've been in this forest many times."

Nancy pointed in the direction that Old Joe had indicated. "I guess we'll have to return to our other campsite, then travel down the mountainside from there."

"It's too late in the day to go to the swamp now,"

Ned told her. "How about going early tomorrow morning?"

Nancy nodded. "But," she added, "suppose the flying saucer takes off in the meantime? We may miss an opportunity to solve the mystery."

"We'll just have to take that chance," he said.

Bess suggested, "Why don't a few of you start out now? I'll stay here until morning. I can't walk too far and I still don't feel up to riding a horse. Too many bruises," she added with a rueful smile.

"I know what you mean," Nancy said kindly. Undecided about what was best to do, she then appealed to Jan and Hal. "We're in your hands. You know more about this forest than we do. What do you advise?"

Since all their supplies were still with the pack-horses, the couple suggested they set up camp at the spot where they had left the two animals.

"That way we can all stick together tonight," Jan added.

Bess groaned.

Jan said quickly, "You won't have to walk a step if it bothers you. These husky boys can carry you. I only hope the horses and the food are safe."

Ned grinned. "Shall we draw lots?"

"Not on your life!" Dave replied. "I'll carry her alone."

"Piggyback?" Bess giggled.

When the group was ready to leave, Bess suddenly shrieked. The others whirled around and stared at her.

"*Now* what's wrong?" George asked, a little annoyed at a further delay.

Terrified, her cousin motioned toward the trees. "There he is again!" she said. "The Indian!"

All eyes turned toward the clump of trees. Indeed, the mysterious man was standing there, motionless, staring at them.

"Oh!" the campers gasped.

His right hand, held high, clasped a huge rock. Was he about to throw it at them?

6

Sign Language

The Indian stood quite still. He did not lower his upraised arm or throw the rock he held.

"He's weird," Bess whispered.

For a few seconds the campers continued to stare at him, fearful of his next move. He was muscular, and though the Emerson football players felt they could put up a strong battle, they wondered if he might defeat them by some unusual strategy.

Nancy was the first to make a suggestion. "Let's try to be friendly and approach him with our hands outstretched."

Bess was not so sure this was a good idea. "Suppose—suppose he's from outer space," she said. "There's no telling what magnetic power he might have. He could mesmerize all of us."

This struck George as a funny idea. She said, "Oh, sure, and a killing bolt of electricity may come shooting out from his body at any minute—z-z-z—look out!"

Burt muffled a chuckle, adding, "Do you think that's his spaceship down in the swamp? He looks too big to live in it."

Bess knew they were teasing her but ignored it. She had seen the Indian before the saucer arrived. Then a thought struck her: Maybe the spaceship came back for him. He might even be planning to kidnap us and take us away in it!

As the Indian continued to stare at the group, Dave glanced at Bess, as if reading her thoughts, and exclaimed, "Watch out! He may hypnotize you!"

Bess made a face at Dave, then said, "Okay, Nancy. Why don't you and Ned approach the man?"

The couple walked forward, slowly. Nancy held a shining gold disc on a chain which she had removed from her neck. Perhaps, she thought, the Indian would be interested in the necklace.

Inch by inch, she and Ned continued toward him. The Indian remained immobile. He stared at the jewelry but did not take it. Finally he let the rock drop to the ground.

Ned sighed in relief. "Maybe he intends to be friendly," he murmured.

As Nancy stepped closer, she smiled and said, "Hello."

The girl detective repeated the greeting several times as she and Ned came right up to the man. He still did not move, but just looked straight at them. Would he attack? The onlookers watched with bated breath.

Now Ned pointed to himself, saying over and over, "Ned. Ned. Ned."

Finally the Indian gave a slight smile and then pointed to Nancy. Ned complied with the sign language. "Nancy. Nancy."

Everyone was delighted and started to applaud, but Jan signaled for silence.

A hush fell over the group as the man pointed to himself and said, "Shoso."

The campers were thrilled. Again they wanted to clap, but Jan shook her head. She was afraid that loud applause might frighten the man away and send him racing off into the forest.

Now Shoso laid a finger gently on Ned and repeated his name several times. In turn, he and Nancy pointed at the Indian and said, "Shoso." He nodded and smiled broadly.

He looked up at the sky and said something unintelligible to them.

"What's he trying to tell us?" Ned asked Nancy.

The young sleuth admitted she was puzzled. "Maybe he'll tell us some more in sign language."

Presently Shoso twirled quickly with his arms above his head. Still the couple looked puzzled. Shoso repeated the motion.

"I think I get it," Ned remarked. "He's trying to imitate the windstorm."

Nancy agreed. "But I just can't figure out his message."

Shoso seemed disappointed and thought a few seconds. Then he leaned down, put his hands on the ground, and galloped about. Suddenly he ran off a short distance into the trees.

Nancy snapped her fingers. "Ned, I think Shoso is trying to tell us something about our horses."

"We'll soon find out," he replied, "if we use some sign language of our own."

He leaned over the way Shoso had done and told Nancy to hop on his back as if she were riding a horse.

As Nancy did this, she laughed and said," I sure feel silly, but if it works, I don't mind."

By this time the other campers, no longer afraid of the Indian, began to roar with laughter.

"You two ought to join the circus," Burt called out.

George scoffed. "A kindergarten circus."

Ned and Nancy played their parts well, ignoring the jibes. Shoso nodded happily and pointed in the direction where the boys had left the horses.

"Something must have happened to them!

Maybe they've been injured!" Nancy exlaimed, jumping off Ned's back.

"Or perhaps they ran away," he replied. "We didn't tie them all. We let a few graze."

"Yes," Burt agreed. "They may have injured themselves being loose in this forest. I've noticed plenty of trailing vines."

"Don't say that," Bess pleaded. "I can't stand to see an animal hurt."

Without wasting another minute, all the campers and Shoso rushed toward the spot where the saddle horses had been left. *Two of them were gone!*

"Oh, what'll we do?" Bess wailed.

"I blame myself," Dave said. "I suggested we let some of the animals graze."

"We're all guilty," Burt added. "We didn't have to take your advice."

Nancy noticed with relief that her lovely Susan B was still there with Goalpost standing next to her. Unfortunately the horses Burt and Dave had been riding were missing. Hal suggested that possibly the animals had gone back to the original campsite.

Jan said, "I have a hunch they may have rejoined the packhorses."

"Oh, I hope you're right," Bess answered. "They have all the food and I'm starved."

Hal said that he was less concerned with their supplies. He hoped that the great wind and the blinding bright lights of the saucer had not frightened the packhorses so much that they yanked themselves loose from the tie ropes.

Although the campers had had little to eat that day, they knew their main job was to find the horses.

Shoso seemed to feel sorry for the group. He beckoned them to follow him. Burt and Dave rode double with George and Bess.

The Indian led them directly toward the campsite where they had left the packhorses. The route was much shorter than the one the group had taken that morning while heading for Old Joe's.

"Oh, thank you," Bess called to him, then remembered that he could not understand her words. He waved and disappeared from view.

Nancy and her friends rushed to the area where the packhorses had been tied. To everyone's dismay, the missing saddle horses were not there. Moreover, both packhorses were gone and so were the supplies!

7

Old Joe's Secret

"Four of our horses gone!" George exclaimed, sighing deeply.

"And all our food and clothes!" Bess moaned.

The campers were nonplussed. What were they going to do without them?

Hal remarked, "Judging from the frayed ropes, I'd say the animals went wild."

"Then there's no telling how far away they went," Nancy commented. "Maybe Shoso knows."

The Indian, however, was not in sight.

"He's the most elusive man I've ever met," Bess commented.

Nancy visualized the tall, erect figure stalking through the forest. Except for the deeper color of

Shoso's skin, his black hair and dark eyes, he was the same type of outdoorsman as Old Joe. The girl wondered if all naturalists were similar in stature.

Hal, in the meantime, was trying to reassure the campers about their horses. "Sometimes they return to their riders."

"That's right," Jan agreed. "We'll manage somehow. If Old Joe can subsist in this forest, so can we."

Nevertheless, Nancy was disappointed. "I was so hoping all of us could go to Dismal Swamp. After all, my main reason for coming here was to investigate the flying saucer. By now, it may have left."

"I doubt it," Ned remarked. "I'm sure we would have seen it take off."

Nancy was not so certain of this. Perhaps the mystery ship had unknown powers that allowed it to depart silently and invisibly.

"We'll get to the swamp somehow," Ned assured her.

They both looked for hoofprints to see which way the missing horses had gone. The search indicated that the pack animals and riding horses had run off in separate pairs. But the hoofprints of all four led to the bank of a small stream where the prints ended. Evidently the horses had walked through the water. It was growing too dark, however, to continue the hunt.

Jan said, "Let's fix a good meal. That will liven our spirits."

"Fix it out of what?" Bess asked.

"The forest," Jan replied. "I suggest we split up in couples and forage for food. In an hour I would bet we'll have a great dinner."

George laughed. "I'll feel like a foraging cow. *Moo moo.* Come on, Burt."

Jan asked Bess and Dave to stay nearby in case any of the horses came back. She smiled. "This time, please tie them."

"You bet," Dave promised, still upset about being partly responsible for the two runaway animals.

Hal and Jan went off in one direction, Nancy and Ned in another. To the young sleuth's delight, she discovered a huge patch of wild blueberries. "But what can I put them in?" she asked.

Ned pulled a large brown handkerchief out of his pocket, filled it, and tied the four corners together. Before the hour was up, the couple had gathered wild scallions and grapes as well.

When they joined their friends, Nancy and Ned were amazed at the variety of food the others had brought back. George and Burt, both mushroom experts, had collected and peeled a large quantity of mushrooms. Hal had chased and caught two rabbits which he had dressed and cut into pieces. He had skewered them onto a sturdy branch broken from a sapling and was now cooking the meat over a small fire Dave had built.

He and Bess had discovered a sassafras tree and chipped off pieces of bark which they mixed with water in a camper's abandoned canteen. Bess set it over the fire to brew into tea.

The meal was enjoyable and satisfying. The group discussed the day's events and finally the conversation turned to the missing horses.

George said, "I think we shouldn't dismiss the possibility that they were stolen."

The remark shocked everyone. If this were true, they might never get the horses back!

"But who would steal them?" Hal asked. "Very few people roam this mountain and I saw no footprints where the horses were tied. Besides, the frayed ropes seemed to indicate that they yanked themselves loose."

Bess asked, "Even if you found footprints, how could you tell that the person who made them had ridden away?"

Hal smiled. "You don't step over a horse's back. You hoist yourself up so you'd make more of a depression in the ground."

Bess giggled. "I guess I still have a lot to learn about horse detective work."

It was decided that Hal and Burt would start to hunt for the missing animals after breakfast the next morning. Hal said they would pick up the search where the hoofprints ended, ride through the stream, and try to find out where the horses had left the water.

"We'll take one of the walkie-talkies along," Burt said, "so you can let us know if any of the animals return, or if we find any of them we'll contact you."

Dave called, "Big game hunters, bring 'em back alive!"

"Shush!" said Bess. "You make me shiver."

That night the group collected pine needles and slept on refreshing beds of pine. The next morning, as daylight filtered down through the trees, Burt and Hal rode off. The campers who were awake wished them well.

"Watch out for wildcats and snakes!" Bess warned.

Burt laughed. "I dare any snake to try biting through these hiking boots."

The searchers were gone several hours but did not call in a report. Then suddenly George exclaimed, "Listen! I hear hoofbeats."

To be sure, she lay down and put her ear to the ground. "Yes, I hear at least two horses coming," she announced.

Everyone expected to see Hal and Burt, but to their amazement Old Joe appeared. He was leading the two lost saddle horses!

"How wonderful!" Nancy called out as she ran to pat them. "Old Joe, where did you find the horses?"

Her new friend grinned. "They came to my cabin. Guess they were hungry for something sweet and thought maybe I'd feed them, which I did. I gave them maple syrup candy. How'd they get away from here?"

Nancy and Ned told him the story, adding that Hal and Burt had gone off to look for the four runaways and the supplies.

Old Joe became philosophical. "Horses are funny creatures. You never can be sure what they're thinking. Sometimes they don't do anything unusual for a long, long time, then something will frighten them and they'll take off like they'd gone clean beserk."

As the campers crowded around the kindly man, Bess asked him if he would like a drink. "We have water and cold sassafras tea." She giggled and told about the campers' supper the night before.

The naturalist chuckled. "You'll be forest folk before you know it." Then he thanked them and said he had had a good breakfast. "But I brought you something. I keep a few hens in a cage near my cabin. Trixie stands guard, of course. She chases the wild animals away. I have some hard-boiled eggs for you."

As each person took an egg to eat, George remarked, "Too bad Burt and Hal aren't here. I think we should try to contact them on the walkie-talkie and tell them that the two saddle horses are back."

Nancy tried to signal the two searchers, but there was no response. Again and again she called in vain and finally asked Dave to examine the instrument.

"It seems okay," he reported. "I'm puzzled why Hal and Burt don't answer."

Old Joe spoke up. "Maybe your friends have gone out of range. Or maybe there are too many trees in the way of the signal."

When the old naturalist said he ought to be leaving, Nancy remembered that they had not yet heard about his mystery. She asked him about it, and he was delighted that she remembered.

He began by explaining that he and his parents lived in the city when he was a boy.

"However, my father was a great nature lover and used to bring me to this forest. I grew to love it as much as he did. After my mother's death my father and I came here more often. In fact, we once spent several months in the forest. That was when the mystery began.

"One day soon after we arrived, my father seemed worried. When I asked him what the trouble was, he told me that he was carrying a lot of money and valuable secret papers in his wallet.

"He said to me, 'Son, there's a man who is an enemy of mine. He would like nothing better than to get his hands on all of this. But I don't intend for him to do so. He must never learn the secret.'

"That night we were very tired and went to bed early. I slept soundly and when I woke up in the morning, my father was gone. At first I figured he was fishing or picking berries or maybe trying to catch a rabbit for some stew. But he did not come back for hours. I became alarmed.

"When he finally returned, I asked him where he had been. He said, 'Oh, just out for a long hike.'

"I was puzzled, but he didn't explain. Then suddenly one morning he announced that we were going back to the city. I asked him why and he told me he had business affairs to take care of.

"We never again came here together. Soon after returning to the city, he had a stroke. He wasn't able to walk, talk, or write. He lived only three more years.

"Just before he died he looked up at me and managed to say, 'F-forest. Mon— b-bur—'"

Spellbound, Old Joe's listeners now began to ask questions.

"Do you think your father was saying he had buried the money in this forest?" Nancy asked.

Old Joe nodded. "I came here many, many times and searched but never had any luck. Finally I decided to leave the city and live here permanently. This forest is more like home to me than any other place. All these years I've hoped to find the wallet and my father's great secret."

Nancy was tingling with excitement. If she could only find that wallet! The girl detective wondered, however, what condition it might be in.

I hope for Old Joe's sake it's intact, she thought. Aloud she suggested, "Let's talk about clues."

8

Pyramid of Rocks

All the campers had questions for Old Joe. Bess asked him, "Did your father have any special places in the forest he liked to go?"

"None that I recall," the naturalist replied. "He loved everything in it."

Ned inquired next if the elder Mr. Austin had any favorite trees.

After thinking over this question for a couple of minutes, Old Joe said, "The taller the tree, the more he admired it. I'd say perhaps the sky-reaching pines were his favorites."

"Then we'll examine those first," Nancy told him.

Jan said she wondered if Old Joe's father would have bothered to make it difficult for his son to find the wallet. "Perhaps your father had some cozy nook where he liked to spend time. Do you know of any?"

The old man told her the forest was full of wonderful small hideaways. "But so far as I know, there are no deep caves or overhangs of rock. I'm afraid I'm not much help to you."

Nancy was not discouraged. She asked Old Joe where he had looked for the wallet.

He smiled. "Hundreds of places," he told her, "but there are thousands more just waiting to be explored."

Nancy had a strong hunch that Mr. Austin had hidden his valuable wallet in a well-protected place. She suggested that Old Joe accompany the group on a new search.

"I'd certainly like to find that wallet," he said longingly. "Okay, I'll go with you."

Before the group had a chance to start off, however, they became aware of prolonged, frantic barking from Trixie. She had been left to guard the cabin.

"Uh-oh, trouble," Old Joe said worriedly. "Some unwanted visitor, I'll bet. I must go right back."

Nancy offered him one of the saddle horses. "Thanks a lot, but I can make better time on foot," Old Joe replied and hurried off.

Ned remarked, "I hate to see that old man go by

himself. I think I'll follow and see if I can help." Dave decided to go along with him.

As the barking continued, George said, "Ned and Dave may be gone a long time. Nancy, if you want to start the search, I'll be glad to go with you."

The young sleuth was eager to begin. She mentioned the idea to Jan and Bess, who felt that they should stay behind to guard the camp.

"We don't want any more trouble with the horses," Jan said.

"Please watch your step," Bess added.

Nancy and George took flashlights to explore the hollows of trees and other possible hiding places. They had been searching half an hour for Mr. Austin's wallet when George found a tree with a deep hole in the trunk.

Excitedly she flashed her light inside, then exclaimed, "Nancy, there's something at the bottom that looks like leather." She laid down the flashlight and reached in. Almost immediately George cried out in pain and yanked out her hand.

"What happened?" Nancy asked, running to George's side.

"Something bit me! Oh! Ow! It hurts!" George replied. She danced around, shaking her hand.

Quickly Nancy flashed her light on the tree. The beady-eyed head of a small snake was visible at the top of the hollow in the trunk. Blinded by the brightness, the reptile instantly slithered down into its den.

Was it a poisonous species? Nancy had no idea but decided not to take any chances. She whipped out a handkerchief and tied it tightly around George's wrist. Then she grabbed a sharp-pointed twig and made a tiny hole in the end of her friend's thumb. By now George's hand was swollen.

"I'm sorry I'll have to hurt you a little," Nancy told her friend, "but we must get that poison out before it spreads."

She hunted for a sharp stone. After cleaning it off with a green leaf, Nancy drew it across the end of George's thumb. Blood flowed out and, she hoped, all the poison as well. Soon the swelling subsided, and George said the severe ache was gone.

"Thanks a million, Nancy," she said gratefully. "I was really scared."

Now that George felt better, Nancy removed the tourniquet. "Do you want to continue the search?" the girl detective asked. "Or would you rather go back to camp for further first-aid treatment?"

George said she was feeling fine. "The bleeding has almost stopped. Maybe we can find a stream where I can bathe my thumb."

The two girls went on, looking intently for places where the Austin wallet might be hidden. Shortly they came to a babbling brook. While George swished her hand in the icy water, Nancy looked closely at the surroundings. She noticed an extremely tall pine tree, perhaps one admired by Old Joe's father. There was no opening in the trunk, however.

"Before we leave," she said to George, "I think I'll climb the tree and see if there's anything ahead."

Hugging the thick trunk, Nancy started to shinny up the tree. George merely looked on, chiding herself for her sore thumb, as Nancy climbed higher and higher. She was examining every inch of the main trunk and looking at each limb and branch. Nothing indicated that a wallet was hidden among them.

Finally at the top Nancy scanned the surrounding countryside and shouted down to George, "I can see Dismal Swamp from here. Oh, no, I can't believe it. The flying saucer is gone!"

"What a rotten break!" George said. "Let's hope it'll come back while we're still here."

Nancy felt miserable because she had lost her chance to see the flying saucer close up. Was her trip in vain?

I should have gone to the swamp as soon as the UFO landed, she thought. It was little consolation to her that the missing horses, Bess's accident, and darkness had compelled her and the others not to ride to the swamp.

Nancy descended the tree. When she reached the ground, George said, "Don't feel too bad. That flying saucer is bound to come back." She grinned. "I just had one of your hunches."

Nancy smiled wanly. "I hope it won't take a hundred million light years, though," she replied.

The girls walked on in silence. Despite their keen observance of many trees, short and tall, they found nothing in any of them to indicate a hiding place. George remarked that perhaps they would have to start digging.

Nancy nodded. "Next time we'll bring spades and picks. You know, George, we aren't very good woodsmen, not to have brought even a trowel!"

In a short while they came to another mountain stream, wider than the other and rocky. Water was rushing rapidly over the stones.

"Isn't that pretty?" George remarked. "It looks like a picture for a calendar!"

"It really does."

As Nancy stood on the bank, she noticed a pyramid of rocks about eighteen inches high in the middle of the stream.

"That's strange," she said. "I wonder what it's for. A marker of some sort?"

"A marker for what?" George asked.

Nancy shrugged and did not reply. She decided to investigate. She took off her hiking boots and socks and waded in. Not only had the stones been cemented together, she discovered, but the foundation reached a foot below the bed of the stream.

Very excited, Nancy asked herself: Could Old Joe's father have made this pyramid of rocks? Were his valuable wallet and secret papers inside?

9

The Black Deluge

Eager to communicate with Old Joe, but having no idea which direction to take to his cabin, Nancy and George decided to return to camp. Bess and Jan were glad to see them.

"We've been so worried about you. You were gone a long time," Jan said.

Suddenly Bess saw her cousin's finger. "George, whatever did you do to yourself?"

"A snake bit me," George replied, and she told them about her painful encounter.

Jan took a protective plastic finger from her first-aid kit and gave it to George to wear over her thumb. Then she said, "Now tell us about your search for Old Joe's treasure. Any luck?"

"Yes and no," Nancy responded.

She told Bess and Jan about the pyramid of rocks—a possible hiding place for the valuable wallet.

"It certainly sounds like a good guess," Bess remarked.

Knowing Jan was knowledgeable about woodlore, Nancy asked her if the pyramid might have been used for something else— perhaps to ward off some superstitious fear.

Jan shrugged. "Possibly. Or maybe someone erected it as an art object. It must have been pretty with the stream splashing around the pyramid."

"It was," George replied, then asked, "Jan, do you think it could have been a marker for fishermen?"

"Could be," Jan replied. "But I doubt that anyone would place one way out there in this wilderness."

Jan said she felt Nancy's guess was a likely one. "You should tell Old Joe soon."

Then Nancy described how she climbed the tree and learned that the flying saucer was gone.

"Did you hear it take off?"

"No."

"Feel any wind?"

"No."

"See any lights?"

"No."

"It's gone," Nancy said sadly. "I wonder if it will ever come back."

"Let's hope so," Bess said and gave Nancy a hug.

When Ned and Dave returned a short time later, Trixie was with them. She jumped around, delighted to see the campers.

Nancy asked what had happened at the naturalist's cabin. To her dismay she learned that the interior was almost wrecked.

"Old Joe found footprints of a bear that got in somehow," Dave reported. "Evidently Trixie couldn't scare him away. The bear ate most of the food he found. Besides that, he emptied the contents of a jar of honey and another of maple syrup.

"He made a shambles of the place," Dave went on. "We helped Old Joe fix things up as best we could. We left him repairing the cabin door which the bear apparently broke down. He must have been hungry."

Nancy and George related their adventures. When Nancy finished, she said, "I'll write a note to Old Joe about the pyramid of rocks and have Trixie deliver it. That might make him feel better."

Hastily she wrote down what the girls had discovered, then tied the note to a small piece of rope which she secured around the dog's neck.

"Take this right to Old Joe," Nancy instructed the

animal. "It's very important." Trixie understood and hurried off.

Without warning a brisk wind sprang up, and it started to rain. The campers put on their rain gear, wishing that the tents were with them and not with the missing packhorses.

"This is more than a rainfall," Bess remarked presently. "It's a deluge."

"A black deluge!" Dave added.

The campers huddled together under a maple tree as heavy drops of rain pelted through the spreading branches.

"I'm really beginning to worry about Hal and Burt," Jan remarked. "They're long overdue. And this weather won't help them any."

"Probably it's too dark for them to proceed," Nancy suggested.

"I hope they've found the horses," Bess remarked. "Then at least they could have something to eat and drink from the packs."

The conversation was interrupted when the forest suddenly lit up with a strange, bright glow.

"Maybe the flying saucer is coming back!" Nancy exclaimed. "Oh, I hope so!"

Ned offered to shinny up a tree to find out. Before he reached the top, however, the mysterious light was gone. Once again it was pitch dark. Gingerly he climbed down.

"This is positively spooky," Bess said.

Nancy stated firmly that she was not going to miss another chance to see the flying saucer.

"Ned," she asked, "are you game to go down to Dismal Swamp with me?"

"Sure," he replied. "Let's take two lantern searchlights with us."

Jan begged the couple not to walk. "You should ride, and take some candy in case you get hungry." Quickly she took two chocolate nut bars from her pack. "I almost forgot I had these," she said.

Nancy put a poncho over her rain gear while Ned took one out of his backpack. They swung the saddlebags across the animals' flanks, then put on the saddles and vaulted into them, covering the saddles as best they could with their ponchos.

"Keep close," Ned advised Nancy and nudged his horse to start off.

Nancy pulled her rain hood snugly forward and followed him. If only the rain would stop, she thought, we could make better time.

But it continued to beat hard, creating slippery craters of mud through the unbroken forest. When the riders reached a small clearing Goalpost picked up speed. He kicked up mud, splashing Susan B's forelegs and causing Nancy to rein in sharply. The mare, however, did not obey. She dug her hooves faster through the wet grass, sinking, then skidding and almost throwing Nancy out of the saddle.

"Whoa, Susan B!" the girl detective ordered. "Whoa!"

Ned heard Nancy's frantic cries. Instantly he swung Goalpost in her direction. The horse whinnied and stumbled toward Susan B. By now the mare was reluctantly under Nancy's control.

"Are you all right?" Ned shouted to Nancy.

"Yes, I'm fine," she replied, though still a bit shaken. "Let's go on."

As the couple started out again, a slight mist began to rise. Oh, no, Nancy thought. We don't need this. I must see the mystery spaceship.

It was only a short time later that she and Ned, shining their lantern searchlights ahead, picked up the dim outline of the flying saucer. It was resting in the center of the swamp in complete blackness.

"It really smells as horrible here as Old Joe said," Ned remarked. "Do you want to stay?"

"I sure do," Nancy replied. "Let's go the rest of the way on foot. We can leave the horses tied to trees up here."

By now the rain had almost stopped, although it continued to drip steadily from the trees. The ground in Dismal Swamp was spongy but passable. What almost stopped them, though, was the rank, gaseous odor. They wondered: How much of it was from the swamp and how much emanated from the flying saucer?

The craft itself was completely silent. Nancy

whispered, "If any creatures are aboard, they're either asleep or keeping quiet to avoid detection."

Ned agreed. "And we'd better watch our step so we don't run into any surprises."

He and Nancy sloshed through the swamp, shining their powerful searchlights on the mysterious craft. They walked around it, but saw no windows or doors.

"How does anybody get in or out of this saucer?" Ned asked. "It seems to be sealed up tight."

Nancy suggested that perhaps no one was aboard. "The craft may be operated by remote control," she said.

"Just the same," Ned remarked, "I'd like to go inside. Who knows what we'd find—maybe someone dead!"

Nancy was as curious as her companion to find out. "Let's pound on the hull," she said. "Maybe we'll get a response."

10

Space Trip

The rain had started to fall again and within seconds was coming down in torrents. Nancy and Ned, however, paid little attention to the deluge as they pounded on the flying saucer. Though they knocked until their knuckles were sore, no response came from the interior of the mysterious craft.

Finally Ned remarked, "Maybe we ought to try communicating by mathematical signals. Suppose I try a few that I've learned in my courses."

He took a key from his pocket and tapped it against the spaceship. First he indicated a simple triangle. There was no response. Next he tried a more complicated geometric formula. Again there was no answer.

Nancy was astounded that although the hull seemed to be made of metal, Ned's tapping made no metallic sound.

That's strange, she thought, and mentioned it to Ned.

"You're right," he agreed. "This ship has some kind of soundproof shell. Even if there's an intelligent being inside, it probably cannot hear my signals."

Wondering what the ship was made of, Ned tried to scrape the surface with his key. He was unable to chip off anything.

"This is incredible!" he exclaimed. "I'd like to know what kind of outer material this is. Possibly some substance from a distant planet."

He sighed, regretting he had not brought chemicals and testing equipment with him.

"Even if we could get in touch with some scientists nearby, they might not be able to reach here before the saucer takes off again."

He and Nancy speculated on the spaceship's source of energy.

"Whether it's programmed or remote-controlled," she remarked, "I'm inclined to think the ship is solar-powered. Perhaps the reason it's stuck here in the swamp is that we've had so much cloudy and rainy weather. The saucer may not have stored up enough solar energy to lift itself off the ground and back up into the air."

Ned said he wondered if the swamp itself exuded special gas that gave the ship buoyancy. "It smells bad enough around here to launch anything." He grinned. "I hope you and I don't suddenly take off!"

She laughed. "In this mud? No chance."

Suddenly aware that they were standing in a deep quagmire of mud and water, Ned asked Nancy if she were ready to go back to camp.

"Are you kidding?" she replied. "I want to see what happens! Whoever or whatever controls the ship may decide to leave suddenly."

"In that case," Ned said, "why don't we get those chocolate nut bars out of our saddlebags?"

"Good idea," Nancy agreed.

First, they retethered the animals so they could reach down to nibble on grass and roots, and even sleep until the couple was ready to leave. They removed their rations from the saddlebags and returned to the flying saucer where they ate the chocolate bars.

"Amazing how satisfying one large piece of candy can be," Nancy commented, leaning against the ship. She yawned.

"I feel better too," Ned remarked sleepily.

Suddenly Nancy felt the spaceship vibrate. She was startled and noticed a side door opening slowly. A mechanical hand reached outside and beckoned her and Ned to come aboard.

"Shall we go?" she whispered to him.

He did not reply. To her surprise, he walked, as if dazed, toward the doorway. She followed.

When they reached the spaceship, the mechanical hand helped them step inside, then retracted. The door slammed shut.

The interior of the craft was brightly illuminated but not by lights that the couple could see and there was no sign of anyone—human or humanoid.

The walls were lined with flashing lights and many kinds of buttons, gadgets, and tools. Some of them Nancy recognized as hammers, screwdrivers, and wrenches; others were totally unfamiliar to her.

She tried to ask Ned what some of the unusual ones were. To her utter astonishment, no sound came from her throat.

We must be in a void, she surmised, but we're not having any trouble breathing. How strange!

More baffling was the fact that all her rain gear was gone. Ned's was missing also. What had happened to it?

Did it evaporate? she asked herself, completely puzzled.

A feeling of fear crept over the young detective. Was she locked in the flying saucer? Were she and Ned about to be kidnapped by unseen space beings and taken away from the earth forever?

Ned, less frightened, began to examine the odd gadgets. None was labeled to give a clue to its use. Curious, he pushed a button on one wall. Sparks flew toward both him and Nancy, slightly scorching the backs of their hands.

Ouch! Nancy cried out, but again she made no audible sound.

The flying saucer vibrated convulsively and lifted from Dismal Swamp. Instantly it turned into a glass cage, climbing higher and higher at a terrific speed. Within seconds it soared above the mountaintop and spun into space.

Although the flying saucer twirled rapidly as it flew, Nancy and Ned managed to stand with ease. Strangely, they forgot their fears. Both of them tried to figure out what had caused the ship suddenly to become transparent. As they gazed outside, the misty sky changed to clear dark blue.

I'm—I'm getting dizzy, Nancy said, reaching for Ned's hand.

Of course, he did not hear her, and she noticed that his eyes were closing. He too was becoming dizzy. Was it from the height or the speed? In a moment he lost his balance.

Poor Ned! Nancy thought. I—I hope—

Both of them toppled onto the deck. As they fell, the flying saucer swirled jerkily. They realized that it was descending. Where was it about to land?

Nancy and Ned tried to stay awake and to get up and look outside to see what was happening. Their efforts were in vain. They could not move. Within seconds both of them blacked out!

11

Human Birds

Nancy and Ned had no way of knowing how long they were blacked out. When they became conscious, they were no longer in the flying saucer.

Instead, Nancy and Ned were lying on luscious green grass. The cloudless sky above them was a beautiful blue and the sun was shining.

The spaceship was not in sight. Where did it go? Nancy asked herself, feeling a chill sweep over her.

She realized it was very cold where they were. Nancy turned on her side to speak to Ned.

Where do you think we are? she asked him. To her utter dismay she knew that still no sound came from her throat.

Ned sat up and looked at Nancy. He asked with concern, Are you all right?

The identical phenomenon had happened to him. He was uttering a thought but not out loud. Suddenly Nancy became aware of what Ned was thinking. The two of them were communicating by thought waves!

This is fantastic! Nancy decided.

The couple stood up and gazed around. Again Nancy asked silently: Where do you think we are, Ned?

He shrugged and replied, Maybe we're somewhere on earth or marooned on another planet. My guess is we're out in space.

For a few moments she and Ned were terrified. They had enjoyed their lives on earth so much that they were not ready to say good-bye to parents, relatives, and friends. Nancy chided herself for being so eager to solve the mystery of the flying saucer in the first place.

Ned thought-waved to her: Don't panic! It may be nice here.

Alone and not knowing what else to do, the couple walked around, trying to warm up. The ground was spongy, and for the first time Nancy and Ned looked fully at each other. They were no longer wearing their own clothes!

Both of them had on tight-fitting military-type

pants and coats in a silver color, with a matching helmet that fit snugly. There were no buttons or zippers.

How does one get into and out of these clothes? Nancy wondered.

Ned did not speak, but he smiled broadly. Nancy could not hear him laugh, but understood what he was thinking.

This is weird! he was saying to her silently.

There was nothing in sight. No buildings, no trees, just a rubberlike expanse of green grass.

Nancy thought-waved to Ned: If we're not in heaven, but on some other planet, do you think the flying saucer will come back, pick us up, and take us home to earth?

Ned shrugged. I'm freezing in this silly costume, he responded. I feel like a person acting a part in some play, like *Earth Man Lost in Space*.

Nancy smiled. I do too, she told him.

The eerie silence had been nerve-racking. By chance the couple happened to look up at the sky. Not far above them a huge bird was flying. It looked like a combination eagle and airplane. As it passed overhead, the bird dipped its wings as if signaling to the couple below, then turned and repeated the gesture.

Was that a message for us? Nancy wondered, glancing at Ned.

At the same time she looked down at her feet. To her amazement the military-type silver pants ended in footgear that looked like bird's claws.

I can't believe it! Bird's feet! She was puzzled by the whole thing.

Ned grinned. Maybe we've become birds! Human birds! You look pretty nifty at that, he told Nancy.

Are we supposed to fly? she responded, still amazed.

Automatically she pictured Ned as a bird and looked at the back of his broad shoulders. There were two retracted wings!

We are supposed to fly! she thought-waved to him. That's what the bird was trying to tell us.

She pulled out the wings. They opened wide and in a few moments Ned was ready to fly.

Here I go! he announced.

Wait! Nancy pleaded. Don't leave me here alone. She felt her own back, found a pair of wings like Ned's, and asked him to pull hers out.

Nancy's wings spread apart too. She wondered what she should do next in order to fly.

Ned solved the problem by indicating that she should run her fingers through the ends of the wings and hold on. He helped her do this, then put his own fingers to his feathery gear.

Ready! Set! Go! he signaled.

The couple ran as fast as they could over the uneven ground stumbling several times, then began to pump their arms. Within seconds they were airborne! Nancy loved her newfound freedom, as she and Ned soared over the landscape.

Isn't this fun! she thought-waved to Ned who flew alongside her.

He replied, I wonder if I'd ever want to be an earthling again. Maybe it would be better to fly than to walk.

It dawned on Nancy that the two of them were moving at an incredible speed. She expected her arms to tire, but they had no feeling in them.

She pumped her wings a little harder and gathered speed. Strange! She did not feel wind rushing across her face. There was no sensation of any kind.

This is really contrary to everything I learned in science, she thought. Ned nodded that he, too, was puzzled.

After they flew without seeing any sign of life, they wondered what kind of creatures might be able to live in this environment. The place was entirely unpolluted.

Nancy smiled. People at home would like it here. There's no smoke, no streams of water containing trash, no debris or poisonous chemicals.

Ned thought-waved to her, If anyone does live here, how do they survive? Nothing at all seems to be growing here except grass.

His flying companion speculated, Maybe it's a planet of intelligent birds. But what do they live on? Everything needs air, food, and water.

Ned suggested with a grin that maybe the birds imported it all in capsules from another planet.

Nancy giggled at this idea. Bird importers!

After a long flight, the couple finally saw a cluster of buildings ahead. Was it a settlement?

They're all shaped like flying saucers, she remarked, and Ned nodded.

Surely somebody would be around. But as the two friends flew over the extensive terrain, there was no sign of movement anywhere in the city.

After flying some distance out of the area, the travelers came to a large section of green grass. Ned thought-waved to Nancy, Let's go down. I'm getting tired of flying.

I am too. Can you help me retract my wings?

Ned drew alongside her, reached out to hunt for some kind of gadget on her back. He could find none. Nancy also tried to locate a similar device on Ned's wings, but she, too, came up with nothing.

The couple panicked. Were they doomed to fly throughout eternity?

Nancy tried to overcome her fear. It suddenly dawned on her that maybe the wings were thought-controlled.

She closed her eyes tightly and concentrated on Ned. Suddenly his wings retracted. He plummeted to the ground.

Within seconds she had drifted beyond him. She tried to retract her own wings but could not.

I must do something—and fast! she told herself. I mustn't fail!

Nancy pleaded for Ned to help her. He anwered, Turn around and fly back toward me.

Nancy dipped her left wing but found herself flying in a circle. Next she tried to stop by lifting the wings so they were parallel to each other. The flying girl wobbled uncontrollably. Was she going to fall?

Again Nancy was headed away from Ned and flying alone very, very fast!

12

Where? What?

Nancy was desperate as she soared above the uninhabited terrain. How could she retract her wings and glide back safely to the ground?

I mustn't let myself be stranded out here, she thought anxiously. I have to get back to Ned. But how? Oh, this is the worst thing that has ever happened to me!

Once more the young sleuth tried to gain control of the situation. By maneuvering carefully, dipping one wing, then the other, she managed by an erratic course to turn herself around. Relieved, she headed in Ned's direction.

I hope he's safe. Nancy sighed. He has to be. Finally she spotted glints of silver far below her.

There he is! Nancy thought excitedly.

She sent him a mental message: Please help me get down! My wings are out of control. Even when I stop pumping my arms, I keep going.

In reply, Ned suggested that Nancy hold her arms back as far as possible. She complied and gradually began to descend. As she neared the ground, Ned caught hold of her to break her fall and pinned her down to keep her from taking off again.

The entire experience had exhausted Nancy. The sky, the landscape, even Ned began to spin in front of her eyes. "Ned, Ned, I'm afraid I—" she mumbled before blacking out.

It was some time later when Nancy awoke. To her astonishment, the girl detective was lying in Dismal Swamp of Shawniegunk Mountain, U.S.A. Ned was nearby. He too was regaining consciousness and stirred slightly.

Through hazy vision Nancy thought she saw the Indian Shoso kneeling beside her. Then she became aware that there was a large leaf in her mouth. It tasted bitter.

How did this get in my mouth and why? she wondered.

As Nancy started to take it out, Shoso shook his head vehemently and pushed the leaf back inside. He pretended to chew, indicating she should do the

same. Too groggy to refuse, Nancy obeyed and was surprised that she soon felt much better. Now she sat up and looked around her. The flying saucer was gone!

Had the spaceship brought Nancy and Ned back to the swamp, then flown off again? Maybe Shoso could tell them.

Using sign language, she asked him if he had seen it leave. He held out his arms in a circle, then pointed to the sky. Next, he fluttered his fingers up and down, implying that rain or rays of some sort had begun to fall. Shoso pointed to the sky again, then finished by making another circle with his arms.

I believe Shoso is trying to tell me that it rained hard, but after the sun came out the flying saucer took off.

Nancy looked up at the sky. The sun was shining brightly and it was hot. The swamp was steaming and the rank, nauseating odor was stronger than ever.

Ned sat up. He was chewing a leaf. As he swallowed it, the couple looked at each other and smiled.

"What an incredible trip we had!" Nancy exclaimed.

"We?" Ned gulped. "You weren't with me."

"Part of the time I was," she told him.

The boy shook his head. "You must have been dreaming," he said.

Nancy's blackout scene was so vivid in her mind she found it hard to believe him. She glanced at the backs of Ned's hands: neither was scorched. Nancy looked down at her own; they were all right, too.

"But I was so sure—"

The girl detective next noticed that she and Ned had on their rain gear—their own clothes! What happened to the fantastic bird-flying suits they had worn? And what about the grotesque bird's claws that had covered their feet?

Nancy shook her head and laughed. "Ned, I've just awakened from the most incredible dream I've ever had. I still can't believe that it was all my imagination."

"Tell me about it," Ned requested.

As she related the story, Nancy kept including him in it. He roared with laughter when she described the two of them in flight through the windless air of an unknown planet.

"Human birds, eh?"

However, he sobered when she mentioned that at one point she wondered if they had died and gone to heaven.

"Too bad you didn't bring back a pair of angel wings," he teased.

She chuckled and took a deep breath. He told

her that in his dream he had not left the forest. "But I became some kind of knight, slashing a sword at wild beasts. I knew what some of them were, but others looked strange—prehistoric."

Nancy and Ned decided that gas from either the swamp or the flying saucer had put them to sleep.

"It's a shame the flying saucer left before we had a chance to investigate it more thoroughly," Nancy remarked.

"It may come back," Ned told her, trying to cheer up the young sleuth. "I'd say the ship was in some kind of trouble when it landed. Otherwise, it wouldn't have stayed so long and put up with our hammering, trying to learn its secret."

"Don't forget that the ship may have been programmed. Maybe it landed and took off exactly when it was supposed to," Nancy suggested. "Who knows what its owners planned to do with it?"

Ned suggested that Shoso might know when it left. "Let's ask him."

The couple stood up and looked around. The Indian was not in sight. They called his name again and again, but he did not appear.

"Too bad," Ned commented. "Now what?"

Nancy suggested that they search for any evidence that the ship might have left. In the center of the swamp was a badly scorched depression which she and Ned noticed for the first time.

Nancy said, "When the flying saucer took off, its antigravity rays may have been so hot they burned the ground. Let's dig up a little of the soil and take it back to camp for a lab analysis."

"Good idea," Ned replied.

Nancy headed for the saddlebags on her horse. Susan B, she was relieved to find, was safe. Apparently the gas from the swamp or flying saucer had not reached the animals. She hugged Susan B and patted Goalpost.

"I'm glad nothing hapened to you," Nancy said affectionately and unfastened one of her saddlebags. She took out a trowel and a small plastic bag.

When Nancy returned to the swamp, Ned dug up a chunk of scorched soil and dumped it into the bag, which Nancy held open. Then she took the mysterious sample back to Susan B, placed it in the saddlebag, and fastened the flap tightly.

She said to Ned, who had followed her up the slope, "Wouldn't it be wonderful if chemists found something in this sample different from anything known on earth?"

"Boy, would it ever!" Ned replied. "It might revolutionize oui whole concept of the universe!"

The couple mounted their horses and set off for camp. They had not gone far, when suddenly Susan B sunfished.

"Easy, girl!" Nancy cried out.

She barely managed to control the horse and stay astride. The saddlebags nearly fell off as the animal dropped down on her forelegs and then lay down on one side. Nancy jumped off. The horse kicked viciously, trying to reach the saddlebag containing the soil sample.

"What's the matter with her?" Ned asked, puzzled by the strange behavior.

Furiously the horse kicked her hooves as the couple watched, helpless.

"She seems to be trying to get at that saddlebag," Nancy observed, keeping a safe distance from the animal. "I'm sure something inside it is bothering her. But what?"

13

A Discovery

Ned jumped from his horse and hurried forward to help Nancy and the distressed mare.

"Thank goodness you weren't hurt, Nancy," he said. "Susan B is really acting up."

"The poor thing's beside herself," Nancy said.

The riders urged the animal to stand up. Then quickly they pulled off the saddlebag.

"Look!" Nancy exclaimed, staring at the horse's flank." Her skin is badly scorched here."

Quickly they flipped over the saddlebag. A large hole had burned through the leather.

"It must have come from the sod we dug up," the young sleuth remarked, alarmed. "Oh, Ned, maybe it's radioactive!"

She unbuckled the saddlebag and dumped the contents on the ground. The plastic bag containing the sample also had burned through.

Nancy and Ned stared at each other as the same thought ran through their minds: Susan B might be contaminated!

"Ned, you and I might be contaminated, too!" Nancy cried out in alarm.

Other articles in the bag did not appear to be damaged, including a jar of healing salve. Quickly Nancy dipped her finger into the ointment and spread a generous amount over the scorched area on Susan B's flank.

She remarked, "Ned, if we've been exposed to radioactive material, I wish this salve alone could cure us. What do you think we should do?"

Ned advised that they bury the chunk of scorched earth, the saddle, and the saddlebag and everything in it.

"Good idea," Nancy agreed.

Using the trowel, Ned dug a deep hole. Nancy dropped in the suspect pieces one by one. After piling dirt over them and marking the spot with a heap of twigs, the campers started off again.

Nancy sat behind Ned on Goalpost, her own horse's lead rope in hand. "As soon as we get to town," she said, "I think we'd better get in touch with some scientists and a vet. Why don't we phone my dad? He might be able to fly up here right away and bring help with him."

"Good thinking," Ned replied.

When the couple rode into camp, they were bombarded with questions by their friends. Before they could answer them, Hal and Burt arrived, leading the two missing packhorses.

"I'm so glad you're back!" Jan exclaimed. "Now we have all the horses again."

"But mine is injured," Nancy announced and told the fantastic story of what happened to her and Ned.

The possibility that she and Ned might be contaminated by radioactive material really horrified everyone.

Dave spoke up. "It's not catching, thank goodness, so we don't have to isolate you two. But we shouldn't use any of the same eating utensils."

Jan offered to ride into town with Nancy, Ned, and the injured mare. "Nancy, you can take one of the other riding horses."

The group ate a light meal, then started off. When they reached the little town at the foot of the mountain, Nancy called her father and told him the amazing story.

"What!" he exclaimed. "Tell me everything. How are you and Ned?"

Nancy gave him all the details, and he replied, "I'll get a plane and scientists and doctors to come up there at once. I'll be with them. Wait right there for us. If we're going to be delayed, I'll phone you in about an hour."

Mr. Drew took the number of the telephone Nancy was using. "By the way, dear," he said, "an excited young woman phoned and wants you to solve a mystery for her. Something about strange identities. I told her you're tied up on another mystery right now, but she begged me to get in touch with you and call her back. What shall I tell her?"

"Oh, I wish I could help." Nancy sighed. "Dad, why don't you suggest she contact our friends the Dana Girls? They're great at solving mysteries."

"I'll do that," Mr. Drew promised. Then he hung up the phone, and Nancy returned to Ned and Jan.

"We're going to have a fairly long wait," she remarked. "Can we take Susan B to a vet?"

Jan nodded. "Follow me."

The three walked to the office-hospital of Dr. Doyle. Fortunately, he was able to examine the stricken animal at once. Nancy told him about the swamp but did not mention the flying saucer. This was to remain a secret until the mystery was solved.

"We thought it might be interesting to have the soil analyzed," she said, "and decided to bring some of it back to camp. The sample was so hot it burned a hole through my saddlebag and injured my horse's flank. I put salve on it." Nancy gave Dr. Doyle the name of the ointment.

"Quick thinking," the veterinarian complimented her.

"What worries us in particular is that part of

Dismal Swamp may be contaminated by radiation and could have affected Susan B. My father is flying here with some chemists to analyze it."

Dr. Doyle looked surprised. "How could Dismal Swamp become contaminated?" he inquired, puzzled.

Nancy shrugged. After the veterinarian had examined Susan B's wound, he said, "I suggest you leave the horse here. This is a pretty bad burn ."

"All right," Jan said, adding that the animal had been rented in town. "But our group will be responsible for your fee."

Before Nancy left the office, she put her arms around the horse that she had grown to love. She whispered in Susan B's ear, "I'm so sorry I got you into this. I hope you'll be okay soon."

After they left, Jan said they would need to rent horses for the new arrivals, a replacement horse for Nancy, and two more packhorses to carry whatever equipment the party might bring. "And we'll buy a lot of food to take back to camp," she added.

By the time the extra horses were collected and all purchases made, Nancy and her friends heard the whir of a helicopter overhead. It did not go to the airfield, but came down in a field on the outskirts of town. Nancy, Ned, and Jan hurried to meet its passengers.

As soon as Nancy saw her father step out of the copter, she ran ahead of the others. Then she stopped short. If I'm contaminated, perhaps I should not kiss him, the girl thought. She blew a kiss from a distance. He laughed, came up, and gave her a hug.

"Let's not be overanxious about this," he said. "I've brought two doctors and two scientists with me. Others will arrive later. Right now the doctors are going to test you and Ned for radioactivity."

After introductions had been made, one of the doctors took from his bag a strange-looking instrument with all sorts of dials and indicators on its face. He held the end of a tube with a knob against Nancy's heart, lungs, and the back of her neck. Was he testing her brain?

"So far everything is negative," Dr. Caffrey reported. "Now, young man," he said, "it's your turn."

Ned, too, was pronounced all right. The doctor shook his head and remarked, "You're lucky." He put away his instruments and the group stowed their gear on the packhorses and set off for camp. They had barely started when Nancy rode up beside Jan and asked if she would please stop the string of riders.

Without questioning Nancy's reason, the leader called out, "Halt!"

Everyone reined in. Nancy said, "It just occurred to me that perhaps we should have Dr. Caffrey examine Susan B for contamination. After all, she was burned by the sod in the swamp, but Ned and

I didn't touch it with our bare hands, or get any mud from the scorched area on us."

"You're right," Jan agreed and called out to the doctor, "Can you give the horse with the burn a radioactive test?"

"Sure. Glad to."

Jan told the others, "Wait here for us. Nancy and I will ride to the vet's and have Susan B examined for contamination."

Everyone agreed to the plan and the three riders galloped off. Twenty minutes later they were back.

"The horse is okay," the doctor reported. "She has a nasty burn but no contamination symptoms. Nevertheless, I think that swamp definitely should be investigated."

"It will be," Nancy said, then added, "Let's go!"

The riders urged their horses up the mountain. When they arrived at camp, their anxious friends were delighted to hear the results of the tests. The newcomers were introduced and they all sat down to a hot supper.

Nancy and Ned asked Hal and Burt to explain how they had found the lost packhorses. According to the boys it had not been easy, but after a fruitless search, they had finally heard a whinny.

"One horse caught a front hoof in a bear trap," Hal said. "Of course he couldn't move, but we managed to get the trap off. Fortunately it had snapped around the colt's hoof, not in it, so he wasn't really injured."

Now it was Nancy and Ned's turn to relate their adventure. The doctors and scientists laughed.

Mr. Drew chuckled also. "I like the part where you two couldn't talk, but were able to communicate by thought waves. From now on I'll have to be careful what I think!"

"That's right, Dad," Nancy said with a mischievous wink.

Early next morning Nancy was awakened by a barking dog. That sounds like Trixie, she told herself, and jumped out of her sleeping bag. She slipped on her jeans over her pajamas and went outside.

George joined her as Trixie bounded into camp and rushed up to the girls.

"Trixie has a note tied to the rope around her neck!" George exlaimed.

Quickly she removed the message and opened it for her and Nancy to read.

14

A Valuable Clue

The two girls read the note aloud. It had been signed by Old Joe.

> Dear Nancy and Friends,
>
> I am still amazed by your finding the stone pyramid. It was a valuable clue. I went to the brook myself; below the waterline I found a marker, and to my amazement my father's initials were on it.

George exclaimed, "How wonderful!" She and Nancy read on:

> There was also an arrow on the marker. I followed its direction for some distance, then I injured my foot.

"What a shame!" Nancy remarked. "I hope it's not bad. Well, let's see what else Old Joe has written."

The note continued:

> I knew I had to give up the search. It was only with great difficulty that I got back to my cabin. Now I have a favor to ask of you: Would you young people like to take up the search?

Nancy and George looked at each other, then grinned. George said, "Would we!"

"It's an exciting challenge," Nancy admitted, but added, "You know that we won't be able to go immediately."

"Why not?" George asked, eager to take up the hunt.

Nancy reminded her that more scientists were arriving and would probably want to ask questions of the campers, especially Nancy and Ned. "I think I should stay here."

George agreed. "Have you any idea when the rest of the experts are coming?"

Nancy shook her head no. "I'm sure it'll be soon. In the meantime, I ought to get some paper and a pencil and answer Old Joe."

In her reply she said that the young sleuths would do their best to find out where the arrow led.

Then she added:

> But I will have to wait at camp a little while before starting. Some scientists are coming here to examine Dismal Swamp. Ned and I discovered it was scorched, apparently by the flying saucer. Incidentally, I'm sorry to say that the ship took off again.

She explained briefly what had happened to her and Ned and how Shoso had put restorative leaves in their mouths.

> Old Joe, do you have any idea what those leaves are?

She signed the note, attached it to the dog's rope collar, and said, "Trixie, take this back to your master." The dog bounded off.

Soon afterward the other campers were awake. Nancy showed the note to Bess and Jan.

"Oh! The poor man!" Bess said. "I'd like to help him. Would somebody go over to his cabin with me?"

Jan offered to accompany her. "I'll pack some medical supplies and see what I can do to relieve Old Joe's pain."

For a few minutes Jan and the girls discussed whether they should ask one of the visiting doctors to go along.

"They would probably prefer to wait for the rest

of the scientists to investigate Dismal Swamp together," Nancy said.

As Bess and Jan gathered supplies, the young detective asked her father to take a walk with her. When they were out of hearing range of the other campers, he asked, "What's on your mind, dear?"

"I was wondering if we should notify the FBI or another top-secret agency about the flying saucer. I have a strong hunch the ship will come back. Wouldn't it be wonderful if the U.S. could capture it?"

Mr. Drew stared at his daughter, then grinned. "It's a great idea but a big order. We don't know if the saucer is from outer space, or the property of some rival country that's spying on us. In any case, I'll ride into town and make some phone calls."

He and Nancy walked back to camp. They learned that Bess had packed some food for Old Joe. As soon as breakfast was over, she and Jan set off for the naturalist's cabin.

On the way Shoso suddenly appeared. He was muttering unintelligibly. Was he trying to tell them something?

Jan said, "I have an idea he's speaking his Indian dialect. It's so strange because, as you know, there are no Indians in this vicinity anymore."

"Maybe he's a wanderer," Bess suggested.

"But Indians usually stay in bands or tribes," Jan countered.

Shoso was gesticulating with his arms, and finally motioned the two campers to follow him.

"Shall we do it?" Bess asked her companion.

"Oh, sure. Why not?" Jan replied. "Besides, I'm curious to find out where he wants to take us."

Shoso seemed to know every inch of the forest. To their surprise he led them to Old Joe's cabin by a completely different route.

"It's about half the distance," Jan remarked. "I hope we can find our way back to camp the same way."

The Indian dropped behind Jan and Bess. Before they could turn to thank him he had, as usual, disappeared.

Bess remarked dreamily, "If I hadn't seen Shoso in person, I'd think he's a spirit. He appears and vanishes so fast, it's like magic."

Jan laughed and said that was a good description of the Indian. They now approached the open cabin door and called inside.

"Come in!" Old Joe responded.

He was sitting up in bed with a huge bandage wrapped around his injured foot.

"Hello," he said. "Isn't this a great way for a forest dweller to treat himself? And I'd just started on an exciting hunt to solve my mystery."

Bess smiled and shook hands with him. "Everybody has an accident once in a while," she said soothingly.

Jan told him she was a nurse. "What have you been doing for yourself, Old Joe?"

"Don't you girls smell what's cooking in my fireplace?"

Jan and Bess nodded. The delicious aroma of pine filled the room. Jan peered into the pot where a combination of pine bark, sap from the tree, and crushed pine needles was brewing. It had cooked down to a thick, jellylike consistency. Old Joe said he had put this mixture on his foot and ankle, then bandaged the whole thing.

Jan smiled. "I couldn't have done better myself. Pine is one of the most healing remedies that exist. I remember an old saying—if anything ails you, go into the forest and lie on a bed of pine needles. It will cure colds or any other type of respiratory disorder. Moreover, it will pep up circulation, and this in turn can cure almost any type of illness a person has except, of course, broken bones."

The naturalist bobbed his head. "I learned the same thing from my father. And let me tell you, it works."

Old Joe brought up Nancy's note. "Please tell Nancy that I don't know what kind of leaves Shoso gave her and Ned. But if you see the Indian ask him to show you where he got the leaves, and give a few to the doctors to analyze."

Bess and Jan prepared the food they had brought and Old Joe accepted it gratefully. When he'd almost finished eating, he called to Trixie.

With a twinkle in his eye, Old Joe said to his visitors, "Don't you think she deserves a little of this good food for doing my errand so promptly?"

"We sure do," Bess agreed. The dog lapped up the remains of the canned beef and wagged her tail in appreciation.

The callers said good-bye and started for camp. Bess and Jan followed the trail which Shoso had shown them. Halfway along they saw the Indian again. He stood before them, arms crossed. First Jan, then Bess, asked him about the restorative leaves. What plant or tree did they come from and could he give them some more? Shoso stared at them blankly. He didn't understand a word.

"I'll try sign language," Bess said hopefully and started a little pantomime for him to watch.

First she raised her arms then flapped them to show that something was coming down from the sky.

She said to Jan, "I hope Shoso won't think that it's a bird. But how do I indicate a flying saucer descending?"

"I haven't the faintest idea," Jan replied.

The Indian watched Bess very carefully as she lay down on the ground and closed her eyes, pretending to be asleep.

Jan caught on to the little act. She pulled a leaf

off a nearby aspen tree and put it in Bess's mouth. The girl chewed it and opened her eyes. She stood up and looked hopefully at Shoso. If only she could get her urgent message across!

Apparently the Indian understood. He nodded and picked several of the same leaves. Then Shoso gave Bess a faint smile and hurried off through the forest.

Jan remarked, "You're quite an actress, Bess. He caught on fast."

"I only hope my message was clear to him," the pantomimist replied. Then she giggled. "Imagine playing charades out here in the forest with an Indian who doesn't speak a word of English!"

Jan grinned. "There's always a first time for everything."

Bess laughed, then she and Jan continued their ride. As they neared their campsite, they heard the loud noise of a helicopter. They looked up but saw nothing. Reining in, they paused to listen and kept their eyes skyward.

"I wonder if the pilot's trying to find us," Jan said. "That certainly would be difficult in this dense forest."

"You mean," Bess asked, "that if he's trying to locate us, he'll land at the foot of the mountain and walk or ride up here to talk to us?"

"Probably," Jan replied.

"What do you suppose he wants?" Bess asked.

"Listen!" Jan ordered suddenly. "The copter sounds as if it's in trouble."

"Oh, I hope not," Bess gasped in fright as the engine sputtered, died, then caught again. Within seconds it repeated the worrisome sound. "It would be dreadful for that poor pilot to crash in the forest!"

15

Lab in the Forest

The helicopter continued to make strange, faltering noises over the camp. Everyone on the ground was afraid it would crash on top of them.

"Why doesn't the pilot try to fly away? Surely he must see us," George complained.

Burt said, "Maybe I can communicate with the pilot by walkie-talkie." He tried to tune in but had no success. "The pilot can't pick up our wavelength, I guess," he said. "Too bad."

The craft dipped and rose, made a large sweeping circle, then flew back over the camp. Again Burt attempted to make contact. Finally he managed to get a faint response. "Come in whoever you are."

"I think I have him!" Burt exclaimed. He yelled

into the speaker, "Standing by in the forest below. Are you in trouble? Over."

"No, but I'm glad I contacted you. We have permission to land in the forest, but can't find a place. Any suggestions?"

Nancy, who had been listening, now spoke up. "Ask them how much room the copter needs."

"Not much," the pilot answered when Burt questioned him. "If we send tools down, can you cut some small trees to make space for us?"

Burt consulted the other boys and the scientists in the group.

"We can do it, but it won't be too smooth," Ned warned.

Burt relayed this to the pilot who said he would manage. "I'll make sure we avoid any leftover tree stumps."

Ned and the men gathered in a small clearing between clumps of trees and bushes. The copter hung overhead and lowered bags on a rope cable. After several of them had reached the ground, the cable was pulled up. The copter circled again.

The bags were opened and axes, saws, and other equipment taken out. The men divided into teams to tackle the saplings.

"Can't we girls do something?" Nancy asked.

Mr. Drew suggested that they pull up the bushes while the men worked on the trees. Soon the stillness of the forest was broken by the chopping sound of axes, the crash of small trees, and the buzz of saws as stumps were cut to the ground.

Whenever a heavier sapling needed to be removed, the men sliced off the branches for the girls to lug away, then either dragged the trunks beyond the immediate area or quickly sawed them into lengths that were easier to carry. Within a short time a landing area was ready for the copter.

As soon as it settled down, men poured from the doorway. First they introduced themselves to Mr. Drew, who in turn presented Jan, Hal, and all the young people.

Among the new arrivals were a botanist, a zoologist, three chemists, and two aerospace experts.

"This copter is not a standard model," said Dr. Halpern, one of the chemists. "It's really a flying lab. We wanted to park it as close to Dismal Swamp as possible."

Dave remarked, "I guess you don't often land in a forest."

"That's for sure." Dr. Halpern nodded, smiling. "What we have ahead of us are perhaps the most unusual experiments we've ever undertaken."

The men brought their own camping equipment and set up near their lab. When they finished, Dr. Halpern asked Nancy and Ned to tell them about their amazing adventure, including their dreams. The couple took turns filling in the details.

When they mentioned the effect of the restorative leaves that Shoso had fed them, Bess spoke up. "He's bringing us more. At least I think so."

The scientists were intrigued. "We'll analyze them," Dr. Halpern said promptly.

"I hope Shoso brings them soon." Bess sighed.

The newcomers were ready to go to Dismal Swamp. They brought masks and heavy gauntlets which they slung over their shoulders. A few carried trowels, others spades, and the rest, acid-proof bags. They borrowed available horses.

To Nancy and the others who stayed behind it seemed like hours before the group returned, but in fact, they were not gone long. As soon as they reappeared, however, all but one of them went to their laboratory to analyze the scorched sod.

One young man stopped long enough to say to Nancy, "You sure were right about the horrible odor from the swamp. I'm glad we had gas masks. I'll take my dreams in more pleasant surroundings!" He hurried after his co-workers.

The young sleuths, together with Mr. Drew, waited impatiently to hear the results of the tests. It was more than an hour later that the scientists rejoined the campers.

Dr. Halpern said, "I assume all of you are eager to know what we found. Frankly we have divided opinions. Some of us think the swamp produced the acid. Others feel the UFO left the acid which may have scorched one area of the swamp."

Nancy asked, "Have you decided yet what the chemical is?"

Dr. Halpern said that the scientists were still puzzled. "All I can tell you is that we've determined it is a strong, nonflammable acid, but very penetrating. One question is, if the flying saucer is responsible, did the acid come from some other planet?"

Dr. York, another scientist, spoke up. "If it's from Dismal Swamp itself, then we have quite a chemical mystery on our hands. To my knowledge, this acid is not found in such concentrated form anywhere else in the world."

The discussion turned to the possibility that the flying saucer sprayed the acid as it took off. Nancy and Ned reminded the men that they were overcome by the fumes before the saucer left.

"That does complicate the matter," Dr. Halpern admitted. "Well, we have many more experiments to make. I hope we come up with some definite answers soon."

Dr. Caffrey, who arrived with Mr. Drew, told the other scientists that he had tested Nancy and Ned for contamination by radiation. "Thank goodness, I found no sign of it," he declared.

Dr. Halpern asked if Dr. Caffrey would mind repeating the radiation test. "I'd like to see how your machine operates."

As before, Nancy was given a clean bill of health.

Ned was about to enter the tent where the test was being held, when he called out, "Do you expect sparks to fly from my head?"

The others laughed. "Not only sparks," Dave replied, "but a pair of antennas!"

When Ned and the doctor failed to appear within a reasonable time, the campers became anxious. Had Dr. Caffrey found something this time?

Nancy felt that she could not wait any longer for an answer and was ready to burst into the tent, when the pair emerged. Both were smiling.

"Everything is okay," Dr. Caffrey reported.

"What took you so long?" Burt asked. "You had all of us worried."

"Sorry," Ned replied. "We were talking about what might have happened to Nancy and me while we were unconscious."

Mr. Drew asked, "You have a new theory?"

Ned wondered if possibly some creature in the flying saucer communicated with the couple while they were asleep.

"How could he do that?" George asked.

Ned answered, "Perhaps he hypnotized us—told us what he wanted us to think, see, and do."

Bess shivered a little. "You mean someone controlled your mind?"

"I suppose it's possible," Ned replied.

"Even—even to make you believe you died and went to heaven?" Bess queried.

"Oh, sure," Ned answered with a chuckle.

By now Bess was absolutely terrified. "Do you realize that those weirdos may come back here and work on all of us?"

When Ned nodded, trying to tease her, she said, "Oh, don't say such things! You've scared me silly!"

Dave felt sorry for her. He sat down next to Bess and laid a comforting hand on her shoulder. "Don't be afraid. Ned is only kidding you."

"Oh, yes?" Ned asked.

Mr. Drew suggested they drop the subject in favor of preparing the evening meal. The newly arrived scientists went to their own quarters in the lab. The rest ate a delicious supper which Jan prepared. There was more conversation until about nine o'clock, when everyone started to yawn. Finally the campers went to bed.

It was a very warm night and Nancy, Bess, and George, who were together in one tent, decided to leave the side flaps halfway up. There was not a sound anywhere except the hoot of a distant owl.

Much later Nancy, sound asleep, thought a voice had called her name. She roused but did not open her eyes. Then she heard it distinctly.

"Nancy! Nancy!"

16

The Eerie Cave

Nancy managed to pull herself out of her deep sleep. She saw a figure standing over her. Instinctively she grabbed the flashlight from under her pillow and shone it into the mysterious face.

"Shoso!" she called.

Without a word he handed her a bunch of leaves, then turned and vanished. Nancy beamed her light on them.

The restorative leaves Bess had asked for! Great! she thought.

Hoping not to disturb her friends, the young sleuth got up quietly, took a plastic bag from her backpack, and put the leaves inside it. Finally she crawled back into her sleeping bag and dozed off.

The next thing she knew it was morning. The sun was shining through the trees, and birds were singing.

When the three groups of campers assembled to plan the day's work, Nancy showed the bag of leaves to everyone and told them about her night visitor.

Bess gaped at her friend in amazement. "And you didn't call George and me? Weren't you scared? Oh, I'd have died if I'd seen that man's stony face staring at me!" The others laughed.

Professor Hendricks, the botanist, asked for the leaves. "We'll analyze them this morning."

"They are unusual-looking," Dr. Caffrey said. "I don't recognize them."

"If you professionals don't recognize them," Mr. Drew remarked, "then I guess nobody would. Do you suppose this mountain forest is the only place in the world where the plant grows?"

"Maybe it's a tree," Bess suggested. "Let's find out from Shoso."

George had an idea. "We don't know where Shoso lives. Perhaps he has a garden and the leaves grow in it."

"Or," Jan said, and paused a moment, "maybe the tribe that once lived in this forest cultivated the plant, knowing its medicinal value."

"That's very possible," Dr. Caffrey agreed. "I'm

curious to see what you chemists come up with."

The botanist smiled. "I may even eat one of the leaves to sample its positive effect for myself!"

Since Nancy's group could do nothing to help, she suggested that the six young people continue their hunt for Old Joe's treasure.

"Where shall we start?" Dave asked, "and what shall we take?"

"I suggest you take hunting knives and that we begin at the pyramid of rocks I told you about," the girl detective answered. "We should see for ourselves where the arrow points."

The young sleuths put on waterproof hiking boots, packed a lunch, collected digging tools, and started off.

Hal called to them, "Bring us some fish!" He ran up to Dave and handed him a bucket with a punctured lid.

"Supper coming up," Dave replied with a grin. "A whole bucket full."

Nancy said, "Let's ride to the stream."

The group mounted. Nancy and George led the way to the marker inscribed with the initials of Old Joe's father. They tethered the horses and waded into the water.

The boys tried to catch trout with their hands. They thought it would be as easy for them as it was for Old Joe's dog, Trixie, but the slippery fish wriggled out of their grasp.

"There's a big one coming!" Dave shouted eagerly. "And I'm going to get it!"

He was about to grab the fish, when he slipped on a rock and fell, splashing water in every direction. The girls burst into laughter.

"Why don't you try it?" Dave said, disgruntled.

Ned and Burt were more successful. They put several fish into the bucket and fastened the lid. But as Ned dived for another speckled trout, he kicked over the bucket by accident. The lid came off and all of the fish they had caught swam downstream.

"We're pretty poor fishermen, I'd say," he chided himself.

Again the three girls giggled. "Maybe we're bad luck," Bess said. "Why don't Nancy, George, and I go on and let you boys catch fish by yourselves?"

The other girls agreed. They stopped to look at the pyramid. By pushing some stones aside they uncovered the initials and the arrow. It pointed directly across the bubbling stream.

When they reached the opposite bank, the searchers decided to separate. "Let's return in ten minutes to this same spot," Nancy suggested, "and report whatever clues we find."

The first time they met they were discouraged. "You don't suppose," Bess said, "that we're on a wild goose chase? Maybe Old Joe's father was a jokester."

"I think not," Nancy said. "I have an idea he was

serious, but wanted to keep his secret well hidden. Let's investigate beyond the immediate area this time."

Once more each girl went on her own, carefully examining every tree and rock. When the trio met again, George was grinning.

"I found something!" she exclaimed. "Follow me. Hurry!"

Bess suggested that they wait a few minutes for the boys. "We're already ahead of them. If we go too far, we could easily lose one another. I don't want us to get lost in this forest."

"Here they come now," Nancy said, glancing back on their trail.

The three boys were trudging up the short path the girls had made leading from the stream. Burt was carrying the bucket gingerly.

"Any luck?" George asked, then added teasingly, "Or did all those small speckled creatures slip away from you again?"

Burt smiled. "I'll show you."

He unfastened the lid partway. The girls gazed inside. To their amazement the bucket was full of trout!

"There's enough fish for everybody at camp," Bess remarked. "What a yummy supper. I can taste it now."

George led the group to a tree on which another

arrow had been carved. Underneath it, almost obliterated, were the initials *JA*.

"Joseph Austin!" Nancy exclaimed. "Super!"

"We're in luck!" Dave said.

The searchers set off in the direction indicated by the arrow. They trekked for some time, looking carefully at everything they passed, but there were no further directions. They kept on straight ahead, but became more discouraged by the minute.

Finally Nancy called a halt. "How about a rest period?" she suggested, dropping to the ground.

"Great idea," Bess replied. "And a good time to have that lunch we brought."

"Is that all you ever think about—lunch?" George replied.

"No," Bess smirked, "sometimes I think about dinner!"

Without waiting for another teasing remark from her cousin, Bess went to help with preparations. The snack was ready in minutes and eaten with gusto. Then the trekkers started off again.

"Wait a minute!" Nancy said. "I think we're going in the wrong direction."

"I agree," Ned told her.

They all returned to the luncheon spot, got their bearings, and started off once more. It was not long before they came to a good-sized tree with another carved arrow on it. They looked carefully for initials but if there had ever been any, they were gone now.

"Maybe Old Joe's father didn't put this arrow mark here," Burt suggested.

Nancy studied it closely. In her mind was a vivid picture of the other arrows.

"I'm sure this was made by the same person," she said. "I counted the number of little featherlike veins on the others. This one has the same amount."

Ned looked at her admiringly. "We didn't even see them, much less count them," he said. "Great sleuthing."

George noticed that this arrow pointed to a steep rise of land. When the climbers reached the top, they saw ahead of them a circular clump of trees that didn't seem part of the original forest, but looked as though they had been planted by someone. "Do you suppose that means something?" Dave asked.

Everyone rushed forward and then the boys squeezed behind the trees. A moment later, Ned called, "There's a cave here. It looks like a deep one."

He had scarcely finished speaking when they heard a nasty snarl and a hiss. The boys shrank back.

"Another wildcat!" Ned cried out, as the animal appeared at the cave entrance.

Nancy had a sudden hunch. "Maybe it's Kitty, Old Joe's friend. This may be her lair." She called out, "Kitty! Kitty! Where are you?"

The snarling and hissing ceased and the wildcat stopped short. Nancy continued to speak to her.

"Kitty, behave yourself! We're not going to hurt you!"

Finally Kitty came toward them. Did she recognize Nancy and Ned? Taking a chance, they patted the wildcat.

Bess was terrified. "You shouldn't do that!"

The animal looked up and for a moment they all panicked. Would she spring at one of them? But the big cat remained passive and quiet.

Nancy said to the others, "While Ned and I keep Kitty happy, why don't you four investigate the cave?"

"Will do," Dave replied.

The two couples walked behind the clump of trees and turned on their flashlights. In the meantime Kitty got a whiff of the fish in the bucket. She pawed at it, trying to push the lid off.

Nancy was afraid she might overturn the bucket and let the water run out. Then the fish would die. "Why don't we give Kitty one of the fish?" she suggested.

"Okay," Ned agreed. He selected a plump trout and threw it to the wildcat. She caught it in her mouth and ran off with the fish.

"I hope she doesn't return for more," Nancy said.

"Me, too," Ned added, with a grin.

Kitty did not come back, and everyone gave a sigh of relief. Ned hung the bucket on a high branch, hoping no other animal would try to disturb the fish. He and Nancy now entered the cave.

"Look what we found!" Bess exclaimed.

She and the others were examining pictures painted on the walls. They had dusted them off so the sketches could be seen plainly. One scene depicted a white hunter stalking toward an enormous tree. An Indian face was carved on the trunk.

George asked the others if they thought Old Joe's father had drawn the pictures, or whether an Indian may have painted them many years ago.

"It's very hard to say," Burt replied. "Whoever painted them was a real artist. The colors are perfect and haven't faded."

"They're great likenesses of Indians," Bess murmured, studying the paintings carefully.

In the meantime, Nancy was looking at another picture beyond the one of the big tree—a half-circle of footprints in front of a cave.

"I think this sketch refers to the cave we're in," she said, "and I think it's connected to the other picture of the hunter. The half-circle of footprints may lead from here to an enormous tree with an

Indian head on it. So let's get going! I have a hunch Old Joe's father really did draw these pictures."

"You mean we may be getting close to the treasure he buried?" Bess asked.

Yes, come on!"

17

Fire!

Undecided how to start hunting for the big tree with an Indian painted on it, Nancy's friends paced aimlessly. Which way should they go? There was no arrow to give them a clue.

Finally Ned broke the silence. "We're wasting time. I have a suggestion. After all, this is Nancy's mystery. Why don't we let her make the decision and we'll follow it?"

The others chorused their agreement.

Nancy smiled. "Thanks," she said. "The pictures indicate that we should half circle the cave until we reach an enormous tree with an Indian face on it."

"So," said George, "we ought to begin with small half-circles and keep making them larger until we find the right tree?"

Nancy nodded. The group spread out into parallel, semicircular formations and walked through the forest, examining every tree along the way.

"I think I found something!" Burt shouted excitedly. "Come here, everybody!"

His friends immediately ran toward him. Nancy was beaming as she darted past the others, hopeful that the search had ended successfully. When she reached him, Burt was on his hands and knees, brushing dirt away from the roots of a tree.

"Where's the Indian's face?" Nancy asked, as she glanced in puzzlement around the trunk.

"No Indian," Burt mumbled, still digging his nails into the soft ground. "Here!" he exclaimed at last.

Proudly he displayed the blunt tip of an arrow.

"Oh," Nancy said, secretly disappointed. "That's very nice."

"Nice!" Burt repeated. "Is that all you can say? It's *great!*"

By now, the others had gathered around the young man.

"So where's the Indian's face?" George inquired.

Nancy pointed to the arrowhead, and George said, "Is that all you found?"

Gradually losing his own enthusiasm, Burt nodded. To ease his regret, Nancy said, "I heard Jan say that Hal picked up a few old arrowheads not far from here. Maybe we ought to add this one to the collection."

Burt dropped the arrow in George's hand. "Be my guest," he said.

"Actually," George interrupted, "I'd like to wear it on a neck chain." She winked at Burt. "If you don't mind, that is."

"Of course I don't mind," he answered, evidently pleased.

The searchers continued their hunt for almost half an hour longer, but returned finally to their starting point. No one had discovered anything helpful.

Again Bess suggested they were on a wild goose chase, and once more the others disagreed with her. "Well, what do we do now?" she asked.

Nancy said that perhaps the half-circle of footprints in the cave picture might be the other half of the circles they had made.

"We'll retrace our steps, but instead of stopping halfway, we'll complete the circle."

George proposed that everyone change places. "Maybe someone else will spot what the others missed."

The group drew lots to determine who would take which circle. Nancy was assigned to the one farthest from the cave.

The search continued and no one spoke. Their

eyes were riveted to each tree they saw. Without discovering anything unusual they soon reached the end of the half-circle and went on to complete it fully.

Nancy had almost finished circling when she paused to gaze at a giant aspen tree. Apparently it had been struck by lightning. Half of it lay on the ground. The lower part of the trunk was still upright. There was no carving on this part.

The eager young detective hurried to the fallen trunk which lay bark side down. She could see part of a carving just above the break.

That looks like the carving of an Indian! Nancy thought, her pulse racing. She could not see it very well. If only she could roll the trunk over! But this was impossible. She called loudly to the rest of the group who flew to her side.

"Look!" she cried out, pointing. "Doesn't that look like the carving of an Indian's head?"

"It sure does," Ned agreed, adding with an obvious twinkle in his eyes, "Some people have all the luck. I knew I should have stuck with you!"

Nancy blushed happily. "I could've told you that," she teased back. "Come on and help me turn the trunk, everybody."

The six young people tried to push the fallen tree, but their efforts were in vain.

"This is aggravating," George fumed. "Especially

since I believe Nancy is about to solve the mystery!"

The young sleuth suggested that they examine the interior of the tree in case something was hidden inside. They combed every inch. The split was clean. There were no bumps or depressions.

"It would take a derrick to lift even half of this tree," Ned complained. "Nancy, what's our next move?"

"I think we should go to Old Joe's cabin and tell him what we've learned."

"This is maddening," Bess said in disgust. "I'm sure we're about to make a great discovery and can't do it because we're not strong enough."

Burt grinned. "Think of all the years this tree has lived here without being disturbed. It must be hundreds of years old. In fact, it might date back to the days of giant men who could lift it with one hand tied behind their back!"

Bess made a face at him, then turned to go with Nancy and the others along a trail they had made to where the horses were tethered. They mounted and, following the stream that Bess had almost tumbled into, headed for Old Joe's cabin.

Old Joe hobbled out to meet them. "Heard you all coming," he said. "You got some news for me?"

"Exciting news," Nancy told him.

The young people took turns telling the naturalist what they had discovered. At the end of their tale, his eyes opened wide in astonishment.

"You've done a magnificent job," he said. "I don't want to wait until my foot is entirely well before we move that tree. How about a couple of you going into town and phoning some lumberjacks to come up here and work on it?"

Ned volunteered. "I'd be glad to go. Tell me who to call."

Old Joe limped back into the cabin and wrote down the name and address of a tree-removal service that Ned would find listed in the telephone book.

"I'll start for town as soon as I get back to camp," Ned promised.

Old Joe told Ned about a shortcut he could take from the cabin to the village.

"Why not?" Ned replied.

Burt offered to go with him. Before the two set off, Nancy said, "Old Joe, how much should Ned tell the lumberjacks to do?"

The elderly man paused a moment. "First, he should let them turn the tree over so the Indian's head shows up. Then the men ought to leave so you young folks can look at it."

"Will do," Ned told him. He and Burt rode off.

Dave gave Old Joe one of the trout in the bucket, and Bess told him, "The boys caught the fish with their bare hands."

The naturalist laughed. "That's pretty clever. As clever as my Trixie, eh?"

Dave and the girls set off for camp. When they arrived, Nancy told only her father, Hal, and Jan what they had discovered.

"We have great hopes of locating the treasure," she explained, "but there's no use spreading the information until we're sure."

Ned and Burt reached camp just as supper was ready. The scent of frying fish whetted the appetites of the hungry campers.

Nancy revealed more of the day's adventure to the group. For a while everyone paid strict attention and asked many questions, but soon one, then another, began to yawn.

Finally Bess stood up. "I'm going to turn in," she announced. "Anybody coming?"

Before she could leave for her tent, some of the scientists joined the group. Nancy asked them if they had found anything new or unusual.

Dr. Halpern answered, "We've learned a couple of interesting things. None of the acid in Dismal Swamp has evaporated from the scorched area. It's very strong stuff."

Dr. York said that the chemists had worked on the chunks of sod that they dug up. We have come to the conclusion that the flying saucer sent out beams containing a combination of natural substances we know about and some secret ingredient. It is quite adhesive and difficult to separate for analysis."

His remark about a secret ingredient gave Nancy an idea. She asked, "Do you suppose the flying saucer came from some rival country and not from outer space?"

Dr. York smiled. "I would hate to think that another country is more scientifically advanced than we are!"

Dr. Caffrey also grinned. "Nancy, I thought you were convinced that you and Ned received thought waves from creatures in outer space. Wouldn't you hate to think that some rival country was able to control your mind?"

Nancy and Ned were horrified, and Ned said, "If men on earth did such a thing to us, I'm going to find them!"

"And do what?" Nancy prompted him.

Ned posed like a boxer. "Fight them, of course!"

Everyone laughed. Then the campers went to their tents and soon were sound asleep.

In the morning they awoke to the buzz of a giant motorized saw.

"Maybe the lumberjacks are cutting up the mystery tree!" Nancy exclaimed.

"How awful!" Bess said. "Why would they do that?"

"I don't know," Nancy replied. "Ned told them only to turn it over."

George jumped up. "But they could ruin the treasure!"

"Maybe even steal it!" Bess added, tears coming into her eyes.

Nancy thought the campers should get to the site at once. "Come on!" she urged. "Every minute counts."

The three boys joined the girls. All of them jumped on their horses and rode up the hill toward the fallen aspen tree.

George complained, "I think this oversized pony had lead feet." She urged him to walk faster.

Before the riders reached the spot, Nancy, in the lead, detected wisps of smoke curling up from the forest. "Look! Up ahead! Fire!" she cried out.

They could hear crackling and smell burning wood. Sparks were flying into the air and being blown about by the breeze; many of them fell to the ground. The fire, still some distance away, nevertheless was moving rapidly toward the valuable tree.

"Oh, this is dreadful!" Bess wailed. "Poor Old Joe! He mustn't be harmed."

Nancy's heart sank. Were Bess's words about to come true? Would a giant conflagration sweep through the forest, burn up Old Joe's treasure, his cabin—and possibly even injure him?

The fire might even destroy Dismal Swamp and the rare medicinal plants in the forest, the girl sleuth thought woefully.

Aloud she called in panic, "We must help put out the fire!"

18

A Rewarding Find

As the riders drew closer to the fire, they could hear men shouting. The young people wanted to urge their horses to go faster, but the climb was too steep. Nancy also feared that the animals might be frightened by the fire. Everyone reined in not far from the treasure tree.

"Fortunately the tree hasn't been harmed," Ned called to Nancy. He dismounted and hurried over to look. The lumberjacks had sawed the fallen trunk into sections and left them bark side down. The Indian's face was barely visible.

Nancy jumped from her horse and ran toward Ned. "Do you think we can turn the piece over?"

"Sure," Ned replied, watching a haze of smoke

drift through the surrounding trees. "But what about the fire?" If it gets too close, it could burn up Old Joe's treasure."

Nancy admitted that this had been her fear all along. "You're right and we must never let that happen. We must try to help the fire fighters at once. The blaze looks bad."

By this time the others had dismounted and were staring at the three girls' discovery. They all peered at what little they could see of the carving.

George said, "We'd better drag this section far away. It's too precious to lose. Hear the crackling of the fire?"

Indeed everyone could. How soon would it be before the flames spread in their direction?

Bess said, "Oh, I hope the fire doesn't get to Old Joe's cabin!"

Dave slipped an arm around Bess's shoulder. "A forest fire can really be frightening," he remarked. "When I was a little boy at camp, one started near us. We had to evacuate in the middle of the night without our daytime clothes. We were told to soak blankets in the nearby brook and put them over our heads as we went through the smoke."

Bess chided him, "Do you have to talk about such horrible things now? Isn't it bad enough that we're practically helpless?"

"Sorry," Dave said.

All the young people worked hard to stand the precious tree section on end. They zigzagged it as far from the fire as possible and laid it down carefully. For the first time the mysterious carving was turned faceup.

"That's gorgeous!" Bess cried out.

Nancy bent down for a close look at the carving. She exclaimed, "Here they are! The initials of Old Joe's father! I'm sure we've found the treasure."

She cut her exuberance short. "But we can't take time to study these clues now. We must help the lumberjacks fight the fire."

Burt suggested that the boys go back to camp for shovels to dig trenches as a backfire.

"And we'll bring axes to cut down underbrush," Dave added.

The smoke was thickening and the sound of burning wood grew frighteningly louder. The fire was spreading rapidly.

"I feel so helpless!" Nancy sputtered, coughing at the same time. "Let's move our horses down to where we dragged the big log. They should be safe there."

"Oh, I hope so," Bess wailed. "This is awful!"

As soon as that was done, the three girls hurried back up the hill. The fire was definitely closer.

"I'm afraid the fire is getting worse," George remarked.

"You're right," Bess added in alarm. "Oh, where are the boys?"

In a short time the three of them returned. They tethered their mounts with the other horses, then the girls helped them carry the shovels and axes to where they were going to start digging the backfire trenches.

"What can we do?" George asked immediately.

Ned suggested that they use the axes to chop down the underbrush and carry it away. "There may be enough dampness under the leaves on the ground to put out some of the flames."

"We'll try it," Nancy said.

While the girls worked diligently, the boys separated to spade up the ground in trenches some distance away from the fire. They lit matches and dropped them into the narrow furrows, igniting a blaze that snaked its way toward the already burning section.

"That should stop some of the spread," Burt declared, "but I think we should work faster."

The girls had already cut down and lugged away heaping piles of brush.

"That's great!" Ned called.

At the same moment they heard a helicopter overhead but could not see it through the dense smoke. No doubt the craft would be forced to stay above or behind the gray billows. In a few moments the group felt sprinkles of what they thought was rain.

Then Dave said, "There must be a forest ranger in that copter. He's pouring water on the blaze."

Bess sighed. "I hope it works!"

The young people continued to work hard even though they were exhausted and filthy. The girls were scratched from the thorny undergrowth they had been dragging away.

"I've never been hotter in my life," Bess said. "The fire must be getting closer."

Unfortunately her words were true. The roar of burning trees was louder than ever and more frightening. Would their work help quench the blaze?

As if in reply, the copter hovered directly overhead. Within seconds they were all drenched with water.

"Whee!" Bess exclaimed, running her hands through her soaked hair. "A free shampoo!"

The others laughed, then Ned remarked, "I guess the pilot missed his target."

"I'm happy he did," said George. "Now I feel cooler. I wish he'd come back and do it again!"

The pilot made no more misses, however, but continued to drench the smoldering trees.

After what seemed like hours of hard work, Nancy's group noticed that the fire was beginning to subside. The welcome deluge from the copter and the joint effort of the fire fighters had, at last, turned the conflagration into a soggy mess. Now they could see how large an area had burned.

"It didn't touch Old Joe's cabin," Nancy said with relief.

As she and her friends laid aside their tools and sank to the ground to rest, they saw two men coming toward them, threading their way among the charred stumps.

They introduced themselves as forest rangers. "We knew someone was helping from this end," one man said. "You young folks did a great job. We're mighty thankful to you."

"It was tough," Ned replied, "but I'm glad our efforts were useful."

As soon as the forest rangers were certain that the embers had died out, they left. Nancy turned eagerly to her friends. "Now we can continue our hunt for Old Joe's treasure."

They hurried back to the big log with the Indian's head carved on it. Nancy paused for several seconds before suggesting how to proceed.

"I think it would be safe to chip around the head and see if we can pry it up intact."

The three boys pulled out their hunting knives and carefully dug a circle around the carved picture. Finally they succeeded in removing it.

"Pretty neat," George remarked. "Nice souvenir

for hanging in your bedroom," she told Nancy.

The young sleuth smiled. "I'd love to have the carving, but I think it should go to Old Joe."

Nancy encouraged the boys to dig deeper. The chips flew as Ned, Burt, and Dave took turns with their strong, sharp knives. Suddenly they struck metal and stopped chipping.

"I think we found something," Ned told the others. Their pulses quickened at the thought that something exciting was about to happen.

Nancy watched closely as more of the wood covering the metal was chipped off. A box was revealed. There was writing on it. Nancy quickly dusted off the top.

On the lid these words were scratched:

For my son Joe Austin

"Old Joe's treasure!" the young sleuth exclaimed, hardly daring to believe her own words.

Ned attempted to lift the metal box from the depression in the tree trunk. No luck!

"Wait!" said Dave.

He and the other two boys burrowed down around the box with their knives until Ned could fix his fingers around it. To everyone's surprise the container was not heavy. Nancy wondered with a sinking feeling if it might be empty! Oh, it mustn't be, she thought.

The box was tightly sealed and there was no way to open it without special tools.

"Stymied again!" said Burt with a sigh.

"We shouldn't open it anyway," Nancy said. "Old Joe should. Let's go down to his cabin as fast as we can."

19

A Strange Reunion

When Nancy and her friends reached Old Joe's cabin, they found him lying on the bed. He complained of suffering a little setback with his foot and said it pained him to walk.

"It was my own fault," he said. "I thought I was stronger that I am. I tried to carry some logs in."

Suddenly he changed the subject. "I'm so glad all of you escaped the fire. Did it get close to your camp?"

Nancy assured him that the area had been miraculously spared and now the fire was entirely out.

Bess added, "The boys dug trenches for a backfire, and we girls cut down brush and dragged it away." She displayed several scratches on her forearms.

Old Joe glanced at the tiny cuts. "You ought to put some salve on those. Anyway, I'm glad nothing more serious happened to you. Personally speaking, I'm right proud of your group. I was really afraid my cabin might burn to the ground."

For the first time the naturalist noticed that Ned was carrying a rusty-looking metal box. Old Joe inquired, "What's that?"

"Nancy will explain," George told the elderly man, who sat up on the edge of his bed.

Ned placed the box alongside him. Old Joe stared at it unbelievingly.

"My name's on it!" he cried, excited. "Where did you find this?"

He cradled it in his hands affectionately as Nancy described their search in detail.

Old Joe shook his head. "To think I've searched this forest hundreds of times and never seen the pyramid of rocks or the cave with the Indian pictures in it!"

A look of fear glazed his eyes as he stared at the small box. "What if the forest fire had ruined everything forever?"

"But it didn't," Nancy said softly. "That's the important thing."

Old Joe nodded. "You're right. How can I ever thank you for saving that priceless log and the carving on it, not to mention what's inside? I'll always be grateful to you."

All this time Bess remained silent. It was clear, however, she was becoming impatient. "Why don't you open the box, Old Joe?"

The naturalist fingered the metal container lovingly. He smiled with tears in his eyes. "I'm almost afraid to open it," he mumbled quietly.

Ned told him that the boys would help lift the rusted lid. Did he have tools they could use? Old Joe pointed to a drawer where Ned found a chisel, a wedge, and a hammer. He used them to pry up the lid while Burt and Dave pushed as hard as they could with their fingers to spring the cover loose. Finally it gave way.

Old Joe peered inside. "Money!" he exclaimed in disbelief. "A lot of it! My father *did* outwit his enemy!"

Nancy was staring too. "And there are a lot of papers. They must be important messages from your father."

The elderly man's hand shook as he lifted out the first one. It was a long letter. He gave it to Nancy.

"Please read it for me. All of you have been so helpful to me the least—the least—"

He broke off, faintly whispering, and slumped back onto his pillow.

"Old Joe!" Nancy cried, letting the paper fall to the floor.

The other young people crowded around the

stricken man while Nancy felt his pulse. "It's very weak," she said. "Bess, please dampen that towel on the sink and bring it to me."

"Sure, Nancy."

George, in the meantime, stroked Old Joe's forehead. It felt cold and clammy.

"Please wake up," she murmured gently.

Within seconds Old Joe's eyes blinked open. A smile spread slowly across his face. "I'm all right," he said hoarsely. "Now help me sit up, will you?"

"Maybe you ought to lie there a little bit longer," Nancy said, patting his face with the wet cloth.

"But I feel fit as a fiddle." Old Joe grinned mischievously. "We'll compromise. You read the letter and I'll sit back. How's that?"

"Okay, if you insist," Nancy said. "But please promise to take a nap when I finish."

The man nodded. "Of course. After all, I don't have any plans to go wild boar hunting right this minute," he teased. "Now don't keep me in suspense any longer."

Without waiting another second, Nancy picked up the intriguing letter and read:

> Dear Son:
>
> This will come as a great surprise to you. At first you are not going to believe it, but I assure you it really happened to me.
>
> Once I came up to the forest by myself.

That one time, an unearthly light suddenly appeared, approaching at tremendous speed from far off in the sky. I finally realized it was a flying object of some sort. To my amazement it slowed down and landed in Dismal Swamp. *It was a flying saucer!*

I rushed to take a close look at it—though the swamp smelled so bad it was overpowering. I heard a voice inside my head giving me orders. That was all I could hear—nothing out loud. The craft flew away almost as soon as it got here. I was terrified. At first I convinced myself that I must be dreaming. The silent voice warned me not to reveal the secret to anyone. Then the voice said the flying saucer would return to earth in ten years!

Old Joe exclaimed, "That's this year!"

The young people checked the date on the letter and confirmed it.

"Incredible!" Dave said.

"Go on, Nancy!" George begged.

The girl sleuth continued:

My son, you may wonder why I buried this information in a tree and carved an Indian's head on it. Now you will be amazed to hear what else I have to say.

I never told you that your mother was a full-blooded Indian. She belonged to a small tribe of the Shawnee nation that used to live in this mountaintop forest. You had an older brother who looked just like her. He was mysteriously kidnapped, and I am sure he was taken away by the Indians, who did not approve of me.

Old Joe's eyes bulged. "An Indian brother! Shawnee!" he cried. "Now I'll never know who he was."

When exclamations of astonishment ended in murmurs, Nancy went on reading the letter.

Two years later you were born. Tragically, your mother died a few hours later. You showed no Indian traits. You look like me. I thought I never wanted you to find out about your mother and brother, but now I believe that in all fairness to you the truth should come out.

Old Joe interrupted to ask, "Does it say what my brother's name was?"

Nancy felt a lump in her throat. As she had been reading, a suspicion had entered her mind. She went on:

Your brother's name was Shoso.

"What!" Old Joe exclaimed. Everyone in the room except Nancy was stunned by the revelation.

Nancy said, "Come to think of it, Shoso and Old Joe do have the same build, and I noticed that their hands are almost identical. The main difference is in the color of their skin and Shoso's Indian face and hair."

Excitement ran high as everyone wondered if perchance Shoso knew the Austin family secret. Was this why he stayed in the forest?

"We must find him at once!" the naturalist announced.

Ned spoke to him calmly. "But how? We have no idea where he may be. We'll make a search, but he has never left a trail we could follow."

While Ned spoke, Nancy noticed another paper folded at the bottom of the box, and said, "More of the secret about your family may be revealed in this."

The elderly man leaned forward to pick it up and spread the paper on his lap. He looked at it for several seconds without speaking.

George, eagerly awaiting an answer, asked him, "What does the paper say?"

Old Joe explained that his father had written down a number of Shawnee Indian words. "Opposite them is the English translation," he said. He ran his finger down the list and exclaimed, "Here's the word for older brother! It's Ntheetha!"

He repeated the word several times as if trying to memorize it. "I hope I'm pronouncing it right," he said.

At this moment they all heard a noise outside the cabin. Slowly the door swung open. To their amazement Shoso was standing there!

At once Old Joe got up from the bed and hobbled across the floor, his arms outstretched in greeting.

"Shoso! Ntheetha!"

20

UFO Capture

A touching scene followed as Old Joe, forgetting his injured foot, hurried toward his newfound brother.

"Shoso!" he exclaimed happily.

The Indian in turn held out his hand, then pointed to himself, and said, "Ntheetha!"

None of the young people spoke as the men clasped each other around the shoulders and touched cheeks, first on one side, then on the other. Finally they backed apart, staring at each other in silence. Old Joe's face broke into a great smile and in response his blood brother grinned, too.

All this time Trixie stood quietly, her ears bent forward as she watched the reunion. Now, apparently feeling it was her turn to greet Shoso, the dog barked and jumped around. First she licked Old Joe's hands, then those of Shoso. Then she sat up between the two, waving her front paws.

The brothers patted the dog while Nancy and her friends laughed. Ned noticed a bone lying on a shelf. He picked it up.

"Okay to give this to Trixie?" he asked.

"Go ahead," Old Joe replied.

He went back to the bed and sat down with a sigh of relief. Nancy and George helped him ease back against his pillow.

"Are you feeling all right?" Nancy asked.

"Yes, yes," he insisted. "I guess the news kind of took my breath away for a minute."

Old Joe now picked up the sheet with the translated words. Using them, he spoke to Shoso. The Indian smiled at him and bobbed his head understandingly.

"Look how happy Shoso is," Bess whispered to her cousin. "Isn't it wonderful?"

"It's great," George said.

Nancy lowered her voice as she motioned to her group. "I think we should let these two brothers become better acquainted."

Everyone agreed. The young people said goodbye to the men.

On the way out Nancy stopped to speak to Old

Joe. "Please thank Shoso for bringing us those healing leaves. Ned and I and the scientists at camp are grateful to him. He may well be responsible for some wonderful new medical discovery."

The naturalist smiled. "It'll be hard to get your message across using the few words on this paper, but I promise to try," he said. "Good luck to you in solving the mystery of the flying saucer. Just remember—if I or Shoso can be of any help, let us know."

When the young people reached camp, Mr. Drew, Jan, Hal, and the scientists crowded around to hear the results of their search. All were amazed to learn not only of the treasure hunt but also the surprising story of the two brothers. "I must remember to call my friends the Dana Girls and tell them the outcome of all this," Nancy said, making a mental note.

"This is all absolutely fantastic," Jan remarked.

Hal added, "It certainly is. As a matter of fact, it's probably the greatest secret this old mountain has ever had!"

Professor Hendricks, the botanist, spoke up. "I'm not so sure that's true, however."

The scientist told his spellbound audience that Shawniegunk Mountain was filled with secrets. "We have men searching all over the place. This is a very special forest, indeed. It is a natural pharmacy filled with rare, unspoiled medicinal plants."

Nancy asked, "What is there besides the leaves Shoso gave us?"

Professor Hendricks replied, "The place is brimming with roots, plants, and leaves that are found sparsely in various parts of the world. Some are nerve medicines. The sap of one tree, if swallowed, is known to give instant relief for heart palpitations. We plan to take samples of these curative plants and herbs and grow them in quantity in other places."

Hal remarked, "It seems incredible that nobody has developed all this stuff."

This gave Nancy an idea. She said to Professor Hendricks, "I'm sure Shoso knows a lot about these plants. He might be a great help to you. Probably Old Joe will teach him to speak English and also keep him from disappearing all the time."

The botanist said he would appreciate the Indian's help. "I doubt, though, that he would ever want to leave this place. From what you've told me, I assume this is his ancestral home."

The day's happenings continued to be the topic of conversation throughout the evening meal. The group had just finished their supper when suddenly a glow of lights flashed brilliantly across the darkened sky. Then came a tremendous rush of wind that shook everything in sight.

"The flying saucer is coming back!" Nancy

gulped. "I don't believe it! Oh, how wonderful!"

Bess was fearful. She had experienced one similar windstorm and did not relish another. She cried out, "Be careful, everybody!"

The others in the camp paid no attention. They were too eager to watch the landing of the mystery ship. Everyone grabbed a flashlight or big camp lantern, and all made their way down the path to Dismal Swamp. They decided, however, not to use the horses and draw attention to themselves.

By the time the group reached the vicinity of the marsh, they saw the flying saucer overhead. It was vibrating convulsively and did not descend at once.

"The saucer must be in some trouble!" Nancy exclaimed.

As the campers watched, all the lights on the ship went out.

"Something is certainly wrong," Ned remarked. "Maybe it's antigravitational beams aren't working."

Within seconds the flying saucer dived for earth and crash-landed in the swamp. The next moment the craft turned on its side.

Dave said, "I hope it won't explode. Maybe we'd better get out of the way."

Everyone except Nancy and her father took his advice and ran into the woods a short way. The girl detective and her father did not move but watched the ship more curious than ever. It did not explode.

Bess, in the meantime, though still wary, edged back toward Nancy. "All we need is for it to catch on fire," she told the others. "Or rather, that's all we don't need."

Nothing happened to the spaceship and the campers descended once more to play their flashlights and lanterns on the mystery craft. It seemed as if the ship had died.

"Now what do we do, Nancy?" George asked.

Before the girl detective could reply, they heard another aircraft coming. Was it a backup flying saucer trying to help its sister ship out of trouble?

As the new craft appeared, the onlookers were puzzled. It was not the shape of the traditional round flying saucer, but was cylindrical, and on one side in large letters the word OPTIMUM was painted. The ship came down like a helicopter next to the disabled flying saucer.

"Wow! What a sight!" Ned exclaimed.

All the onlookers turned their flashlights on the ship. They saw the outline of a door. In a few seconds it opened and steps were lowered to the ground.

A man appeared in the doorway. He was wearing a uniform and the silver eagles of a United States Air Force colonel.

Mr. Drew stared at him, then exclaimed, "Colonel Aken!"

Nancy was dumbfounded. "You know him, Dad? The aircraft belongs to our country?"

"Yes, dear," her father answered, then walked forward to greet the colonel. As he came down the steps, several other airmen appeared. The campers moved ahead and everyone was introduced to the special group of Air Force men chosen to fly the *Optimum.*

Bess admired one young man who was blond and husky like Dave. "Isn't he cute?" she murmured in George's ear.

Dave pulled Bess by the hand toward Colonel Aken and Mr. Drew.

Nancy's father admitted he was surprised to see his friend in Dismal Swamp. "How did you happen to come here?" he asked.

Colonel Aken explained that when Mr. Drew had contacted the head of the Air Force and recounted Nancy's work on the flying saucer mystery, he was chosen to investigate.

"I also asked permission to try out this new American version of a flying saucer."

Nancy asked, "How did you know when the mystery ship was coming back?"

The colonel smiled. "I guess I have to let you all in on a secret—a government secret, actually. This wounded vehicle belongs to the U.S. It was built and launched ten years ago as an experiment, but disappeared shortly after. At the time not much was known about programming this particular type of spaceship. Of course, since then we've learned a great deal. The flying saucer suddenly reappeared at our experimental grounds but gave no clues as to where it had been, and so far as I know no sightings were ever reported."

When Colonel Aken paused, Nancy spoke. "I believe your flying saucer landed here in Dismal Swamp." She told him about the letter written by Old Joe's father.

The Air Force group was astounded. One of the young men, Major Tanner, remarked, "Mr. Austin must have been psychic to prophesy that our saucer would return to the same spot ten years later."

"Is this the identical ship?" Nancy asked.

"Yes," Colonel Aken replied. "It was worked on, reprogrammed, and sent out on a test flight. For a while it beamed back messages that all was going well. Then, as before, all communication ceased. We feared some rival country had captured our saucer."

Bess cried out, "That would have been a—a catastrophe!"

"I agree," the colonel replied.

"Where did you pick up the saucer?" Mr. Drew asked.

"About thirty thousand feet almost straight up. Our radar finally detected it. We felt sure the ship would return here, but its flight pattern was so erratic, it was hard to follow."

"I'd like to ask a question," George interrupted.

"I'll answer it if it's not classified," Colonel Aken replied, his eyes twinkling.

"Before the flying saucer arrived, the wind blew like a cyclone. Everything that wasn't tied down scattered."

"Yes," Bess added, "it actually blew away our picnic, even the fish cooking over an outdoor fire."

The Air Force men laughed. Colonel Aken said, "Young lady, you did hit upon classified information. Yes, the flying saucer caused the windstorm. Sometimes rain follows. How and why, I'm obliged to tell you, must remain a government secret. Sorry to disappoint you."

"But your new ship, the *Optimum,* didn't cause a windstorm," Nancy remarked.

Colonel Aken looked at her searchingly. "You have a very keen mind. It's true. This newer ship was built from totally different plans and will accomplish more than the earlier model. Again, however, I am not at liberty to give you additional information."

Ned admitted he was puzzled about why the old flying saucer whirled as it flew.

The colonel said with a knowing grin, "After you graduate from college, enroll in our technical training school. We'll be happy to teach you some of our trade secrets."

Suddenly Nancy realized the mystery had been completed. The girl detective felt sad to think her work was over. In a short time, however, she would become involved in solving the mystery of *The Secret in the Old Lace*.

She snapped out of her reverie and asked the officer, "Will the old saucer ever be able to fly again?"

"We'll try to find out very soon," Colonel Aken answered, "but first, in honor of your helping us find her, I think we should reward you with a little trip in our *identified* flying object." He smiled. "Tomorrow all of you will have a chance to ride in the *Optimum*. You'll be the first civilians to do so."

Nancy and her friends as well as the scientists were thrilled by the prospect and applauded Colonel Aken for his invitation.

He in turn held up his hand for silence. "Don't give me any credit for recovering the mystery ship. I believe it all belongs to Nancy Drew, her father, and her friends. What do the rest of you say?"

Professor Hendricks called out, "We say yes!"

A great cheer rang through the forest.

THE SECRET IN THE OLD LACE

The Secret in the Old Lace was first published in the UK in a single volume in 1982 by William Collins Sons & Co. Ltd.

1

Crashing Ladder

"Nancy, what are you doing?" asked Hannah Gruen, pausing at the door of Nancy's bedroom. The attractive, titian-haired girl was seated at her desk writing something hurriedly on a notepad.

"Oh, Hannah," Nancy said, turning around in her chair excitedly, "I've just completed the mystery story for the magazine contest I told you about!"

"That's wonderful, dear," the woman said in a motherly tone. "Now perhaps you can get out and enjoy this lovely weather. You've been cooped up here for days." She went to a window and opened it slightly, allowing a warm breeze to rustle the papers on Nancy's desk.

"For days?" Nancy repeated in mock surprise. "Why, it feels like no time at all." She winked affectionately at the housekeeper who had taken care of her since she was three years old.

"No time, indeed," Hannah said, shaking her head. "You're as pale as the paint on the shutters."

"The old paint or the new paint?" Nancy teased. The pungent odor of a fresh coat of paint drifted through the open window, and they could hear the scraping of a ladder as a man in white overalls worked on the trim.

"It's all the same color," Mrs. Gruen quipped. "Ghost white!"

Nancy smiled. "Aren't you even interested in my solution to the mystery story?"

Hannah slipped her arm around the girl's shoulder. "Of course, I am. May I read it now?"

"Mm-hmm, and you know what?"

"What?"

"I'm going to get lots of sun today."

A smile crossed Hannah's lips as she glanced at the penciled page half hidden by several others. "I must confess, Nancy, I'm very happy about this mystery."

"You are?"

"Yes, because it's one you were able to solve in the safety of your own home!"

"Oh, Hannah . . ." Nancy laughed. Although she

was eighteen years old now and well-known as a capable amateur detective, she knew Hannah could not help worrying about her.

Without another word, the girl put the papers in order and clipped them together. "Here you are," she said, handing the manuscript to Hannah.

"Let me get my reading glasses," Hannah said, excusing herself just when the front doorbell rang.

"That must be Bess and George," Nancy said. "I called them while you were out shopping." She dropped the papers on her desk and flew down the stairs, followed by Hannah. "Hi!" She welcomed the visitors. Bess Marvin and her cousin George Fayne were Nancy's closest friends.

"Have you come to rescue the fair maiden from her ivory tower?" Hannah said mischievously.

"Guess so," Bess smiled, revealing deep dimples in her cheeks. "We're taking Nancy to Pickles and Plums for lunch!"

The Drews' housekeeper wrinkled her nose. "Are you sure you won't get indigestion on that diet?" she asked innocently.

"Oh, no!" George giggled. "It's a new health-food restaurant downtown. We can sit outside and get lots of vitamins A and D."

Hannah's eyes brightened. "Health food! That sounds just like what the doctor ordered," she said approvingly.

Nancy kissed the woman's cheek, then ran upstairs, calling to her friends, "C'mon, I want to show you the story I'm submitting to *Circle and Square* magazine!"

"Can't we eat first?" Bess replied, following her cousin to the second landing. "I'm starved!"

"So what else is new?" George teased. Unlike Bess, who tended to be plump, George had a slim figure.

"I haven't eaten a thing today! Really!" Bess giggled as Nancy gave her the manuscript to read.

"Let me see it too," George said eagerly. "I want to learn what happened to the mystery man."

"Just a minute," Bess protested, holding the manuscript away from her cousin and toward the sunlight streaming through the bedroom window.

"Oh, please don't keep me in suspense," George begged.

"For all those terrible things you always say about my figure," Bess declared, "you'll have to wait your turn."

George shrugged. "Beaten again."

"Who's beaten—someone in your manuscript?" Hannah Gruen interrupted, joining the girls.

"No, no." Nancy chuckled. "This is a love story. Actually, it won't make much sense unless I tell you how the whole thing started. The opening of the story appeared in the magazine. It contains a real-life mystery which every contest entrant is supposed to solve."

As Nancy spoke, Hannah sat in the Queen Anne chair opposite the girl's desk while Bess and George plopped at the foot of the bed.

"I gather from the little I read," Bess put in, "that the story takes place in Europe."

"That's right," Nancy replied. "It starts in Brussels, Belgium, in the nineteenth century. A handsome young man whose name was François Lefèvre received a pair of mysterious lace cuffs which he wore with a red velvet dress jacket."

Bess leaned forward with a starry look. "Mm, too bad he isn't living now. I'd love to meet him."

"Believe me," Nancy said, "you would have been only one of many admirers. One of them apparently was too bashful to tell him how much she cared for him."

"You mean he never found out who sent him the lace cuffs?" George asked.

Nancy nodded. "François disappeared suddenly with a rather sizable fortune. Neither his family nor friends ever heard from him again."

"Oh, how sad!" Bess remarked.

"In the fireplace of his bedroom," Nancy continued, "his servants found burned fragments of letters. Among them was a mysterious note in flowery handwriting—"

"Obviously from a woman." George seized the clue.

"It was in French," Nancy said. "Translated the message read:

Turn your face
To the lace
Of the cuffs
A secret—

The rest of it was charred."

"Did the servants find anything else?" Hannah questioned eagerly.

"Yes, on another shred of paper was the word *marry*."

"What a story," Bess said dreamily.

"Does anyone know who sent the lace cuffs to François?" George inquired.

"The story didn't say," Nancy replied. "I guess no one ever admitted to being the lace maker."

"Oh, please tell us the rest," Bess said, "before you hear my news—"

Nancy's eyebrows shot up. "What news?"

"We'll get to that later. Finish your story first."

"Well, what I've told you so far is all that was published in the magazine. Everything else I made up."

Nancy handed the housekeeper her story. "Hannah's first. I promised to let her see it before you arrived."

The woman began reading the manuscript with great interest. Bess was quiet for a while, then became impatient. "Nancy, got your passport ready?" she asked.

"Why, where are we going?"

"To Belgium!" Bess blurted.

"Belgium?" Nancy said in puzzlement. "Now, Bess, I told you François Lefèvre has been dead for more than a century."

Grinning, Bess swept a blond curl off her forehead. "We're not going there to hunt for François," she said. "You remember my telling you about Mother's old college friend, Madame Chambray?"

Nancy nodded.

"Well, about a month ago she moved from France to Brugge, Belgium—"

"Why, that's the name of a city in Nancy's story," Hannah interrupted.

"You're kidding," Bess said.

"No, it's true," Nancy concurred, "but tell me about Madame Chambray."

"She wrote to Mother recently. Here's the letter," Bess said, rummaging through her purse for it. "It seems that Madame Chambray found a valuable antique cross in her house. It's made of diamonds and lapis lazuli. Madame Chambray believes it belongs to someone who lived in her house years ago. Unfortunately, she hasn't had much time to search for the owner of the cross but she's going to put an ad in the newspaper over there."

Intrigued by the story, Nancy glanced at the letter for a moment, then dropped it on the desk. "What about the person from whom Madame Chambray bought the house?" the girl detective inquired. "Isn't it more likely the cross belongs to him or her?"

"Apparently it doesn't," George spoke up. "Madame Chambray checked on that."

Just then Hannah, not taking her eyes from the manuscript, commented, "It's a wonderful story, dear. You know, I'd been hoping you'd be content to work on fictional mysteries for a while, but I can see—"

Before the housekeeper could continue, there was the shatter of glass followed by an earsplitting crash.

"Oh, my goodness!" Hannah shrieked, rushing to the window.

"What was it?" the girls chorused as they ran after her.

"The painter!" Hannah cried. "His ladder must have slipped and he fell!"

All four were staring down at the lawn, where the man in white overalls was dizzily swaying to his feet. The ladder was lying on the grass a few feet away from him.

"I hope he isn't badly hurt," Hannah said. "We'd better go down and find out."

Her words were hardly spoken, when the man quickly hobbled across the lawn to a truck parked in front of the Drew home. Nancy raced downstairs two steps at a time, the others close behind her, and bolted outside along the curving driveway toward the truck.

"Are you okay?" she shouted anxiously to the man.

But he pulled himself into the driver's seat, slammed the door, and roared off. Nancy turned back to the house, meeting her friends and Hannah halfway. The housekeeper still held the manuscript in her hand.

"The ladder must've slid straight down," Mrs. Gruen observed, "and hit the dining room window."

Nancy gaped at the pile of broken glass beneath the opening. "I'm going to call the paint company immediately," she announced.

"That guy sure acted strange, don't you think?" Bess said.

"I just hope he's all right," Hannah said.

Nancy dialed the phone number of the painters, Kell and Kell, and talked with the owner, Oscar Kell. He offered to come at once to see the damage. While they waited, Nancy and the other girls decided to take a second look at the scene themselves.

"Be careful," George cautioned Nancy as she walked gingerly between shards of broken glass.

"What do you think of this?" Nancy said, ignoring her friend's comment. She pointed to a paint can standing on the ground a few feet away from the window.

"It's white paint," Bess said. "What are you getting at?"

"If he was working on my window frame, the can would have fallen and splattered paint on the grass, wouldn't it?" Nancy questioned.

"You're right," George admitted. "He climbed up there without it. I wonder why he did that?"

"I have a hunch he was eavesdropping on us!"

2

The Disappearance

"How much do you think the painter overheard?" Bess asked after Nancy revealed her conclusions.

"Probably only snatches," Nancy replied, "but enough to give him ideas."

"Well, I wouldn't worry too much about it," George said. "He didn't find out your solution to the contest."

"True, but I bet he wanted to," Nancy replied. "He must have heard us talking about the mystery while he was painting near the window. So he scooted down his ladder and moved it right underneath my room, and climbed up again. Of course, by doing that, he missed part of the conversation."

George nodded. "He probably mixed everything

up and figures there's some important connection between your contest and Madame Chambray's story!"

As George spoke, a station wagon pulled into the driveway. A middle-aged man with stocky features emerged. "I'm looking for Nancy Drew," he called to the girls.

Nancy stepped forward. "Mr. Kell?"

"That's me," he said, knitting his eyebrows as he noticed the broken window. "I'm sorry I couldn't get over here faster. I was waiting for Matey to return with the truck."

"Did he?" Nancy asked impatiently.

"Yep, and before I could find out what happened, he quit on me. Said he was tired of house painting. When I asked him what he intended to do, he said he was going treasure hunting. A real smart aleck!"

Nancy, unwilling to reveal her suspicions, innocently asked, "What's his last name?"

"Johnson," Mr. Kell replied. "He used to be a sailor; I guess climbing the mast was good training for the kind of work he did for me."

"Was he with you a long time?" Nancy asked.

"A year. He's been on parole for a while," Mr. Kell said with hesitation in his voice. "But he's okay. A good painter, just a smart aleck."

Bess and George had all they could do to contain their anxiety while Nancy spoke to Mr. Kell. Then

Hannah appeared at the dining room window, and for several moments she and the contractor discussed repairs.

When he left, Bess grabbed Nancy's arm. "I don't believe it!" she said. "That painter is an ex-convict!"

"Matey Johnson was probably a second-story burglar," Nancy concluded.

"To think he could've just squirmed his way into your room and stolen your manuscript!" George exclaimed.

"But he didn't," Nancy pointed out calmly. "Of course, if he had, he could've copied my answer to the contest and sent it in. Then, if his entry had reached the magazine office first, the editors would have accused me of plagiarism."

"How awful!" George said. "But he would have been the plagiarist—the one who stole your idea!"

"I know," Nancy said, "but how could I prove it?"

"We're your witnesses," Bess said cheerfully.

"You're more than witnesses." Nancy smiled. "You're my best friends."

"Say, what about lunch?" George piped up.

"Don't tell us you're hungry!" Her cousin smirked.

The girls went to get their handbags. Nancy saw the manuscript lying in the hallway where Hannah had placed it after she had come back into the house. Quickly the girl put it into the closet before she followed her friends outside.

They climbed into Nancy's car and headed for Pickles and Plums Restaurant. Outside were rows of round yellow tables with floral umbrellas poised in the center of each one. Several of the umbrellas were open; a few were not.

"Let's get a little sun," Nancy suggested, remembering her promise to Hannah.

The girls chose a table with a closed umbrella and within a minute or so a lanky waiter in blue jeans and a floral shirt brought them menus.

As soon as Bess had ordered an exotic fruit and yogurt salad, she leaned toward Nancy. "We never did read the rest of your story so please tell us how it ends."

Nancy said she felt sure there was a message in the lace cuffs that prompted François to disappear.

"What kind of message?" Bess persisted.

"I have a strong hunch that the girl who made the cuffs was in love with François but he didn't love her. Maybe he was fearful his family and the girl's would arrange their betrothal. In those days young people had little to say about such things."

"How horrible!" George spoke up.

"I understand that marriages are still arranged in some countries," Nancy said.

"Well, I'm glad I don't live in one of them," George declared.

Bess saw a chance to tease her cousin. "I'm sure Burt is equally happy about it," she commented.

In reply George wrinkled up her nose. Burt Eddleton was her favorite date.

"Of course," Nancy said, interrupting the banter between her friends, "I don't think François ever left Belgium."

"What!" Bess and George said. They were totally bewildered.

"But the story said he disappeared," George noted.

"He did—from Brussels. But I have a hunch he stayed in his native country. You see, he was very interested in painting. I didn't mention this earlier, but he always wanted to study with Dirk Gelder, a famous teacher in nineteenth-century Brugge. I think François might have gone there."

"But that's not far from Brussels," George objected.

"I know. Yet, in those days people didn't travel as they do now. If he changed his appearance a little and learned how to speak the dialect of that town, he could conceal himself easily enough."

"Don't they speak Flemish there?" Bess inquired.

"Flemish is spoken in Flanders," Nancy admitted. "But the people in Brugge have their own dialect."

As the chatter continued, the lanky waiter placed three large platters of salad in front of the girls.

"You said that François took a fortune with him when he left," George put in. "In those days robberies were as prevalent as today. Did it occur to you that maybe he was overtaken and killed?"

Nancy admitted the thought had entered her mind. "But the magazine story doesn't even hint at foul play. My impression is that François changed his whole appearance and life-style. He could've grown a beard to hide his handsome face and switched to plain clothes, for instance."

"In your story," Bess asked, "what name did he take?"

"Karl Van Pelt."

"I still think it's incredible," George insisted, "that such an attractive man could live no more than sixty miles from Brussels without ever being identified. His clothes alone—"

"Not really," Nancy interrupted. "Don't forget, according to the magazine, he took no clothes other than the red jacket with the lace cuffs. Obviously, he didn't want to be seen with any baggage to indicate he was traveling or moving away. He could've hidden whatever treasure he had in his sleeves, pockets, and shoes and rolled up the jacket into a neat little package."

"In that case," George pointed out, "François's personal fortune must've been in money and jewels."

Nancy nodded. "Exactly. In my story I said he used some of the money to start a successful business and at his death willed the red jacket to a museum."

"Just think," Bess said, digging her fork into a cube of fresh melon, "we'll be able to walk on the same cobblestones François did and look at the same canals he saw and—"

George rolled her eyes upward in mock disgust. "Spare me," she said. "I don't know how Dave stands it." Dave Evans was Bess's boyfriend.

"Okay, you two," Nancy broke in.

"You know I was serious about us all going to Belgium," Bess said. "Madame Chambray has plenty of room and more than one mystery to solve!"

"Really?" Nancy asked eagerly.

"Yes. She found part of an old letter too, which says something about a treasure."

"Is that all she said?"

Bess nodded. "Madame Chambray didn't reveal too many details in her letter to my mother, but she does want us—you especially—to visit. She knows your dad's a lawyer and that you often solve mysteries."

Nancy's heart was beating excitedly. "I'm just flabbergasted," she said. "After working on the mystery contest, the one place I'm eager to see is Brugge!"

"Who knows, maybe we'll find François's red jacket in one of the museums!" George giggled.

"Let's not get too carried away," Nancy said. "After all, my part of the story is only fictional. Speaking of that, I ought to mail it in at once."

George called to the waiter for a bill as Nancy caught sight of someone bending behind the front fender of her parked car. "Is he letting the air out of my tire?" she cried, pushing her chair back and darting toward him. "What do you think you're doing?" she shouted.

For a split second the stranger bobbed into view. He looked like Matey Johnson!

3

Missing Manuscript

"Stop!" Nancy cried, dashing into the street after the man. But he darted away lithe as a cat, skirting several taxis and bike riders before disappearing into an alley.

Stymied by the heavy traffic, Nancy did not attempt to cross the street. George and Bess, who had quickly paid the waiter, were now staring at the front right wheel of Nancy's car. The tire was slowly going flat!

"What a shame!" Bess remarked.

"Who was that guy anyway?" George asked.

"I'm pretty sure it was Matey Johnson. I didn't get much of a look at him at the house but I recognized his reddish-blond hair."

While Nancy removed a tire inflator from her trunk and hooked it to the wheel, she listened quietly as her friends discussed the latest event.

"Why would Matey Johnson let air out of Nancy's tire?" Bess asked her cousin.

"Obviously he wanted to stall us here for a while," George said.

"Well, he sure accomplished that," Nancy sighed, watching the air-pressure gauge slowly creep higher.

"You don't suppose," Bess suggested, "that he's planning to go back to your house?"

"That's exactly what I was thinking," Nancy said. "If only I could speed up the air pump!"

At last the tire was mended. "Keep an eye on everything," the girl detective told the cousins. "I'm going to phone Hannah."

Nancy disappeared into the restaurant again to use the public telephone. In less than five minutes she returned with a glum expression on her face.

"What's the matter?" Bess asked.

"Nobody's home."

"Uh-oh," George commented. Then, out of the corner of her eye, she noticed a River Heights patrol car cruising toward them. "Isn't that Chief McGinnis?" she said.

Nancy waved frantically to him, calling at the same time, "Chief! Chief McGinnis!"

The young police officer at the wheel swung the car behind Nancy's and his superior stepped out.

"What happened?" Chief McGinnis inquired, gazing at the tire. "Did you pick up a nail?"

Quickly Nancy explained, adding her fear that Matey Johnson might be on his way to her house to steal something important.

"In that case," the chief said, nodding to the other policeman, "you stay here with the girls. I'll drive Nancy home."

Nancy gave George the keys to her car and slipped her registration in the glove compartment. When she and Chief McGinnis presently pulled into her driveway, the girl flew to the front door past the ladder which was now standing up against the house again. She fumbled for her key, opened the door, and ran upstairs.

"It's gone!" she exclaimed. "Oh, Chief, the letter I told you about is gone!"

"Are you sure?" the man replied as he reached the landing.

Nancy sorted nervously through numerous papers on her desk, opened all the drawers, and peered behind and under the furniture. There was no sign of Madam Chambray's letter.

"What about your manuscript?" the police chief said.

"Oh, I put that in the hall closet," Nancy said.

"Let me check." She hurried downstairs and opened the closet door.

"Oh, good!" she cried out. "It's still here!"

Chief McGinnis had followed her. "The thief couldn't find it," he deduced.

Nancy nodded. "Matey Johnson must have looked for it in my room. But Hannah brought it down here and I put it away before we went out to lunch."

"Nancy," the police officer said, "I'd like to caution you about one thing. Even though you saw Johnson deflating your tire, you don't have any proof he burglarized this house."

The girl detective agreed. "But I have an idea. The ladder you saw downstairs was moved by somebody. I'm going to check it for fingerprints. If they all belong to Matey—"

Her voice faded as she took a fingerprint kit from a desk drawer and went outside with the chief.

"You know, Nancy," he said, smiling, "I don't think I've ever watched you lift fingerprints!"

"Any chance I can work on the force?" Nancy said impishly, removing a can of spray powder from the kit.

"Just let me know when you're ready!"

The young detective dusted parts of the ladder with powder, then pressed rubberized lifting tape over the latent prints. She peeled off the tape with the powder on it, and sealed the impressions under a plastic cover.

"Would you identify these for me?" she asked.

"As soon as I get back to headquarters," the chief promised.

He backed the patrol car out of the driveway as Bess and George pulled up at the curb.

"Is everything okay?" Bess asked, darting across the lawn ahead of her cousin.

"I'm afraid not," Nancy said grimly. "The letter Madame Chambray sent your mother is missing and I'm practically certain Matey Johnson stole it. I'm waiting for Chief McGinnis to identify some fingerprints for me."

Bess and George were stunned. "What about your manuscript?" George asked. "Was that taken too?"

"Fortunately, no," the young detective said, "and before anything does happen to it, I'd better type up the final draft and mail it to *Circle and Square* magazine."

"This is really exciting," Bess remarked, giving her friend an enthusiastic hug. "I hope you win first prize!"

"Thanks," Nancy said appreciatively. "The magazine is awarding a large cash prize which I'd like to donate to charity."

After Nancy had typed the story and labeled the

precious package, the girls drove to the River Heights post office, where Nancy then suggested they speak to Mr. Kell. "I'd like to get Matey Johnson's address from him."

"You're not planning to visit Matey, are you?" Bess inquired nervously.

"I might," Nancy said and aimed the car toward a small industrial park at the edge of town.

Kell and Kell proved to be a fairly large company with an attractive office. When Nancy greeted the young woman behind the desk and asked to see the owner, the receptionist giggled.

"Oh, you're Nancy Drew. How I envy you trotting around the world and solving mysteries! Do they always start with something simple like a falling ladder?"

Nancy and the other girls laughed. "It's not that simple," Nancy replied.

"But just as startling," Bess added, as the receptionist announced the visitors to Mr. Kell.

Momentarily, he stepped out of an inner office. "No more trouble, I hope," he said warily.

The young detective bit her lip, not wishing to say anything in front of the receptionist. "May we talk to you privately?" she asked.

"Certainly."

As concisely as she could, Nancy told him what had happened that afternoon. "Would you please give me Mr. Johnson's address?" she requested.

"He was staying at a friend's apartment while he worked here," Mr. Kell said. "As a matter of fact, his friend—André Bergère—worked here a few years ago; a real loner and not too friendly to the other people in the shop."

He buzzed the receptionist for the address. It was in a section of River Heights where many European people lived.

"Are you game to go?" Nancy turned to her friends.

"I guess so," Bess said reluctantly, "but I don't relish meeting either André or Matey face to face."

When the girls arrived at the address, neither name was listed in the lobby directory. Bess was relieved. "Well, that settles that," she stated. "Let's go home."

"Not yet," Nancy replied. She decided to knock at the door of a tenant on the first floor. An elderly man answered. "Would you happen to know if a Mr. André Bergère lives here?" she asked.

"No, he doesn't. Moved out a little while ago."

"Did he say where he was going?" George pressed the man.

"I think he said Europe."

"That's very interesting," Bess commented. "You don't suppose he went to Belgium?"

The elderly tenant shrugged. "I have no idea," he replied. "Sorry I can't be of further help to you girls."

"Now what?" George asked.

Nancy said she wanted to discuss everything with her father the next evening, when he was due to return from a business trip.

"Well, don't solve the mystery before we all see each other again!" Bess exclaimed as she and George parted to do errands.

"Don't worry," Nancy said lightly. "There's no chance of it!"

The trio said good-bye in the center of the shopping district. Nancy returned home to find Hannah knitting a sweater and waiting for a cake to finish baking in the oven.

"Something smells delicious," Nancy remarked.

"Your favorite—angel food cake." The housekeeper smiled. "I thought you deserved a little special dessert to celebrate the completion of your manuscript."

"Oh, Hannah, you're such a dear. You always do something to make me feel better."

That evening Nancy went to bed early. She wondered if her priority mail package would reach the magazine office quickly, as promised. What if someone intercepts it? she thought anxiously, then chided herself. Oh, that's silly. Why would anybody—

She drifted off to sleep, but late the next morning she could not resist calling *Circle and Square* to find out if her entry had been received. The young woman on the other end of the line was rather curt. "Entries haven't been sorted yet," she said flatly. "Call back later, miss." She hung up.

To Nancy's chagrin, the answer was equally disappointing that afternoon. The manuscript had not arrived so she made a beeline to the post office.

The clerk on duty offered to put a tracer on the package. "Stop back in a few days," he suggested.

But the contest deadline is tomorrow, Nancy thought desperately. What am I going to do?

Nancy rushed to her father's law office and with the help of his secretary, Miss Hanson, she made photocopies of her carbon copy of the manuscript. Then, taking a chance her Aunt Eloise, who lived in New York City, would be able to hand-deliver it to the magazine, she returned to the post office.

"This package must reach New York tomorrow," Nancy said, "so please send it the fastest way possible."

"I can't promise there is a fastest way," the clerk said. "There's a transit strike in New York, and mail trucks are having a tough time getting through."

"Oh, dear," Nancy replied worriedly.

What if the second copy of her manuscript did not reach *Circle and Square* magazine the next day? She would lose her chance to enter the contest!

4

Clever Caller

Seeing the glum expression in Nancy's eyes, the postal clerk added cheerfully, " 'Course express mail usually gets through no matter what."

Nancy sighed. "I hope so."

That evening before her father arrived home, she telephoned his sister. "Aunt Eloise, would you mind doing me a very special favor?" the young sleuth requested.

"I'd be glad to. Just tell me what it is," Miss Drew replied.

Briefly Nancy told her about the manuscript, how the first copy had gone astray and that she had mailed Aunt Eloise a second copy to be hand-delivered. "I hate to trouble you with this in the midst of a transit strike," Nancy apologized, "but the magazine office is not too far from your apartment. Do you mind very much?"

"Now don't be silly. Of course not," the kindly woman answered. "I wish you could come for a visit. It's been so long since I've seen you, Nancy."

Her niece promised that she would try to spend a weekend in New York soon. "And I'll bring my bike!" she added with a chuckle.

When Carson Drew arrived home later that evening, Nancy was eager to tell him about the recent events at the Drew house. One by one she related all of the problems.

"Don't worry about your manuscript," the tall, distinguished-looking man consoled her. "Your Aunt Eloise will see that your package gets to the proper person."

"I'm sure, Dad," Nancy said. "It's just that—"

"Winning the contest isn't everything, you know," Mr. Drew interrupted. Nancy began to smile as he continued. "I've been doing some serious thinking, Nancy. And in view of everything you've told me, I think you ought to consider some on-the-spot investigation."

"Oh, Dad, do you mean it?" Nancy burst out joyfully.

"Sure I mean it."

The girl threw her arms around her father, hugging him happily. "Bess invited George and me to stay at Madame Chambray's!" she exclaimed and hurried to the telephone.

By next morning the three friends had chatted several times, discussed travel arrangements and clothes, and made a long-distance call to Madame Chambray.

After breakfast, the telephone rang again. This time it was Aunt Eloise Drew.

"Good news, dear," she reported to Nancy. "Your manuscript arrived and I took it immediately to the magazine office."

"Oh, wonderful," Nancy said.

"Well, not entirely." Miss Drew's voice became somber. "I asked to see Mr. Miller, the editor-in-chief of the company, but before the receptionist could buzz his office, another man rushed up to me and said, 'You have Nancy Drew's manuscript? I'll take it.' Of course, I wouldn't give it to him. He was rather unpleasant about it, and I really was afraid we'd come to verbal blows."

"Oh, dear," Nancy said. "Who was he?"

"I don't know. Fortunately, though, Mr. Miller appeared. The receptionist told him I was delivering the second copy of your story because the first entry had been lost en route."

Nancy fastened on every word. "What did the other man do?" she asked.

"Well, Mr. Miller turned to him and said, 'You're not connected with this contest, are you, Mr. Rocke?' Rocke said he wasn't, and that he had merely offered to take the package to the proper person. To tell the truth, Nancy, he gave me an uneasy feeling. I insisted that Mr. Miller look after your entry personally."

"Thank you so much, Aunt Eloise," Nancy said gratefully. "You're a real lifesaver."

After hanging up, Nancy related the conversation to Hannah Gruen, then called her father at his office. He was as puzzled as Nancy. "I can't imagine why there is so much interest in your manuscript," Mr. Drew commented. "It's only a magazine contest."

"That's what I thought, Dad," Nancy said.

Deciding to put her aunt's strange encounter out of her mind, Nancy headed downtown to do some shopping for her trip. On the way, though, she suddenly remembered that she had not heard from Chief McGinnis and stopped at police headquarters.

"I should've called you yesterday," the chief apologized, "but I got bogged down on a couple of things. Those prints do belong to Matey Johnson, so it looks as if he stole that letter from you. Even so, you might have a hard time proving it. I'm waiting for him to report to his parole officer."

"He probably won't," Nancy said and told about

her trip to the apartment house where he no longer lived. "I should've mentioned this as soon as I found out. But I've been worried about sending my manuscript to the magazine and now I'm leaving for Europe."

"Well, have a wonderful trip—"

"It should be a mysterious one," Nancy interrupted, reminding Chief McGinnis about Madame Chambray's story of the antique cross and its missing owner.

After leaving police headquarters, she made a few purchases, including a pretty blue sweater-coat that matched the color of her eyes, then returned home. To her delight, Hannah said Ned Nickerson had called. He and Nancy were special friends; neither of them ever dated anyone else. For a moment a picture of the tall, good-looking athlete from Emerson College swept pleasantly across her mind.

"Nancy," Mrs. Gruen said, interrupting the girl's daydream, "poor Ned has laryngitis. He could hardly talk but he wanted to know how you were and what you were doing. When I told him you were flying to Belgium with Bess and George to solve a mystery, he sounded very downhearted and said he wished he could go along."

"I wish he could too," said Nancy, "but he has a summer job I know he can't leave."

Eager to speak to him herself, Nancy dialed his

number. To her amazement Ned's voice was clear as a bell. He said he certainly had not phoned her!

Fear suddenly rippled through her as she revealed her travel plans. "Then Hannah told a stranger about Bess, George, and me definitely going to Belgium in connection with a mystery."

"That's bad," Ned remarked. "I'm sorry I won't be able to come along to protect you, but I just can't get away right now. I'll see you before you go, won't I?"

"I don't know," Nancy said. "We're leaving as soon as we get our reservations." She admitted she was glad Hannah had not been aware of the details of her flight. "So your impersonator didn't find out anything definite about our departure."

Ned agreed. "But when you find out what flight you're taking, please tell me. Promise?"

"Promise." Nancy blushed.

With so many chores to finish before leaving, the rest of the day flew by. At bedtime she crawled between the covers, checking off in her mind all that was left to do. Then, yawning deeply, she fell asleep.

A strange clipping sound awakened her a few hours later. She listened intently. The noise stopped. Was she dreaming? Nancy closed her eyes again, telling herself to ignore the interruption. Then *clip, clip, clip*.

What is that sound? she wondered, lifting her head off the pillow. She squinted at the open window across the room where a shadowy face was outlined in the moonlight.

A man was cutting the screen with a large pair of shears!

5

Midnight Intruder

Nancy's heart pounded as she watched the blades sink through the screen wire. Desperately she wondered what to do. If she slammed the window down and locked it, the intruder could not enter her room.

But then he'd escape for sure, Nancy decided, and come back another time when I wasn't here to catch him!

Quietly she got out of bed and tiptoed to her father's room.

"Dad!" she whispered hoarsely. "Dad! Wake up! Someone's trying to break into my room!"

Mr. Drew stirred uneasily, mumbling in reply.

"Dad!" Nancy repeated nervously as he blinked

his eyes open. "A burglar is breaking into the house!"

"Where is he?" her father asked. Now fully awake, he followed Nancy back to her room.

There, staring at the girl's empty bed, stood the intruder! Instantly, Mr. Drew pounced on the man, throwing him to the floor. He pinned his arms back to prevent him from pulling out a weapon.

"Let me go!" the stranger bellowed. He tried to wriggle out from under his captor. But Mr. Drew sat squarely on his chest!

"Call the police, Nancy!" her father said, glaring at his prisoner.

The girl detective was already dialing headquarters. She told the sergeant on duty what had happened. "Please hurry over here," she said, ending the conversation. Then she turned to her father. "They're sending two policemen right away."

Once more the captive struggled for release. He pushed his knees up and dug his feet into the plush carpet, trying to get a strong foothold.

"No, you don't," Nancy informed him, forcing his knees down and sitting on them.

"Ou-ouch!" he cried out furiously. "Get off me. You're breaking my bones!"

The rumpus in the room carried into the adjacent one where Hannah Gruen slept. She awoke

and rushed to the scene. Flipping on the overhead light, she gasped. "Oh, my goodness! Who is he?"

"You're Matey Johnson, aren't you?" Nancy responded as she leaned back and noticed the man's reddish-blond hair.

All color drained from his face. His mouth quivered open but shut quickly.

"Well, when the police get here—" Nancy began as the front doorbell rang.

Hannah hurried downstairs. Shortly two officers appeared in the girl's room and immediately handcuffed the prisoner. After advising him of his legal rights, one of the policemen said, "Haven't I seen you around the station?"

The captive tightened his lips angrily.

"This is Matey Johnson." Nancy identified him. "He's been out on parole."

"How do you know th—" the intruder began, then caught himself.

"Why were you trying to break into our house?" Nancy questioned. "You already stole Mrs. Marvin's letter. Were you coming back for my manuscript?"

Matey refused to answer.

"And I suppose," the girl detective went on, "that paint ladder came in handy again, didn't it?"

She pulled a flashlight from her desk drawer and shone it out the damaged window. Sure enough, the ladder was leaning against the house!

"Too bad we didn't think of putting it in the garage," the girl said to her father.

"You're right," Mr. Drew admitted. "We made it easy for Johnson to break in a second time. Only this time he didn't get away with it!"

Johnson glowered as the officers led him out of the house. Hannah Gruen locked the door behind them and yawned. "What a night!" she said.

Nancy nodded. "You know, I'm hungry all of a sudden. Would anyone else like a snack?"

Mr. Drew laughed, following Hannah and his daughter into the kitchen. "I guess I lost a few calories sitting on that character! How about another dish of your rice pudding, Hannah?"

"Coming right up," she said. "I think we all need to eat a little something to settle our nerves." She dished out the rice pudding while Nancy made cups of steaming hot chocolate topped with whipped cream.

"It's too bad you didn't get your letter back from Mr. Johnson," the attorney said to his daughter.

She shrugged, spooning a bit of the cream into her mouth. "I'm just glad we caught him," she said. "The only thing that bothers me is he may have shown the letter to someone else—like André Bergère."

The next morning Nancy told Bess and George all about the midnight intruder and her father's bravery.

"It sounds to me you were pretty courageous yourself," Bess complimented her friend. "I would have been totally paralyzed!"

"Oh, that isn't true," Nancy remarked. "You've been in lots of scary situations with me and done okay."

Bess giggled in embarrassment. "I'm hoping, though, there won't be any in Belgium," she said, leading Nancy to reveal Hannah Gruen's phone conversation with Ned's impersonator. "Oh, no!" Bess panicked. "Maybe we ought to give up the trip!"

"No, indeed," the girl detective replied, "but if *you* want to back out—"

"Oh, I'll go along," Bess agreed reluctantly, "but I know I'll be a wreck the whole time."

George's reaction was quite different. The minute she heard Nancy's story she said, "The sooner we leave the U.S.A. the better off we'll all be!"

"I hope you're right," Nancy commented, "but we might just run into trouble in Belgium."

"You mean we might run into Bergère," George said, adding crisply, "Well, let's talk about something more pleasant. Burt says he, Dave, and Ned want to come here tomorrow to say good-bye. Since we only have a short time left before our trip—"

"Listen," Nancy interrupted, "I want everybody to have dinner here, all right?"

"Fabulous," George replied.

The girls contacted their Emerson friends at once. When the boys arrived the next evening, Dave suggested going to a local show followed by a dance to benefit a home for handicapped children.

Dave, who had driven Burt and Ned to the Drew house, chided himself for not thinking ahead. "I am really stupid," he said. "There are six of us, but my car can only take four."

"That's okay," Nancy said. "Ned and I can use my car."

The three couples drove off in two cars, but Dave and Ned did not follow the same route. Bess, George, and their escorts arrived first. They waited in the lobby for Nancy and Ned.

"I wonder where they are," Burt remarked after a while, glancing impatiently at his watch. "We've been here almost fifteen minutes. Did Nancy say anything about stopping on the way?"

"No," George answered.

She and the others watched the last trickle of audience take their seats. "It's curtain time," Dave commented. "Maybe we should go inside."

"What do you think, George?" Bess asked. "You know it's not like Nancy to be late. I hope nothing has happened to them."

The sound of applause now drifted through the

doors into the lobby which, except for the foursome, was empty. "Oh, I'm sure they'll be here soon," George said, leading the way into the darkened auditorium.

On stage was a beautiful woman with long silky hair that hung over the shoulders of her white sequined gown. She began to sing softly, bringing a hush over the auditorium. Bess, however, could not concentrate on the performance, that featured several popular songs including a romantic ballad she loved. Bess bit her lips anxiously and turned her head now and then to look at the closed doors.

"What's the matter?" Dave whispered to his date, putting his hand comfortingly on hers.

"I have a feeling something dreadful has happened to Nancy and Ned!" Bess answered in alarm.

6

Kid Attack

Nancy and Ned had started to follow Dave's car but soon realized another one was tailing theirs. Its headlights created a glare in Nancy's rearview mirror which caused Ned, who was driving, to push the mirror back.

"At the next side street," Ned said, "I'll turn right and switch off the headlights. If the car passes us, we can stop worrying."

Nancy stared out the back window trying to see who was in the vehicle, but could not discern anyone's face. Ned pressed down on the accelerator and screeched around the corner, switching off his lights as he swung past a truck and swerved over to the curb in front of a parked car.

"I think we lost them," the young man said, pulling onto the road again.

"We can get back to the main street by turning at the end of this one," Nancy observed. But suddenly a roadblock of wooden sawhorses came into view. A sign attached to them read:

BRIDGE OUT. ROAD CLOSED.
WATER AHEAD. DANGER!

"Sorry," Nancy said to her friend. "I guess the old twenty-twenty vision is failing."

Ned chuckled lightly as he put the transmission into reverse to turn around. Just then the car that had been tailing them pulled up directly behind the couple!

"Oh, no!" Nancy cried, as four teenage boys, all wearing jackets with sinister-looking spider patches on them, jumped out and swarmed around her car!

They grinned maliciously at the couple. Nancy and Ned hastily locked their doors and started to roll up their windows. One of the boys, however, was too quick for Nancy. He reached into the car before the pane was all the way up, shoved her hand aside, and pulled open the door, dragging Nancy out.

Ned, unable to prevent this, frantically pressed the horn, trying to attract the attention of anyone near enough to hear him. Just then, another boy pulled him away from behind the wheel and, with the help of one of his friends, lifted him out of the car.

Ned struggled furiously and quickly regained his balance. He dived at the two boys, as another young punk swung at him from behind.

"Ned, watch it!" Nancy cried. She stood next to the boy who had dragged her out of the car. Apparently convinced she was too scared to move, he left her unguarded and joined in the fray.

Ned, hearing her warning, ducked and, gripping the legs of his attacker, pulled him to the ground.

Nancy knew she would be unable to assist Ned in the fight. She turned and ran down the street as fast as she could!

"Hey! Stop her!" one of the gang members shouted. The boy who had dragged Nancy from the car dashed after her. His long legs carried him closer and closer to the fleeing girl, when Nancy turned a corner. Her pursuer followed suit, but suddenly he cried out in pain! He had stepped into a pothole and fallen headlong onto the pavement.

Nancy looked over her shoulder and realized that he was unable to get up. Relieved, she ran on, calling loudly for help.

Ned, meanwhile, had been overpowered by the three young hoodlums who remained behind.

Panting and exhausted, he stopped fighting. "What do you want?" he asked his attackers.

"We're going to take your car apart, wise guy!" one of the boys replied. He ran to the trunk of his own car and got out a box of tools. "Here," he said to one of his companions, "you disconnect the radio. I'll get the hubcaps."

The third boy, who was the smallest and looked about fifteen years old, stood guard over Ned.

While his friends were busily working on Nancy's car, he released his grip on the athlete somewhat. Ned, perfectly still, tried to regain his strength. Suddenly he twisted his body and grabbed the boy, lifting him up and dragging him toward the road barrier.

"Let me go!" the boy screeched, trying to get away from Ned.

The captive thrashed his legs, allowing his body to fall like dead weight toward the ground. But Ned tightened his grip on the boy's arms and, kicking over one of the wooden horses, he dragged him to the dark, swirling water.

"Tell your friends to quit or I'll dump you in the river!" he panted.

By now the boy's companions had come after Ned and his captive, ready to pounce on the young athlete again, when they heard police sirens in the distance.

"The cops!" one of the young punks yelled. "Let's get out of here!"

The two ran up the street, too scared to come to their friend's help.

"Just who are all of you?" Ned asked his captive.

"Friends!" the boy hissed, squirming and trying to kick Ned in the shins.

Ned sank his fingers into the boy's arm.

He bellowed in pain, but did not answer when Ned repeated the question.

"As soon as the police get here," Ned said, "I'm going to tell them you were responsible for this whole mess."

"But that's not true. Sammy Johnson made us do it," the boy blurted out.

"Who's he?"

After a slight hesitation, the answer came. "He's Matey Johnson's brother!"

By now, a patrol car flashing blue and red lights had pulled to a halt behind the two cars. Two officers and Nancy emerged. She rushed to Ned's side.

"Are you okay?" she inquired, noticing a slight bruise along his cheekbone.

Ned grinned. "I feel as though I just scored a touchdown—"

"I hate you," his captive snapped at Nancy.

She stared at him in surprise. "I don't even know you! What did I ever do to you?"

Before he could answer, the police officers interrupted. "Come on, we're taking you down to headquarters," one of the men said.

Immediately Ned related what the boy had told him. "I guess the kids were trying to get even with Nancy for catching Matey Johnson," he concluded.

"Incredible," the girl detective said. "Was Sammy one of the gang members?"

The boy, who was now handcuffed, glared. "Well, you won't catch him!"

Staring at her car stuck between the roadblock and the gang's vehicle, Nancy replied, "I guess I won't."

Before long, however, a tow truck was on the scene to move the boys' car. As soon as Nancy's hubcaps were replaced, the couple was ready to leave.

"Too bad the radio was ripped out," Ned said, looking at the hole, the wires dangling under the dashboard. "But at least they didn't take it with them. I'll have it put back for you while you're away."

"That's really nice of you," said the girl, adding, "I couldn't get over how you tackled all those kids. You were terrific."

Prompted to tell Nancy the full details of the final capture, he said, "I just dragged that little squirt to the goalpost—I mean the river!"

Ned turned the car around and drove toward the

main street once again, while Nancy looked at her watch.

"It's too late for us to go to the show," she said. "Why don't we go straight to the dance and meet everybody there? I'm sure Bess, George, and the boys are really worried about us."

Ned agreed. As Nancy had predicted, their friends were extremely anxious when they arrived.

"Where have you been?" George questioned, observing their disheveled attire. "Were you attacked by a monster?"

"Four of them," Nancy replied, urging Ned to tell the story.

When he had finished, George remarked, "Being captain of the football team sure comes in handy sometimes. But I never knew they trained you for multiple attacks."

Ned grinned. "We might not have fared so well if it hadn't been for our fleet-footed Nancy. Man, can she sprint!"

"But I'd rather dance!" Nancy laughed, as the orchestra music swelled in the hall. Ned took Nancy's hand and led her onto the dance floor. "Do your bones ache too much to dance?" she asked with concern.

"Never!" He laughed, sweeping the girl toward the center of the room.

The other two couples followed them. Bess,

however, was more perplexed than her cousin about Nancy's casual attitude.

"Look at them," she said, keeping her eyes on Nancy and Ned. "They're dancing and laughing as if nothing happened."

"Maybe," Dave chuckled, "Ned's feat did wonders for their relationship!"

As they found themselves dancing near Nancy and Ned, Bess said to her friend, "You ought to call your father and tell him you're all right. I phoned him, thinking possibly you went home for some reason."

Taking Bess's advice, Nancy excused herself for a few moments. Her father and Hannah Gruen were relieved to hear that she and Ned were safe after the attack.

"Those boys must be punished," Carson Drew declared. "The people in this town won't tolerate such nonsense." He paused, adding lightly, "Have a good time, dear, but stay together as a group on your way home." Nancy promised they would.

In the course of the evening, the young people discussed Nancy's manuscript and the mystery involving François Lefèvre's lace cuffs. "I'd also like to know who owns that diamond cross," Burt Eddleton spoke up. "You'll sure have plenty to keep you busy in Belgium."

"They'll be so busy, they won't even have the

time to send us postcards," Dave remarked.

The day the girls were to leave for New York, the boys drove them to the airport, stopping briefly at the post office on the way. To Nancy's amazement a copy of the signed receipt for the manuscript had just been received. But the signature was illegible. The young detective showed it to her friends, then put it in her purse.

"Besides that little gem," Ned said, "did you pack your toothbrush, your clothes, and a picture of me?"

"I did—in just the reverse order," she said, kissing Ned good-bye. "I'll bring you back a surprise!"

"Make it a solution to the secret in the old lace!"

When the threesome reached New York City, they took a taxi directly to Aunt Eloise Drew's apartment house. She welcomed the girls with hugs and kisses. After they were settled, Nancy told her aunt everything that had happened so far.

Aunt Eloise was shocked. "Terrible, just terrible!" she exclaimed. Then, looking fondly at her niece, she said, "I'm sorry to tell you this, Nancy, but the editor-in-chief of *Circle and Square* magazine wants to see you as soon as possible."

"Did he say why?" Nancy asked.

"Well, yes," Aunt Eloise replied, unsure of what to say next. She took a deep breath.

"I can take it," Nancy insisted.

"It seems there's a serious charge against you!"

7

The Stolen Bag

"What kind of charge?" George asked. "Nancy hasn't done anything wrong."

Aunt Eloise put an arm around her niece. "Of course she hasn't. My brother phoned me a little while ago with the message. He said Mr. Miller, the man to whom I gave your manuscript, didn't give any details, but he stressed he must see you personally."

"It's almost five-thirty," Nancy said. "The magazine office is probably closed now. I'll have to go there first thing in the morning."

The following day, she set up an appointment to see Mr. Miller.

"I'm going with you," Bess insisted. "After

what's happened to you, I don't think you should travel *anywhere* alone."

"Bess is right," George agreed. "I'll come along too."

Nancy's face creased into a broad smile. "With two bodyguards to protect me, I guess I ought to be fairly safe."

"And if all else fails," her plump friend teased her, "we'll call Ned to the rescue!"

Aunt Eloise, who taught school, had already left so the visitors tidied the apartment before leaving for the office of *Circle and Square* magazine.

Once outside, the girls headed west past a small private park toward Madison Avenue, one of New York City's busiest streets. It was filled with taxis, passenger cars, and crowds of pedestrians walking at a faster clip than any vehicle could move that morning.

"I just love New York," Bess swooned, gazing into the window of an Italian dress boutique. "The clothes are gorgeous, the people are gorgeous—" She paused to stare at a sleek, black-haired girl in the shop. She was wearing a fine lemon-colored knit suit. "Boy, I wish I could look like that."

George nudged her cousin away from the window. "You could if you stopped eating!"

Bess pretended not to hear the remark. "Nancy, wouldn't it be great to see a few shows and concerts too?"

"I hardly have enough time to see Mr. Miller," Nancy said, her thoughts miles away from Madison Avenue. "But maybe we can catch up with New York when we return."

Soon the trio reached the entrance of a tall building where they found a wall directory next to a bank of elevators. *Circle and Square* magazine was on the twelfth floor.

As they rode up in silence, Nancy steadied her eyes on the floor indicator. When the light stopped at twelve, the doors slid open slowly and she took a deep breath.

George leaned toward her. "Don't worry," she said, as they entered the magazine office. "Everything will turn out all right."

Mr. Miller proved to be a handsome man with light brown hair and cheerful blue eyes. Nancy judged him to be close to her father's age.

"I have an eighteen-year-old daughter too," he volunteered. "She looks a little bit like you, Miss Drew, but I'm afraid the resemblance ends there. She would never plagiarize someone's story."

The accusation stunned the girl detective. "Well, I wouldn't either," she replied evenly, trying to check her rising temper.

"That's right," Bess said in support.

"Why don't you let Mr. Miller explain what he means," George suggested.

The editor-in-chief said that his readers had

found two identical entries to the contest. "One of them is yours," he stated. "Your solution to the mystery is the same as the other contestant's."

"Word for word?" Nancy inquired.

"Well, no," he replied, "but it certainly looks like a clear-cut case of plagiarism or mental telepathy. Which is it?"

The girl detective gritted her teeth as she proceeded to answer. She told about Matey Johnson and his attempted break-in.

"But now you say he's in jail," Mr. Miller replied. "Did he manage to steal your manuscript?"

"No," Nancy admitted, suddenly realizing Johnson had had no opportunity to see her entry. "But he overheard me talking about it! Then I mailed you my original, which your office claims never arrived. Yet I have a receipt that says otherwise. Then my aunt delivered a copy of my story several days ago."

Nancy opened her purse and took out the receipt with the illegible signature on it.

"Strange, very strange," Mr. Miller said, frowning. "This doesn't look familiar to me. I'm sure it didn't come from here."

"What?" George cried. "But the receipt was returned to Nancy by the River Heights post office!"

"You'll have to leave it with me," Mr. Miller said abruptly. "This is most irregular."

Worried that she might lose an important clue to

the identity of the plagiarist, Nancy asked for a photocopy of the tiny paper.

"Don't you trust me?" the editor quipped, showing the first sign of friendliness.

Ignoring the comment, Nancy said, "Can you figure out the signature? We can't."

"No, but I'm inclined to think it belongs to someone who doesn't work in this office."

"Possibly my rival in the contest," the girl sleuth concluded. "Who is it, by the way?"

"A man named Paul Frieden." As Mr. Miller stared at the illegible signature, he added, somewhat embarrassed, "I may owe you an apology for my attitude when you walked in here this morning. But I'm afraid that until this matter is resolved, we cannot enter either your manuscript or Mr. Frieden's in our contest."

"Oh, that's awful!" Bess burst out in Nancy's defense. "She wrote every word of the story herself. She didn't steal anything from anybody!"

"I admire your loyalty," Mr. Miller remarked, "but rules are—"

"Nancy's an amateur detective," George interrupted, "so naturally that's why she was able to make up such an interesting ending to the story of François Lefèvre."

"I'm sure—" Mr. Miller started again, but George would not let him finish.

"Nancy hoped to win first prize and give the

money to a very worthy charity," she said pleadingly.

Mr. Miller led the disappointed visitors to the door. "I'm truly sorry about this whole thing. Look, here's what I'll do. I'll request my staff to hold both manuscripts until the very last minute of the deadline, which has been extended a bit. Perhaps we'll know by then what really happened."

Nancy smiled faintly. "Thank you very much."

"That's the best I can do," the man said, shaking her hand.

Hopeful that Mr. Drew might be able to work on Nancy's case while they were away, the girls left New York on a night flight to Brussels, Belgium. From there they planned to take a train or drive to Brugge, since the small city had no airport of its own.

As the plane's wheels touched down, George stared out the window at the sun-soaked terminal building. It was noon in Belgium which meant it was only 6:00 A.M. in New York.

The travelers passed through Immigration and Passport Control quickly, then headed for the baggage area. One by one, pieces of luggage appeared on the moving conveyor. First George, then Bess saw their suitcases and pulled them off. Nancy also spotted hers, a sturdy green bag, but waited for it to come closer before taking it. Suddenly, to her astonishment, a man at the head of the line reached out, grabbed the bag, and hurried away.

"Did you see that?" Nancy cried out. "A man stole my suitcase!" She dashed through the crowd of passengers. A guard stopped her abruptly at a doorway leading to the exit. She could not pass through until her luggage was cleared by a customs official.

"But someone just took my bag!" she exclaimed indignantly. "He went through this door!"

"Well, evidently he works here and has proper identification. Maybe the bag just looks like yours."

Nancy rejoined Bess and George, hopeful that another green bag bearing her initials would appear. None did. Completely frustrated, Nancy spoke to the guard again, insisting she had seen someone take her luggage.

"If so," the guard replied, "I suggest you report it to our lost and found office. Most likely, the person will return it when he realizes he has the wrong bag. Come back tomorrow morning and check."

Following the man's instructions, Nancy and her friends went to the lost and found desk and reported the theft. Afterward they decided to stay in Brussels overnight.

"Oh, well," Bess said, "look at the bright side. This is where François lived!"

She and George tagged after Nancy to a shuttle

train which was headed for the heart of the city. They chose a quaint hotel listed in Nancy's pocket directory that was within walking distance of the station.

"Belgium is a three-language country," Bess said. "People speak either French, Dutch, or Flemish depending on where they live. Many, of course, speak all three."

Despite the beauty of the city and her friends' attempts to cheer her, Nancy's thoughts were solely on the missing luggage.

Somebody wants to keep me from going to Brugge! she thought as she crept into bed that night. *But who?*

8

Detective Trouble

Nancy slept fitfully and awoke early the next morning. She showered and dressed before her traveling companions had awakened, then went for a short walk until George and Bess were ready for breakfast. In the dining room, the girls discussed their situation.

"I have a hunch that someone is trying to stall our visit to Brugge," Nancy said, sampling one of the sweet rolls on her plate.

Bess gulped down a cup of tea. "Can't," she said.

"What do you mean 'can't'?" George questioned.

"If Nancy's bag doesn't show up today," her cousin replied, "we'll go on to Brugge and tell the airline to forward it to Madame Chambray's."

To Nancy's disappointment, the green suitcase had not been returned to the airport. She gave the address she would be staying at in Brugge and begged the airline representative to deliver the luggage as soon as it arrived.

"Frankly," Nancy said to her friends, "I doubt it will ever come. I'm positive that the person who took my bag did so on purpose."

Noticing a policeman standing outside the main entrance to the terminal, Nancy walked up to him.

"*Monsieur*," she called. "Do you speak English?"

"*Un peu*—a little."

The girl detective explained that her suitcase had probably been stolen.

"Can you describe the man—slowly, please?"

Nancy said he had been too far away for her to give a thorough description. "But I can tell you this. He was tall and thin and wore a dark blue suit or uniform. When I reported him to the guard, he said the person probably worked here."

The officer paused a moment before speaking again. "Can you point the guard out to me so I can question him?"

The girl ducked back into the terminal, glancing in the direction of the baggage area. A different man was on duty there. When she returned to report this, she added one more identifying clue—the initials *ND* on her suitcase.

"Perhaps all your trouble is simply based on coincidence," the officer said. "The man who took your bag may, in fact, own one just like yours."

"And his name begins with the same letters as mine?" The young sleuth completed the policeman's deduction. "That would certainly be a coincidence."

"Well, I will file a report for you and maybe your suitcase will be found."

"If so, could you forward it to Brugge? We'll be going there today." She gave the officer Madame Chambray's address and thanked him for his help. Then the girls took the shuttle train to the railroad station.

The ride to Brugge was uneventful. The girls watched the flat, green landscape and talked little. Finally, after a stop in Ghent, they reached the medieval town of Brugge. It was quaintly picturesque with lots of narrow streets and three- or four-story old stone houses often separated by canals.

"This is like traveling back into history to the Middle Ages," Bess remarked.

Her cousin was intrigued by the canal boats. Several of them were open motorboats while others were canopied with colorful awnings. "No wonder Brugge is called the Venice of the North."

Rather than take a land taxi, the visitors chose a boat. The *schipper*, a man whose ruddy complexion indicated he spent many hours at the wheel, stowed their luggage and started the motor.

It chugged loudly, causing Bess to whisper, "Maybe this is a medieval motor!"

Nancy smiled halfheartedly. "I hope the dress shops aren't," she said, wishing she had worn her new sweater-coat on the plane. She wondered if she would ever see it again.

As the *schipper* steered the boat from one canal into another, it passed under a small stone bridge with a Gothic hump in the middle. Beyond was a fieldstone house evidently built centuries ago. The narrow back windows were set under arches beneath a triangular roof.

"That must be where Madame Chambray lives," George announced, as the boatman tied the craft to a post.

He helped the girls out, and unloaded the larger pieces of luggage. Then he grabbed the smaller ones, including Bess's cosmetic bag. She held her hand out to take it, but the bag slipped through the man's fingers, splashing into the water.

"Oh, no!" Bess cried out. "There go all my lipsticks and nail polish!"

The *schipper* jabbered something unintelligible.

Nancy caught the word *droevig*, which she figured probably meant "sorry."

"Do be careful!" Bess pleaded while the man hopped back into the boat and picked up a pole with a grappling hook at one end. He slid it into the water and fished slowly for the handle of the case. In a few moments he nodded happily. He had caught the little bag!

"Thank goodness," Bess sighed.

"You and your makeup," her cousin needled her. "Why wear rouge at all when you know I can keep your blood pressure sky-high!"

By now, the boatman had picked up their luggage and was leading the way to the door of the house. It opened, revealing a tall, slender woman with silver-gray hair wound into a knot at the nape of her neck.

"Madame Chambray?" Nancy inquired.

"*Mais oui*," she said in French. "Yes, and welcome."

The girls introduced themselves, and Nancy paid the *schipper*. Once they were seated in the living room, the visitors were struck by its charm. It contained numerous pieces of intricately carved furniture and heavy brocade draperies. Many of the paintings on the walls had been done by very fine artists, some of them famous.

Nancy was eager to see the diamond and lapis lazuli cross but decided to wait for Madame Chambray to mention it first.

"I am so glad you could come," the woman said. "You know I've been living in this house only a very short while but already it has produced—how you say—a mystery?"

"Yes, you wrote to Mother about it," Bess said.

"Then you understand I am looking for the owner of a beautiful cross," Madame Chambray continued.

Nancy felt obligated to warn her not to tell her story to too many people.

"No?" the woman replied, raising her eyebrows. "But how will I ever find the owner? I must tell you I put an article in the newspaper about it. Let me show it to you." The well-meaning woman excused herself for a moment and returned with a news clipping which she handed to Nancy.

Immediately the girl detective's eyes fell on her own name. "You mentioned my visit here as well," Nancy said in disbelief.

"It isn't every day that a famous young detective comes to Brugge." The woman chuckled.

"Oh, dear," Bess moaned. "All your chances of working under cover, Nancy, just vanished into thin air!"

Madame Chambray caught the look of disappointment on Nancy's face. "Is there a problem?"

she asked. "Did I do something wrong?"

George replied first. "No, but—"

"But what?" Madame Chambray said anxiously.

"Nancy may not be able to solve your mystery," Bess declared boldly.

9

The Ghost

Nancy was less pessimistic than her friends and smiled at Madame Chambray. "Let's just say you've given me—all of us—quite a challenge," she said. "The more people who know about the diamond cross and your search for its owner, the more chance there is that someone will put in a false claim."

The woman chided herself. "How stupid I am!" she exclaimed. "That never occurred to me."

It was obvious to her visitors that Madame Chambray was scrupulously honest and very trusting. No doubt she could be easily swayed by the sympathetic tale of a con artist.

"Where did you find the cross?" Nancy inquired. She gazed toward the narrow hallway where steps led to the second and third stories and tried to imagine how Madame Chambray had stumbled upon the glittering piece in some medieval nook upstairs.

"It was in a most unlikely place," the woman said, pausing. "In the cellar."

"The cellar?" George repeated in surprise. "Was it in a box or just lying on the floor somewhere?"

"Actually it was wrapped in a piece of linen that was caught in the stonework—"

Madame Chambray stopped speaking for a moment and went into another room. When she returned, she held a small purple velvet box in her hand. "You must see it—it is so beautiful," she said, giving the box to Nancy to open.

Bess and George gathered near the young detective as she lifted the cover. Inside lay the dazzling cross.

"It's exquisite!" Bess exclaimed while Nancy removed the piece from the box to examine it closely.

The oblong diamonds and lapis lazuli stones were set in solid gold. But there were no unusual markings on the setting.

"The linen I found it wrapped in," Madame Chambray said, "is folded under the mount in the box."

George took the cross from Nancy, enabling her to remove the linen. "There's something stitched on it," Nancy commented as she stared at the line of French words embroidered on the soiled material. Below them was the name *Antoinette Tissot*.

"Maybe the cross belonged to King Louis XVI," Bess suggested with a grin.

Madame Chambray interrupted the conversation, asking Nancy if she could interpret the message.

"I think so," the girl detective replied. "Doesn't it say, 'God protect you wherever you go'?"

"That's correct," the woman said with admiration.

"Have you shown this to anyone else?" Nancy questioned.

"Other than some friends, I did ask an expert appraiser of antique jewelry to look at the cross. He estimates it to be more than one hundred years old."

"Which means," George said, "Antoinette is not living anymore."

"Possibly," Nancy put in, "but not necessarily. After all, the cross could have come into her possession years after it was made." She stifled a yawn, suddenly feeling extremely tired after their adventure in Brussels.

"I can see you are a very smart detective, Nancy," said Madame Chambray, "but I don't want you to trouble your mind about all of this right now. You need your sleep. You all do."

She took the little velvet box from the girls and replaced the linen and beautiful cross.

"I am having a small dinner party this evening to introduce you to my friends. They are so eager to meet all of you," the woman went on. "So—"

"But I have nothing appropriate to wear," Nancy murmured worriedly. She told Madame Chambray about her missing luggage, adding, "Is there a dress shop nearby?"

"There are plenty of shops," Madame Chambray replied. "But you must rest. I will find something for you to wear. Don't worry."

Madame Chambray led the girls upstairs to their rooms, each one charmingly decorated with silk-covered beds and matching drapes. George lent Nancy a robe which she changed into before collapsing on her pillow.

The girl detective's mind whirled endlessly about the new, exciting mystery. To whom did the antique cross belong? Someone—apparently Antoinette—had given it to someone else, but when and why? There were few clues to go on, fewer than those about the secret in the old lace.

When Nancy awoke, she felt a surge of energy. We ought to investigate the cellar, she decided, quickly getting out of bed. Maybe we'll find an important lead down there.

Except for the sound of an approaching motorboat, the house was very quiet. Nancy pressed her nose against the casement window. She noticed Madame Chambray at the dock, waiting to board the boat. Maybe she's going shopping for the party tonight, the girl thought, then went to the room next door.

"Wake up, Bess!" she called. "We have work to do!"

Her friend was sleeping peacefully, oblivious to Nancy, who was jostling her now. "Wha-what is it?" Bess finally mumbled.

"Come on, lazybones, get up. We're going on a hunt for clues!"

Next Nancy knocked on George's door, then went back to her own room where she put on her skirt and sweater. The young detectives, their flashlights in hand, gathered in the corridor at the top of the steps.

"Where do we start?" Bess asked.

"In the cellar," Nancy said, "since that's where Madame Chambray found the cross."

The girls noticed a heavy wooden door off the kitchen. It creaked noisily as Nancy swung it back on its hinges and saw that it led below. Before descending, Nancy thought she heard something underneath the stairwell but dismissed it when the noise was not repeated. Step by step she guided her friends into the eerie darkness.

"I'm scared." Bess shivered. "Nancy, why don't we wait for Madame Chambray to return before we go any farther?"

"Sh!" George quieted her cousin. "Stop pretending to be a chicken detective."

"Who's pretending?" Bess laughed nervously.

As they stood in the musty, dark room, they beamed their lights on the stone walls, looking unsuccessfully for a switch to turn on an overhead light.

"Oh!" Bess cried out suddenly while Nancy and George walked ahead of her.

"What's the matter?" Nancy asked.

"I hear weird noises. Don't you?"

"No," the other detectives whispered back.

"Stick closer," George said, but her cousin continued to lag behind.

Nancy swept her flashlight across a deep stony crevice in one wall while George examined the floor beneath it. "Swing your light over here, Bess," George requested, unaware that her cousin was not with them. But when no response came, George spun around. "Bess, where are you?"

Instantly Nancy flashed her light toward the cellar steps where they had started their investigation. Bess was nowhere in sight. A couple of tense minutes later, they saw a ghostly figure in white standing beyond the fringe of light!

Nancy turned her flashlight on the mysterious apparition, noticing it wore leather boots. "Who are you?" she cried out.

There was no answer.

"Let's get him, George!" Nancy hissed, feeling the two girls had a good chance to overpower the lone ghost, who seemed to be a tall, slender man.

"Right!" George said, and both charged toward the figure, diving for the sheet that covered him. The ghost threw out his arms and with a powerful thrust flung both girls to the floor. Their lights fell out of their hands and went out. Now they were in total darkness.

George screamed, expecting the ghost to pounce on them at any moment. All they heard, however, were a few shuffling noises that quickly faded.

A bit shaken, the young detectives groped for their flashlights. George found hers first and beamed it toward Nancy, who had noticed a small hole right next to where she had fallen. "I—I think my light rolled in there," she said.

"Where's the ghost?" George asked, now beaming her light in the direction where the apparition had stood. All she could see was the cellar wall.

The ghost had vanished. Was he hiding nearby

ready to attack them again? And where was Bess?

Had he kidnapped her?

Panic-stricken, both girls shrieked, calling out, "Bess! Bess!"

10

The Water Tunnel

Nancy and George called Bess's name several times but there was no response. "What could have happened to her?" George asked in bewilderment.

Then they heard a muffled sound. Keeping quiet, Nancy took George's flashlight and edged toward the cellar steps. There, under the staircase, was a door made of heavy wood and painted the color of the stonework.

"George, help me!" Nancy said, tugging on the iron bolt. Her fingers, wet with perspiration, slipped.

George grasped the bolt firmly and yanked it back. The door swung open, revealing a small closet. Inside was Bess, a gag stuffed across her mouth, her wrists and ankles bound tightly. She sat on the floor, leaning against the cold stone wall, where spiders had fastened their cobwebs.

"Oh, Bess!" Nancy gasped.

"Are you all right?" George cried, quickly bending over her cousin to remove the gag from her mouth.

"Who did this to you?" Nancy asked as she went to work on the ropes that were tied around the girl's wrists and legs.

"A—a man!" Bess murmured. "He was dressed like a ghost. Oh, it was horrible!"

"Poor Bess," George said sympathetically, massaging the red welts where the rope had cut into her cousin's wrists.

"He—he came out of that closet," Bess went on. "He grabbed my flashlight, then put the gag over my mouth."

"Did he say anything to you?" Nancy asked.

"No, nothing."

"We must report this to the police," George said resolutely as Bess slowly stumbled to her feet.

Despite the ache in her ankles, the girl insisted on climbing the stairs without help. "I don't want to stay down here one more second."

When they emerged into the kitchen, the girls heard the back door open and close.

"That must be Madame Chambray," Nancy said, calling out her name.

"Yes, dear, I'm home," the woman replied, joining her young guests. Madame Chambray's smile quickly changed to a deep frown when she saw the smudges on Bess's face and the stains on her skirt. "Did you fall?"

Tears welled up in the girl's eyes as she said no and explained what had happened.

"*Ma pauvre chérie,*" the woman said, hugging Bess briefly. She rinsed a small towel in lukewarm water and patted the girl's face. "There, there, you will be fine again."

"Oh, thank you," Bess said. "I do feel better."

"How did this terrible man get into my house?" Madame Chambray asked. "Maybe we should call the police."

"Well, he's gone now," Nancy said, adding, "Is there some sort of connection between the basement and the canal?"

"Not that I know of. I haven't lived here very long and I am still learning about the house. It seems to be full of little doors and nooks and crannies so there may well be an underground passage."

That was all the young detectives needed to hear. "Are you game to go back down?" Nancy asked George, knowing that Bess was not up to it.

"Why not?"

"Please don't," Bess pleaded. "The ghost may try to stick you both in that awful closet!"

"We'll be careful," Nancy promised. "And we'll send up a report every ten minutes. Okay?"

As she and George hurried below, Bess asked to be excused.

"By all means," Madame Chambray said. "Take a good hot bath and relax. You want to look your prettiest tonight!"

She winked at the girl, causing Bess to wonder if she was planning to introduce her guests to some charming young Belgian men. "Oh, I will!" Bess giggled, leaving her hostess alone in the kitchen.

Madame Chambray busied herself with some last-minute dinner preparations. Then, glancing at the package she had brought home for Nancy, the woman smiled happily.

I think she will like it, Madame Chambray thought. I'll put it on her bed, so when she comes up she'll find a nice surprise.

She stepped out into the hallway and was about to go upstairs when she spied someone staring through the living room window.

"Who's there?" she called out.

The figure ducked quickly out of sight, prompting Madame Chambray to drop the package and run to the door. She opened it and stuck her head outside.

"Is anyone there?" she repeated.

But the only response was the water of the canals gently lapping against the walls of the house.

How strange! she said to herself.

Nancy and George, in the meantime, were exploring one end of the cellar where they discovered another door. It opened onto a short tunnel of water.

"I'm sure this is how the ghost got in," Nancy remarked. "I wonder how deep the water is. Maybe he waded in and out."

"Did his boots look wet to you?" George questioned.

"I couldn't tell—they looked dark to begin with."

"I'll go upstairs and get a yardstick," George volunteered. "That way we can find out how deep it is." She rushed off.

Nancy, however, became impatient and went down to the lowest step. Maybe I can tell by sticking my hand in, she thought.

She kneeled down, lowering her arm into the water. Her fingers did not touch bottom. Guess I'll have to stretch out, she decided.

The stone step shifted slightly as she lay flat, then slipped forward ready to sink into the murky pool!

Oh, no! Nancy panicked, trying to hold her position until George returned. "George!" she cried loudly. "Help me!"

George could not hear her friend from upstairs where Madame Chambray was telling her about the stranger at the window.

Oh, why doesn't she come? Nancy thought in alarm as she tried to grab the dry step above her, praying it would not also give way.

Fortunately, George had not lingered too long in conversation with Madame Chambray and was on her way back downstairs. She raced to the tunnel door, shouting to Nancy, "Wait until you hear what—" and then broke off when she saw Nancy's predicament.

George dropped the yardstick on the top step and gripped Nancy's arm, helping her up, as the stone step crumbled into the water.

"Where would I be without you, friend?" Nancy said gratefully.

"Swimming," George quipped.

Nancy laughed as the other girl lowered the yardstick into the water. It was shallower than she had estimated. When George pulled the stick out, it was covered with weeds and muck up to a foot and a half.

"That man could have waded out of here very easily," Nancy concluded. "And a boat could have been waiting for him out on the canal. Of course, the big question is why— Why did he come here at all?"

Had he planned to burglarize Madame Chambray's house while she was out? Was he pursuing the diamond cross or something even more precious? The girl detectives tried to piece the puzzle together.

"But what could be more valuable than the cross?" George said to her friend. "Of course, the furnishings and paintings must be worth a lot—"

Nancy snapped her fingers. "Didn't Madame Chambray mention in her letter to Mrs. Marvin something about a document and—and a treasure?"

"Yes, you're right. I completely forgot about that."

"I almost did too."

"But how would the ghost know the contents of the letter?" George asked.

"He wouldn't unless he's André Bergère," Nancy said grimly.

"Not necessarily," George said after thinking for a moment. "Since Madame Chambray talked so openly with her friends about these things, they may have inadvertently passed the information along to another would-be thief!"

Nancy was eager to ask their hostess about the mysterious treasure and stepped toward the tunnel door. The chugging sound of a motorboat stopped her midway.

"Look!" she cried, pointing toward the canal.

The boat was entering the tunnel. Who was steering it? Had their ghostly attacker returned?

11

Fantastic News

The oncoming boat drew closer. George clicked off her flashlight, waiting for the single occupant to reach the steps.

"When he gets here," Nancy whispered, "shine your light right in his face. We'll be able to capture him then!"

The boat, however, stopped some distance away. A man who was carrying a large bundle hopped out and entered another door at the base of the tunnel.

"I guess he lives next door," Nancy remarked with a giggle.

George also laughed in relief. "I'm glad he wasn't our ghost after all," she said and seized the chance to relate Madame Chambray's story about the stranger at the window.

"I wonder if he and Mr. Ghost are one and the same," Nancy commented, leading the way back to the kitchen. "We have so much to talk about with Madame Chambray." She glanced at her watch. "But it's nearly dinnertime."

Upstairs the girls found the woman peering into a large kettle on the stove. The aroma of delicate spices filled the air.

"What are you making?" Nancy said. "It smells absolutely delicious."

"*Waterzooi*." The woman smiled. "One of our traditional dishes—poached capon in a light creamy sauce. The rest of the menu is a surprise. And so is the package on your bed, Nancy. Now go up to your room and get ready. My guests will be arriving soon."

Excitedly the girl dashed upstairs and opened the bundle. Folded carefully inside was a beautiful ecru linen dress trimmed in fine lace!

"Oh, it's lovely!" the girl detective exclaimed happily.

She held up the dress in front of her and gazed into the full-length mirror in the corner of the room. Around the neckline and fitted cuffs of the long, tight sleeves were ruffles of lace. I wonder if François Lefèvre's lace cuffs were like these, Nancy said to herself. Then, hearing Madame Chambray come up the stairs, the girl hurried out of her room. "Oh, thank you so much, Madame—"

Embarrassed, the woman cut her off, telling her to dress quickly. "Everyone will be here in a few minutes!" she said with a smile.

To her delight, the three girls were ready to greet the guests when they arrived. Madame Chambray introduced Professor Philip Permeke and his daughter Hilda, a pretty blond who looked about twenty. With her was a young man with sturdy features and brooding green eyes.

He's cute, Bess thought, but he looks so sad. I wonder why.

"And this is Joseph Stolk," Madame Chambray announced as Bess shook his hand. "He and Hilda went to high school together. Now Joseph is studying art history in Brussels."

"Oh, how interesting!" Bess said eagerly. "I bet you know a lot about all the museums of this wonderful old town. Perhaps you could take us on a tour sometime." She flashed him a dazzling, flirtatious smile.

"Yes—uh—perhaps I could," Joseph replied shyly.

Hilda seemed less than delighted with that suggestion, and George tugged on her cousin's arm, signaling her not to pursue the conversation any farther. "You're about to set off a little quarrel between those two," she whispered to Bess. Then, turning to the professor, she said, "Dr. Permeke, I understand that you are an expert on the history of Brugge. Would you tell us a little about it?"

"Gladly," he said, "but stop me when you get bored."

His remarks during dinner were fascinating. "Did you know that the original town of Brugge was on the seacoast? The name of our ancient town means city of bridges. Long ago it was a thriving port. But storms were so devastating, even the dikes could not save it. The merchants moved inland—to the spot where we are today—and dug a canal to connect the town with the ocean."

"That was quite an engineering feat," Madame Chambray commented. "It's about ten miles from here to the coast."

The jovial gray-haired professor nodded. "When this new town was built, its predecessor on the coast took the name of Zeebrugge which means Sea Brugge."

While he paused to take a sip of wine, his daughter continued the tale. "This was a very fashionable place in the fifteenth, sixteenth, and seventeenth centuries. Merchants were rather successful and able to buy the finest of everything, including the best clothes from Paris. If you like, I'll give you a tour tomorrow."

"Perhaps I can go with you too," Joseph suggested, looking over at Bess for a moment.

Hilda's suspicious glance trailed from him to Bess, who was beaming prettily. "I think not," Hilda said firmly. "Don't you have a term paper to finish before the end of the week?"

"Yes, but I—"

Poor Joseph is trapped under Hilda's jealous thumb! Bess decided.

Seeing the fire grow in the young Belgian woman's face, George quickly changed the subject. "Maybe Hilda can take us to a gift shop where I can buy something for Burt and you can buy something for Dave and—"

"I can buy something for Ned," Nancy chimed in.

"Are they your brothers?" Hilda inquired with interest. "Or, as you say in America, your boyfriends?"

Nancy grinned. "They're our boyfriends," she said, happy to see a smile return to Hilda's face.

"In that case," their new friend went on, "you must buy them very special gifts—and, of course, you will want some lace for yourselves."

The mention of lace prompted Nancy to reveal one of her reasons for coming to Brugge. She mentioned the magazine contest and the story of François Lefèvre."

"What?" Madame Chambray said, electrified. "What was that name you mentioned?"

"François Lefèvre."

The woman stared at her, unable to speak for a moment.

"What is it, Madame Chambray?" Nancy asked anxiously. "Is that name familiar to you?"

"*Mais oui*—yes, indeed," the woman cried out. "It is one of the names mentioned in the document I found. It was written by one Friedrich Vonderlicht, also known as François Lefèvre!"

"I don't believe it!" George blurted out. "You mean, François once owned this house?"

"Apparently he did!"

"Then maybe the secret in the old lace is hidden right under this roof!" Nancy deduced.

"I doubt it," Madame Chambray remarked. "After all, François lived here a long time ago. Others have come and gone since and I'm sure that whatever secrets he had were discovered by later occupants."

"Could we see the document, please?" Nancy urged.

"I locked it in my desk upstairs," Madame Chambray said. "I've been looking for my keys but can't seem to find them."

"Oh!" Bess said anxiously. "Do you think they were stolen?"

"No, dear." The woman smiled. "I always misplace them. I'm sure they're in the house somewhere and I'll find them tomorrow. No one would have any reason to steal them, so don't worry."

"But what does the document say?"

"It was a small part of a will, actually. It said that Friedrich Vonderlicht, also known as François Lefèvre, was leaving his fortune to his wife. But the part telling where he left it has been torn off."

"Too bad," George said. "I'm afraid it won't help us much then."

"Well, it's helped already," Bess pointed out. "Now we know that François lived in this house!"

The group discussed the strange coincidence at length, and the rest of the evening proved enjoyable as everyone moved into the living room to taste Madame Chambray's surprise dessert, a delectable lemon meringue pie.

"I'm stuffed," Bess admitted at last.

"Well, tomorrow we will walk off all the calories!" Hilda chuckled.

But before the visitors were ready to leave Madame Chambray's house the next morning, there was an impatient knock at the door.

"Will you answer it for me, please?" Madame Chambray asked Nancy. "I want to keep an eye on the toast."

The girl hurried out of the kitchen to the hallway and flung open the door. To her surprise, it was a *schipper* holding a piece of green luggage in his hand.

"That's my suitcase!" Nancy cried gleefully.

12

At the Lace Center

"Where did you find my suitcase?" Nancy asked the boatman.

But he spoke no English. He merely smiled and waved good-bye, leaving the girl dumbstruck. Immediately Nancy looked through her bag to see if anything was missing. Nothing appeared to have been stolen. She told the good news to everyone before changing from the travel clothes she had worn since leaving New York, then called the airline for details.

"Someone found your bag in an alley behind a hotel in Brussels," a clerk told her. "Although your luggage tag was taken off, the airline tag wasn't. And we knew your initials, which helped us identify it."

Nancy repeated the conversation to her friends. "Now I'm totally convinced someone took it, hoping to keep me from leaving Brussels," she said. "Whoever it was is probably in Brugge this very minute."

When the threesome met Hilda, they asked her to take them to a lace shop. "I'd like to learn as much about lace making as possible," Nancy said.

"Then I know just where to go," the young Belgian woman said.

She led the girls to the Lace Center where supplies were sold and lace makers could take courses in their craft. There were two types of lace, Hilda explained: bobbin lace which originated in Belgium and needlepoint lace which developed at the same time in France.

"Those are bobbins," Hilda said, pointing to a tray of wooden objects which resembled miniature bowling pins. "They are attached to linen threads and serve as weights when the threads are combined in intricate patterns. But first, the *kantwerker* or lace maker chooses a wooden mold to work on. Like one of these."

She indicated a stack of disks about a foot and a half in diameter. One side of each disk was a mound covered with canvas. "They're called pillows and are filled with seaweed," the girl continued. "After the *kantwerker* chooses her pattern, she copies it with pins which she sticks into the pillow. The threads are woven around the pins and then the pins are pulled out."

George noticed sheets of transparent plastic. "What are these for?" she asked.

"The lace maker covers her pillow and the finished lace with a piece of plastic, leaving open just enough space for her to work on. The plastic helps keep the lace clean."

Nancy and Bess discovered a bin of linen threads. "Hannah would love these," Nancy said. While she purchased three spools, George wandered toward the rear of the shop. A chubby boy about eight years old was dipping his hands into another barrel. He pulled out a bunch of bobbins, and threw one at the window and the other at a small statue on a shelf.

"Stop it!" George exclaimed, rushing toward the boy and grabbing his arm.

"Says who?" he answered stubbornly.

"I do," George said, quietly challenging the boy.

He yanked away from her. As she dived for him again, he threw a bobbin at her, hitting her neck hard. Furious, George gripped him by the shoulders and shook him.

"Mommy! Mommy!" the boy yelled frantically.

"What's going on?" A woman suddenly appeared out of the crowd milling about the Lace Center.

"Your son just threw that at me!" George defended herself, pointing to the bobbin lying on the floor.

"Did you do that, Peter?" the boy's mother asked, grabbing the child's hand. The small boy started to protest but at his mother's stern look, lowered his head guiltily.

Meanwhile Nancy and Bess dashed toward their friend. "What happened?" Bess asked, noting the red spot on her cousin's neck.

"Lets just say I hope the next time I get this close to a bobbin I'll be making lace with it," George replied dryly.

"I apologize," the boy's mother said softly. "My husband and I have been dragging Peter with us everywhere and he's getting very cranky, though that's no excuse. I think we'll take him back to the hotel now." Still holding the little boy's hand she exited quickly.

Meanwhile, Nancy asked the shop owner if she had any ice on hand. The woman flew toward a back room and returned with a small bowl and cloth.

"This should prevent any swelling," Nancy said, wrapping the ice in the cloth.

George held the compress against her neck, insisting her friends continue their tour of the store. In a back room about twenty women were making lace. Their nimble fingers moved the bobbins with dizzying speed.

Nancy spoke to one of the lace makers who was seated in one corner, studying a book about lace.

"Could you tell us a few facts about your craft?" the girl detective asked.

"*Oui*. I'll try," she said, speaking slowly with a soft accent. "In the sixteenth and seventeenth centuries, lace was worth much money. It was very valuable as trim for clothing. Many people sold their homes and other belongings just to buy it."

"That's incredible," Nancy commented.

"Incredible but true. There are old papers that say Charles I of England bought forty-four yards of lace trim for a dozen collars and a dozen cuffs, and six hundred yards of bobbin lace for just his nightwear!"

The girls giggled. "Can you picture Dave or Ned wearing ruffled shirts and pajamas?" Bess said, as the woman handed her book to Nancy.

There were numerous photographs of lace patterns throughout. Birds and flowers predominated but there were geometric designs as well.

"Judging from these," Nancy said, "it wouldn't have been too difficult to hide a message in a pair of lace cuffs. It could have been easily woven among flowers and leaves or fantastic-looking birds, like this one." She pointed in the book to a picture of a bird with a striking fantail.

Bess agreed. "I can just imagine a young woman spending endless hours weaving a message for François like 'I must meet you soon in the garden of my home.' Or, 'A moonlit night would be best.' "

The girl's reverie was quickly interrupted, however, by her cousin and Hilda, who had been chatting with George. "My neck's a hundred percent better and we're ready to move on; are you?"

"If you say so," Nancy replied. "Where to, Hilda?"

"Well you did mention you'd like to go to the museums so I suggest the *Gruuthuse* next."

As the girls left the shop, however, Nancy sensed that somone was watching them. Across the street stood a man in a raincoat and hat. He glanced at the girl detectives, then disappeared down the street and around a corner.

Wondering if he had been waiting for them, Nancy decided not to mention this to the others until the pleasant tour was over.

Hilda, meanwhile, directed them to the large old building with minaretlike towers and a store facade. "This used to be the home of the Gruuthuse family. By our standards, it was a palace more than a house."

Inside, the visitors were impressed by the beautiful tapestries, china, and furniture. "How do you like these old beds?" Hilda asked when they reached the second floor. "Notice they are short and narrow. In the old days many people were small."

"Guess they didn't take their vitamins." George laughed.

Bess followed Hilda to the top floor where the Lace Room was. "What gorgeous centerpieces!" she exclaimed, gaping at the large display case. "It would be a real shame to put one of those on a table and then cover it up with a lamp or something."

Nancy was equally awestruck by the collection of lace collars. They were designed to stand up stiffly around the neck, some up to six inches high!

"Those are ruffs," Hilda explained. "They were very fashionable all over Europe in the seventeenth century."

George flinched. "I'd hate to wear one of those. They must have been very hot and uncomfortable."

There were also handmade children's dresses, hats, and handkerchiefs on exhibit. "Several of these things," Hilda remarked, observing Bess's admiring glance, "are worth many thousands of dollars—they are irreplaceable."

"Oh, my goodness!" Bess said. "And I was just

thinking how nice it would be to buy one to show everybody at home."

Hilda now suggested they go downstairs to see the guillotine. Bess trailed after her down the stairway while Nancy hung back, talking to George.

"Don't turn around," Nancy said in a low tone. "There's someone in this room who's been following us. I don't want to lose him."

"Well, you won't if he's following us," George said wryly.

She and Nancy stepped out of the room for a moment and pinned themselves against the outside wall behind the door. Surely the man would go downstairs now. The next few minutes ticked by slowly as the young detectives waited.

"You were wrong," George whispered to her friend when the stranger did not appear.

Nancy peered through the crack below the door hinge. "He's gone!" she cried, racing back into the empty room. Her eyes circled quickly to a balcony doorway. "He must have escaped through there!"

She dashed toward the opening and peered over the railing. Hand over hand, the man was lowering himself on a rope!

"He stole some of the lace!" the young detective gasped, seeing fringes of ruffles sticking out of his pockets.

Instinctively she leaned across the balcony and

grabbed the rope, pulling on it as hard as she could. But the man's weight was too much for her to budge. Suddenly Nancy's foot slipped and she lost her balance. She slid forward over the railing, ready to tumble over the edge!

13

The Thief

Instantly George rushed toward Nancy and grabbed her around the waist, pulling her back fast. "That man mustn't get away!" Nancy cried.

But the thief was already halfway down the rope and was now dangling only a dozen feet above the ground.

"Oh, look! The rope's splitting!" George cried out.

Indeed, the strands were fraying rapidly until the last few threads snapped and the man hit the ground hard. His legs gave way underneath him, and he fell, letting out a howl of anguish.

"We're about to lose him!" George exclaimed, watching the thief try to get up.

"Maybe not," Nancy said. "He seems to have

hurt his ankle. Let's hurry downstairs. Chances are he won't be able to run away!"

The girl detectives flew down the stairway toward the front door and rushed around the building. Hilda and Bess, who were in the Weapons Room, were unaware of what had happened and wondered why their friends were taking so long to join them.

When Nancy and George reached the spot where the frayed rope lay, the man was gone.

"There he is!" George shouted, pointing to the thief as he desperately hobbled toward a bridge spanning a narrow canal between the *Gruuthuse* and another museum. Nancy darted ahead of her companion, yelling at the top of her lungs.

"Stop! *Arrêtez! Halt!*" But he kept limping on as fast as he could.

Halfway across the bridge, however, he paused to rest his hurt ankle. Nancy dived toward him, grabbing the lace centerpiece hanging out of his pocket. Instinctively, he snatched it back, causing the beautiful piece to tear in half!

"Get away from me!" he shouted at Nancy in English. Then he scooped her up in his arms, ready to push her over the stone railing into the water!

"Stop!" Nancy exclaimed just as George caught up to the pair and seized the man's arms.

Should she give him a judo flip into the canal?

No, she decided. He would drag Nancy along with him.

Instead, George continued to hold him while Nancy slid from his grasp and began to empty his pockets that were bulging with lace. Angrily, the man shoved the girls aside and darted across the bridge.

Her arms full of beautiful lace, Nancy called out, "George, go after him while I take this stuff back to the museum!"

George nodded and rushed after the man. Just as he stepped off the bridge, a group of visitors arrived, completely filling the narrow walkway. All of them were young men, laughing and joking with one another. When George tried to push past them, one caught her in his arms.

"Don't run away, pretty girl!" he said in a lilting Irish brogue. "Why don't you join us on our tour? We'd love to have something lovely to look at!"

"Please excuse me!" George said, trying to get away from him.

"Ye look like ye're running away from someone," another fellow said.

"No, I'm running *after* someone!" George cried in utter frustration. "A thief, if you want to know. Now please let me pass!"

The young man looked at her with big eyes. "A thief!"

By now George had wriggled out of his grip and slipped past the other young men. In a few long leaps, she crossed the bridge.

There was a narrow alley to her right and a park-like courtyard to her left. The man was nowhere in sight!

Some distance ahead of her was the other museum. Would he try to hide in there? George wondered. If I were he, where would I go?

In answer to her own question, she raced down the narrow street. But when she turned the next corner, there was no sign of the fugitive. Disgusted, George walked back to the museum. I've lost him, she said to herself. What bad luck!

She met Nancy in the lobby, surrounded by guards. They were excitedly jabbering in Flemish, and the woman from the reception desk walked up and translated for the girls.

"You stole these things from the exhibit upstairs!" she accused Nancy.

"I didn't steal anything!" the girl dectective said evenly. "Someone else did. He let himself down from the balcony on a rope. I caught him and got all the stuff back. But one piece ripped when he tried to hold on to it!"

The guards continued to converse loudly. Finally the woman said, "Jacques here said he saw you walking *into* the lobby with the lace, not running away with it. Will you please tell us exactly what happened?"

Nancy did, and George verified her explanation. Bess and Hilda, meanwhile, had left the Weapons Room and were looking for their friends. They were just in time to hear Nancy's story.

"Did he take the pieces from the glass display cases?" Nancy asked as she finished.

The receptionist shook her head. "No. We just received a new shipment which Jacques was bringing upstairs. Apparently the thief saw him and decided it would be easy to steal as long as he could get the guard out of the room."

"How did he manage that?" Bess asked.

"He told Jacques he was wanted in the lobby. So the unsuspecting guard put the box of lace behind one of the display cases and hurried downstairs. The thief then must have waited until you girls left the room before he made his next move and escaped over the balcony."

"But what about the rope?" George asked. "If he hadn't planned to steal the lace before he arrived, where'd he get the rope from?"

"Unfortunately, it was lying on a chest of drawers in one corner of the room," the receptionist said. "We had men working on the chimney, and they forgot to take the rope when they left early this morning before the museum opened. The thief saw it and realized it was long enough to help him down from the balcony."

The receptionist turned to Nancy. "What did the thief look like? I will call the police and ask them to look for him."

"He was tall and thin," Nancy said, "and wore a raincoat. He had a hat pulled low over his forehead, so I couldn't see his eyes too well. But his face was narrow, his lips thin, and his coloring was very pale, almost gray. He looked like a man who rarely went outdoors."

"He also limps because he hurt his ankle," George added.

"Thank you," the woman said. "I shall pass this information on to the authorities. Will you give me your names and addresses in case the police find the man and need to get in touch with you?"

The girls provided the information and then stepped out into the sunlight again.

"Phew, what an experience!" George said.

"That man was watching us at the Lace Center," Nancy told her friends. "He must have followed us all the way from there. I didn't want to say anything before, because I wasn't sure and didn't want to worry you. He might have been the same man who stole my suitcase at the airport. I didn't see his face then, but he had the same build as the lace thief."

"But if he wanted to know what we were up to, why would he draw attention to himself the way he did?" Bess asked.

"Perhaps he thought the cuffs with the message in them were among the antique lace pieces the guard brought upstairs for display," Nancy guessed.

"Well, unfortunately he got away," Hilda said. "There is nothing we can do about it. We might as well continue our tour." She paused briefly. "We'll go to an art museum—yes, I know just the one!"

The gallery she had in mind was filled with numerous paintings that depicted life in Brugge since the sixteenth century.

"As your father said, Hilda, not many things have changed, have they?" Nancy commented.

"No, they haven't. But we love the old charm of our city."

Suddenly an oil painting caught Nancy's eye. It was a striking portrait of a gallant young man with a mustache. He was wearing a red velvet jacket with a lace jabot and cuffs.

"Bess! George!" Nancy called out. "Look over here!"

Eagerly the girls joined her. "My goodness, that looks just as I imagined François Lefèvre." Bess gaped in surprise.

"But who's that behind him?" George asked.

In the scene the handsome young man was posed on an arched stone bridge. He was leaning forward, his hands on the edge of it. In back of him was the menacing shadow of another figure. Cloaked in a full black-hooded robe that covered his face and body completely, he was peering over the young man's shoulder. Two hands emerging from under the robe were ready to attack the unsuspecting victim.

"I wonder who the artist is," Bess said.

"There's no name on the picture, only initials," Nancy replied, "but maybe Hilda can tell us what they mean."

The Belgian girl said she was not familiar with this particular painting. "I've been here many times but I don't recall ever seeing it." Aloud she read the small gold plate underneath the picture. "*Le Cavalier et le Spectre Noir*. Translated that means *The Cavalier and the Black Ghost*. It must be a rather recent acquisition."

When she asked the curator, he replied, "It was found in somebody's attic. So far as I know, the museum did not pay very much money for it."

"Do you happen to know who sold it to the museum?" Nancy inquired.

The curator rubbed his chin with uncertainty. "Mm—no I don't, but even if I did I would not be able to answer your question. The museum keeps information about its purchases strictly confidential."

"Well, then," George put in, "perhaps you can tell us who the painter is."

"Yes. It was done by a man named Dirk Gelder, a well-known art teacher in his day. The story goes that the cavalier's girlfriend commissioned the painting, because her beau was an ardent admirer of Gelder."

"Do you know her name?" Nancy asked eagerly.

The curator shook his head. "Sorry. Now, if you'll excuse me," he said, "I have some business to attend to." He turned on his heels and walked away.

"Did you hear that?" George said excitedly. "The man in this picture was an admirer of Gelder, and so was François Lefèvre! I'll bet they're one and the same person!"

"If so," Bess added, "perhaps there's a hidden clue in the artwork that would help unravel the secret in the lace cuffs!"

Nancy nodded eagerly. She opened her handbag, took out her magnifying glass, and trained it on the lace cuffs.

"There's a clue in one of these cuffs!" she exclaimed.

14

A Threat

"What's the message, Nancy?" Bess asked eagerly.

"Here, look for yourself," the girl detective replied, handing the magnifying glass to her friend.

"Oh, I see it!" Bess exclaimed, playing the glass over the lace cuff. "It says, '*Je vous aime*.' "

"Doesn't that mean 'I love you' in French?" George asked Hilda.

Hilda nodded, causing Bess to look dreamy-eyed. "How romantic!"

Nancy, in the meantime, was studying the intricate pattern in the lacework. Woven around the words was a scene of some sort. A geometric figure seemed to be the focal point. It was oblong with vertical stitches that curled into a knot at the top. Above the figure was a diagonal design that formed a baseless triangle. Nancy thought it was very strange.

"Is there anything in the other cuff?" George asked.

Nancy shook her head. "Unfortunately, the details are blurred. Maybe the artist deliberately chose not to paint them."

"Remember the piece of paper that was found in François's bedroom fireplace," George reminded her friends. "Wasn't the word *marry* on it?"

"So possibly the same word appears in the other cuff," Nancy said. "Of course, there must be more than one word. Perhaps the message was 'Marry me' or 'Don't marry anyone else.' "

"Or," Bess suggested, " 'Will you marry me?' "

"Or 'Marry Harry?' " George snickered.

Soon they were all laughing so hard the curator asked them to be quiet or leave. Hilda was already eyeing the door.

"My mother and father want all of you and Madame Chambray to come to dinner at eight o'clock," Hilda told her new friends. "Afterward, we'll watch the procession on the canal. Does that sound all right to you?"

"Oh, how exciting!" Bess replied promptly.

When the girls returned to Madame Chambray's house, there was only a short time to bathe, dress, and exchange news. Madame Chambray had found her desk key and used the opportunity to show the girls the letter she had written to Mrs. Marvin about.

The paper was yellow and splitting apart in the folds so Nancy held it carefully under a lamp. All that remained readable was part of a sentence, written in French, which Madame Chambray translated.

"I, Friedrich Vonderlicht, also known as François Lefèvre, leave to my wife, Elaine Warrington, the treasures of my family protected by our golden—"

Nancy stared at Madame Chambray. "Where did you find this?" she asked.

"Under a loose floorboard in one of the bedrooms."

George shook her head incredulously. "Isn't it odd," she said, "that none of the previous owners of this house ever discovered the will?"

"Not so odd," Madame Chambray replied. "I only came upon it because I was having the old floors refinished. The vibration of the sanding machine moved the loose section a little. I was helping the man who was about to nail it back into place when I noticed something yellowish underneath."

As she spoke, Nancy and George continued to study the document closely. "What are you thinking?" George asked her detective friend.

"The name Elaine Warrington sounds very familiar to me. Wasn't she a well-known actress in her day?" Nancy replied.

"I believe she was," Madame Chambray said.

"In that case," Bess declared, "we ought to be able to find out about her easily. Maybe she was married to François!"

"I wish we could start looking into that right now, but we've really got to get ready for dinner." Nancy sighed. They all agreed, and a short time later were seated in the Permeke home while the professor entertained the Americans with more historical stories about Brugge.

"Did you know," he asked, "that the *Gruuthuse* where you were today was once the refuge and hiding place of an English king?" Dr. Permeke explained that King Edward IV of England was forced into exile there for political reasons.

"Speaking of our tour," Nancy said, "we saw a most interesting portrait at one of the galleries."

Hilda repeated the name of the picture in French. "Joseph, have you heard of it?" she asked the student, who had joined the group for dinner.

"Yes. I believe it was painted by a man named Dirk Gelder. A young Frenchwoman, who was a friend of the man in the painting, asked him to do it."

"That's just what the curator told us," George

remarked. "Do you remember her name?"

"I read it somewhere," Joseph said. "Tissot—yes, that's it. Antoinette Tissot."

Nancy, Bess, and George were struck with the same startling thought. Was she not the same person whose name was stitched on the linen wrapping around the diamond cross?

"Do you know anything else about Antoinette Tissot?" Nancy inquired.

Joseph shook his head. "No. Sorry. I only saw her name in an article I once read about the painting."

Nancy's mind was racing. Perhaps Antoinette had given François the cross! If so, it now belonged to his descendants. But where were they? First thing the next morning, she and her friends would check the local telephone directory.

"There is another famous picture," Dr. Permeke told his guests. "The subject is a stout gentleman wearing breeches which just covered his knees. He has on long white stockings and at the top of them is a three-inch flounce of lace! Can you imagine dancing with him?"

Peals of laughter rang across the table. Bess, however, stopped giggling abruptly when the Permekes' housemaid placed a plate of eels in green sauce in front of her. The girl lifted her eyes from the dish and turned to her cousin. George was smirking.

"I dare you to try them!" George whispered in Bess's ear.

Bess poked her fork into the slippery meat, cutting off a small portion and popping it into her mouth. "It's delicious," she announced with a gulp.

Later, when everyone was seated at the edge of the canal waiting for the procession to pass by, Bess admitted to her friends, "I hope we don't have to eat again tonight. I'm not feeling very well."

"It's all in your mind," George said.

"Uh-uh, it's in my stomach."

The rest of Bess's remark was lost in the din of motorboats chugging past. Each craft was decorated with strings of lights rigged from pole to pole. Passengers on board wore all kinds of costumes, among them clowns, giants, monkeys, robbers, and even Dracula.

"Some of them are really scary," Bess commented, as another boat swung into view.

A ghostly figure was standing near the helm. He was completely covered by a sheet, only his feet were sticking out, and in his hand he held a small package.

Bess laughed. "Look, a ghost in cowboy boots!" she said, pointing to the man's footgear.

"He reminds me of that creep in Madame Chambray's basement," George declared. "He wore boots, too, only it was too dark to see much of them."

Soon the craft swerved close to the canal edge where the girl detectives sat and the strange figure hurled the package toward them. It fell a couple of feet away from them.

"I'll get it," Hilda volunteered. As she picked it up, she glanced at the writing on it. "Nancy, your name is on this!"

"My name?" the girl replied in surprise.

Quickly she opened the package. Inside was a small toy dagger and a note printed in bold letters.

"What's wrong?" Hilda's father asked, seeing the deepening frown on the detective's face.

"It says, 'Stop interfering or you will get this,' " Nancy said.

"How dreadful!" Madame Chambray exclaimed.

Everyone began talking at once and hardly noticed Nancy excuse herself and follow the route of the slow-moving boats in hopes of catching up with the ghostly stranger.

She hurried along the towpath and through the adjoining park that bordered the canal which curved just ahead of her. For a moment she lost sight of the boat, but caught up to it a few minutes later. Suddenly she gasped. The mysterious ghost had vanished!

"Where is your passenger?" the young sleuth

asked the boatman as she ran alongside his craft.

"I do not know," he replied in halting English. "He made me pull over and jumped out."

"Thank you," Nancy said in disappointment, and hurried back to her group.

When they heard her report, Dr. Permeke suggested that Madame Chambray lock all the windows and doors in her house. "And please," the professor urged, "do not go out of your house alone."

Everyone agreed that was a good idea. Madame Chambray and her young guests thanked the Permekes for the delightful evening and took a taxi home. Upon arriving at the house, they discovered an open window on the first floor.

"I don't understand it," Madame Chambray said. "I'm sure I closed everything before we left." Fearfully she slipped her key into the front door lock.

"Let me go in first," Nancy suggested.

Cautiously she stepped into the hallway. A lamp was burning dimly in the living room. At first glance none of Madame Chambray's belongings were missing, but everything looked slightly out of place to Nancy. Thinking of the diamond cross hidden in a corner cabinet, Nancy ran up to it and opened the middle drawer. The purple velvet box was missing!

15

Cowboy Suspect

The diamond cross was stolen! Heartsick, Madame Chambray crumpled into a chair. "It's all my fault. I was so stupid to tell the newspaper about it!"

While Bess and George tried to comfort her, Nancy darted to the telephone and called the police. She gave a full report of the theft and the earlier events of the evening.

"I'm positive that the man who threw the package at me stole the antique cross," she said.

The *politieagent* at the other end promised to send a patrol to the area immediately. Before going to bed, Nancy checked her bureau drawer for the old document Madame Chambray had entrusted to her. Fortunately, it was still there.

Nancy had much to report when her father

phoned the next morning. Upon hearing the name Elaine Warrington, he said, "She appeared in some very fine plays in this country in the late eighteen hundreds. I may be able to track down some information about her for you, if you like."

"Oh would you, Dad?" Nancy asked gratefully. "Then all I'll have left to do is figure out what the mysterious something is that's mentioned in the will!"

"By the way," her father went on, "Mr. Miller from *Circle and Square* magazine told me that the unfriendly editor, Herbert Rocke, left New York a few days ago to go on vacation."

"I have a feeling that he intercepted the first copy of my manuscript," Nancy declared.

"I'm sure he did, because Mr. Miller found out that Rocke is a friend of your contest rival, Mr. Frieden!"

"What!"

"Of course, the magazine would never have permitted a friend of one of its editors to participate in the contest; but as Mr. Miller said, he didn't know of the connection until recently. Anyway, Miller has been trying to reach Mr. Frieden about his entry ever since he saw you but hasn't been able to."

"Interesting," Nancy said. "Rocke must have given Frieden my original to copy and submit to the magazine as his own."

"Nancy," Mr. Drew said slowly, "a lot of these

things don't make sense. Why would Rocke and Frieden get involved in something like that? There's no big money to be made. Other factors must be involved that we don't know about yet. That's why I want you to be very careful."

"What do you mean, Dad?"

"It's possible both Frieden and Rocke might turn up in Brugge. I want you to watch out for them."

"What do they look like?"

"I don't know about Frieden, but Rocke is tall and thin, with a narrow face and thin lips. His complexion is very pale."

"That's the man who followed us from the Lace Center and then stole the new shipment from the *Gruuthuse!*" Nancy exclaimed.

"He may be," Mr. Drew said cautiously. "Unfortunately, I can't send you a photograph for a more positive identification. Are the police looking for this man?"

"Yes. I gave the people at the museum a good description."

"I'm glad," Mr. Drew said. "And I have another piece of information you'll be interested in."

"What's that?"

"Frieden's address is the same as André Bergère's."

"Oh, dear!" Nancy cried out. "Maybe they know

each other and Frieden read Madame Chambray's letter to Mrs. Marvin!"

"It's quite possible. So please be extra careful!"

After Hilda arrived that morning, Nancy confided her father's report to everyone.

"So Rocke's the lace thief!" George declared.

"And maybe the ghost who threw the dagger," Bess added, "and stole the diamond cross!"

"Or," Nancy pointed out, "Frieden or Bergère could be the culprit!"

Despite the recent theft, Nancy decided to find out if any descendants of François Lefèvre were living in Brugge. A quick scan of the local telephone directory revealed nothing.

"Dad's going to let me know what he can about Elaine Warrington, but I thought we ought to do some digging ourselves about her," Nancy said. "Why don't we go to the library and see if we can find anything?"

"Good idea," George and Bess agreed.

On the way to the library, Nancy noticed a tall man peering into a shop window. He was wearing a ten-gallon hat and a well-tailored cowboy suit. On his feet were beautiful leather boots much like the ones worn by the ghostly intruder!

"Come on!" Nancy told her friends and hurried toward the man.

"Hello! You're from the United States, aren't

you?" Nancy asked boldly. "So are we."

"Well, I'm sure glad to meet you all," the cowboy replied, extending his hand to shake theirs.

"We've been here a few days," Nancy said. "When did you arrive?"

"Only a little while ago. I flew in with a charter group."

The man seemed genuinely friendly. Either the girls' suspicions were unfounded or he was putting on an act!

"Your boots are pretty fancy," George said pointedly.

Still unflustered, the cowboy thanked her for the compliment. "They're straight from Dallas, like me."

"You don't by any chance know two men named Frieden and Rocke?" Bess asked.

The cowboy shook his head

George glared at her cousin for blurting out such revealing information. "Do you travel much?" she asked, changing the subject abruptly.

"Not a whole lot," he said, "but I may be doing some more if I land a part with a summer playhouse—" He stopped talking when a young woman emerged from the shop. She trotted past him, clearly annoyed. "Nice to meet you," he said quickly to the girls and hurried after the woman.

As they watched him disappear down the street,

Nancy wondered if he really was their suspect and if they should alert the police.

"If he changes his shoes and his outfit," George said, laughing, "they'll never find him."

The foursome headed for the library, and with Hilda's help found a large book about the history of the theater. Among the names listed in the index was Elaine Warrington's. There were several references to her, including mention of her marriage to Friedrich Vonderlicht after her family had disowned her.

"Where was she from?" Bess inquired.

"According to this," Nancy replied, "she was born in France but lived in the United States. Apparently she lived in Europe most of her married life but returned to America abruptly after her husband's death and died penniless—so she must not have known about François's will or the treasure."

"Or if she did, she never found it, or maybe he died while she was on tour, and he never had a chance to tell her," George said. "Was Warrington her real name?"

"I doubt it," Nancy replied, shutting the book. "It must've been her stage name."

"And François must have changed his name to Vonderlicht when he settled in Brugge!" Bess declared.

"Well," Nancy replied, "let's go back to Madame

Chambray's house. Some of the answers have got to be hidden there."

Hilda admitted she had never done any detective work before but was eager to help. She even agreed to search the basement where the ghostly intruder had captured Bess.

"You go ahead," Bess said. "I have no desire to be thrown into a closet again."

"You won't," George insisted. "We locked the tunnel door so no one can get in there."

"Even so, I prefer to stay up here in the safety of the kitchen."

"You just want to be near the refrigerator," her cousin teased, following Nancy and Hilda down the cellar steps. They had found extra flashlights and beamed them ahead as they descended.

Fascinated by the depth of the room, Hilda said, "Centuries ago I imagine this place was filled with boxes and barrels of food. People used to import it from many parts of the world—luscious bananas from the warmer climates and olives, too—"

Her light now shone on the tunnel door, prompting Nancy to interrupt.

"George, wasn't there a key in that door?"

"Yes."

"Well, it's gone."

George hurried forward and turned the handle. The door swung back freely.

Distressed, Nancy examined it for evidence of force. "The door isn't damaged; it's been unlocked with a key. But how? Did someone enter the basement from upstairs or from the tunnel?"

"There's no way to tell," George said.

"But I'm sure it was Mr. Ghost again!"

Hilda expressed alarm as well. "No one in this house is safe!" she said.

16

Exciting Clue

While the other girls were in the cellar, Bess decided to do her own investigating, but was at a loss as to where to begin. She remembered seeing a door at the end of the hall on the second floor and, not knowing if it led to the third story or another closet, concluded she'd start there.

Bess shivered nervously as she approached the door. "I refuse to be called 'Chicken Marvin' any more," she murmured, opening the door.

Before her was a twist of stairs that rose steeply upward toward a small landing. She took a few steps, then paused, listening to a shuffling noise above her. It sounded as though someone was in the room overhead.

Bess froze temporarily but continued the climb. To her surprise there was no door at the top—only a window opposite an unevenly papered wall.

Hmph, that's odd, the young detective thought. A bunch of steps that lead nowhere!

She pressed her ear against the wall. The shuffling sounds had stopped, at least for the moment.

It must have been my imagination, Bess concluded, turning to leave.

But suddenly she felt something settle on her forehead. It moved, tickling her skin. Quickly she brushed it to the floor, shrieking and jumping flat against the wall as a spider crawled into a corner. At the same time Bess's hand detected a crack in the wood. Was it the work of termites or of an eccentric architect? she wondered.

Curiously, the girl sleuth ran her fingers along the depression. The wallpaper crackled as it tore apart—revealing a panel!

Bess's heart pounded hard. She tugged at the wood but it was warped. Now what'll I do? She sighed, her mind racing. Well, at least, I know one thing. If I can't get through this wall, Mr. Ghost couldn't either!

She flew downstairs to the kitchen, shouting to her friends in the cellar. They rejoined her immediately and told her about the missing key to the tunnel door.

"Uh-oh," Bess said. "Then maybe there is somebody upstairs." She revealed her discovery and the shuffling sounds on the third floor.

The girls locked the door between the kitchen and the cellar in order to prevent an intrusion through the tunnel. Then, armed with flashlights and a thin steel wedge they found in an old toolbox, the young sleuths followed Bess upstairs. Nancy worked the wedge deftly into the crack in the wall, forcing the panel back slightly.

"It's coming," she said, and stuck her fingers through the opening.

George and Hilda placed their hands around the wood as well. Inch by inch they moved it back. "There's another wall behind this one!" George exclaimed as Madame Chambray's familiar voice called to them from below.

"Girls!" she shouted. "Where are you?"

Bess hurried down to the second floor landing. "We're up here! We found a hidden panel!" she called loudly.

"I'll be right there," the woman said, dropping the packages she had brought.

When she saw the partly open wall, the torn paper and steel wedge, Madame Chambray gasped. "What are you doing?"

"We think there's a hidden room on the other side of this wall," Nancy explained.

"A hidden room? How interesting. How did you find it?"

Bess explained how she had discovered the crack. "That spider really was helpful, even though I hate the things." she concluded.

"Well, someday I'll have to explore that room," Mrs. Chambray said.

"I think we should do it right now," Nancy urged. "The treasure might be hidden in there!"

Madame Chambray nodded absentmindedly, and Nancy wondered why the woman did not share the girls' excitement. Instead, she almost seemed sad.

"We might even discover a clue to the owner of the diamond cross!" Nancy went on.

"I've found him already," Madame Chambray said.

"You have? Where—"

Nancy was interrupted by the ringing of the telephone. It was Mr. Drew.

"Hi, Dad," Nancy said. "Any news?"

Nancy listened eagerly as her father told her his startling discovery. A relative of Elaine Warrington, her great-grandson in fact, was traveling in Belgium!

"That's fantastic!" Nancy exclaimed. "What's his full name—of course, his family name is Vonderlicht."

"He changed it to Vaughan . . . Cody Vaughan," Mr. Drew said.

Nancy laughed. "He sounds like a cowboy," she said.

"He is. Well, not exactly. He's an actor who's been working at different jobs to prepare for roles he hopes to get. He moved to Dallas not long ago—"

"I think," Nancy cut in excitedly, "we may already have met Mr. Vaughan!"

She told her father about the cowboy they had spoken to in town, then added, "But Madame Chambray claims she's found the owner of the antique cross."

"Did she say who he is?"

"No. We were interrupted by the phone."

"Well, maybe she ran into Mr. Vaughan also," Mr. Drew said. "Let me know what's happening, Nancy, and take care of yourself."

"I will, Dad."

After the girl hung up, she found Madame Chambray in the living room with her face buried in her hands. Nancy darted to her side, slipping one arm around the woman's shoulder.

"What's the matter, Madame Chambray?" She asked softly. "Don't you feel well?"

The woman lifted her eyes dolefully. "You must leave this house at once, dear," she said. "It isn't safe for you to stay here any longer."

Nancy sensed that something had happened that was troubling Madame Chambray a great deal.

"Has someone threatened you?" she inquired.

"N-no."

"Are you sure?"

"No, I mean, yes, I—uh . . ."

"Madame Chambray, we can't leave you alone," the young sleuth said. "Please tell me what is bothering you."

The other girls kept silent, allowing the woman to speak. Haltingly she said, "This came in the mail."

She pulled a letter from her skirt pocket and handed it to Nancy, who read it aloud. "Dear Madame, your visitors have put a curse on your house. They must leave immediately or it will burn!"

"This is only an empty threat," Nancy said.

"How do you know?" Bess spoke up.

"It sounds like a real one to me," Hilda agreed.

"But this is a stone house," Nancy retorted. "No one can burn it."

"Not the shell, perhaps," Madame Chambray said, wiping her eyes. "But inside there is wood everywhere. Oh, you must go back to America! I cannot be responsible for your safety any longer."

The girls begged the woman to reconsider but she remained firm. "Besides, someone called me just before I left here today. He claims to be the owner of the diamond cross. He's coming here later."

"But the cross is gone," Bess observed.

"I told him that. But he still wants to see me," the woman replied.

"Did he give his name?" Nancy asked.

"No."

"Did he speak with a Texan drawl?"

"No."

"Then I'm positive he's an impostor!" the girl detective said resolutely.

17

Hidden Treasure?

"Madame Chambray," the girl detective said, trying a new tack to convince the anxious woman to let them stay, "I believe the secret in the old lace is buried here. If you want us to leave tomorrow, we will; but please give us till then to continue our search."

The woman did not answer immediately. She glanced at the pleading expression on her visitors' faces, then spoke. "All right, you have until tomorrow, but for your own sakes, I can't permit you to—"

"Oh, thank you!" Nancy interrupted, hugging her.

George sighed. "I hate to admit defeat," she said,

"But if François Lefèvre's secret has been hidden for more than a century, how can we find it in less than twenty-four hours?"

"Think positive!" Nancy grinned.

Reluctantly Madame Chambray gave permission for the girls to open the panel on the third floor. "I suppose I ought to put new wallpaper up there anyway," she said.

"I'm sorry I won't be able to stay and help you," Hilda spoke up. "But Joseph is taking me to a concert this evening. Perhaps all of you would like to join us . . . if this is to be your last evening in Brugge."

"We would love to," Bess said, "but it sounds as if Nancy has other plans for us."

The girls thanked Hilda for her invitation but said they expected to spend every minute left on the mystery. After saying good-bye, they hurried upstairs, and in less than half an hour slid the double panel fully open.

Beyond, drenched in sunlight streaming through a skylight, was a strange-looking room framed by high beams. It was cluttered with antique furniture, china, pictures, knickknacks of all kinds, and an old trunk thick with dust like everything else.

"What should we tackle first?" George asked, spying a pile of boxes in a corner.

"That's exactly what I was going to ask," her

cousin replied. "Maybe we ought to split up our investigation."

Bess headed toward a delicate silk screen that stood near the center of the room, and peered behind it. On the floor lay an old tarnished birdcage which she set upright.

"Find anything of interest?" George called out from her corner of the room.

"Uh-uh, just a birdcage without a bird."

Nancy, in the meantime, was drawn to the big trunk. She raised the lid, revealing bundles of newspapers and letters.

"These are all addressed to François!" Bess observed excitedly. She opened one of them. "Here's an invitation to a ball in Brussels! Oh, I wish I could've gone too. It must've been fabulous!"

"And this is an invitation to a big party," George said, pulling out another letter. "I'd say François had a terrific social life!"

As the girls continued to sift through the papers, Nancy suddenly discovered a leather-bound book beneath them.

"Look, I've just found his diary!" she exclaimed and read several passages aloud, translating them from French into English.

Bess hung on every word, gazing moonstruck toward the skylight where a face pulled suddenly out of sight!

"Oh!" the girl gasped, causing her friends to look at the window.

"What is it?" Nancy asked.

"A-a man—" Bess stuttered.

"You're imagining things," her cousin said. "There's no one—"

"But I saw him—"

Nancy laid the diary on the pile of papers in the trunk and slid a chair under the skylight. "I don't see anybody," she said, after climbing on the chair. "But the skylight isn't locked. I wonder if someone's been using it as his access to the attic. He could have made the noise Bess heard."

"We should report this to the police," George suggested, and left to make the call.

Meanwhile, Nancy read more of the diary. It revealed that François was in love with an actress. "And guess who she was?" Nancy asked.

"Elaine Warrington, of course," Bess said.

"Uh-uh. It was Antoinette Tissot!"

"What! But I thought he married Elaine Warrington."

"He did," Nancy said. "Originally her name was Antoinette. It seems that her family disapproved not only of her interest in François but also of her desire to become an actress. I guess they thought François was a playboy and insisted Antoinette not see him. She refused to obey."

Nancy read and translated one of the passages. " 'I cannot permit her to be disowned. I can't do it. I'm going to disappear and change my name. François Lefèvre will be no more.' "

"Amazing," George broke in. She had overheard the girls' conversation as she climbed the stairs. "I gather Antoinette followed François to Brugge—"

"And changed her name to Elaine Warrington when she joined an acting troupe," Nancy said, "since she did not wish to disgrace her family name."

"But if she and François got married," Bess went on, "why didn't Antoinette simply work under his new name?"

"Because they didn't get together right away," Nancy answered. "According to this diary, François tried to send her back to her family—"

"But she was in love with him," Bess sighed. "Isn't it wonderful?"

Meanwhile, Nancy continued to flip through the book and settled on another long passage. "Joseph Stolk was right," she said. "Antoinette did ask Dirk Gelder to paint that picture of François. It symbolized the end of Monsieur Lefèvre. From then on, he would be known as Friedrich Vonderlicht."

Bess opened a fair-sized box near the trunk. "Look, everybody!" she exclaimed, holding up a red velvet cavalier suit with a lace jabot and detachable lace cuffs. "This must have been François's!"

Excited, Nancy dashed to Bess and took the cuffs, examining them inch by inch. They were intricately woven, but to the girls' chagrin, there was no message in either of them.

"They are beautiful nonetheless," Nancy said, dropping the cuffs back in the box.

Now she picked up the diary once again, wondering if she had overlooked anything else of interest. A few pages from the end she discovered a description of a beautiful statue in a tiny walled-in garden, and tied to the last page with pale blue ribbon was a painting of a man with a golden face and hair. He was wearing a close-fitting gold suit. One hand rested on a low pedestal fountain in the garden.

"Maybe this is where the treasure is hidden!" Nancy exclaimed. "The will mentioned it was protected by something golden!"

When she told Madame Chambray about her discovery, the woman said, "I know where that statue is. It's right here on the grounds!"

She led the way to a small garden behind the house. In the center stood a gold statue!

"May we move it to see if anything is buried underneath?" Bess asked Madame Chambray.

The woman nodded slowly. "I will get some

tools," she said as the girls loosened the base by hand. Within moments the marble figure and pedestal had been pushed carefully aside and the girls had started digging.

"It's such an unlikely place to hide a treasure," Madame Chambray insisted. "After so many years, it would be ruined by now."

But the diggers continued, filled with anticipation. They failed to see a man peering over the garden wall. His snakelike eyes glistened eagerly as George's spade struck something hard.

"Hold everything!" she cried out.

All work stopped while George's fingers probed the dirt. She yanked on something, prying it free.

"A stone!" she exclaimed in disgust and threw it aside.

The work went on for several minutes until Nancy jabbed the soil hard with her shovel. Almost instantly water began to seep through the soil. She pulled the shovel out and a needle-sharp geyser shot up toward her face!

18

The Spy

Quickly Nancy dodged the geyser of water. As she did, she happened to glance at the top of the garden wall. A man with shiny black hair was staring ominously at her. Was he the same person Bess had seen through the skylight? Before Nancy could attract her friend's attention, the spy slithered out of sight. Meanwhile, the groundwater continued to gush.

"I must have punctured a water pipe with my shovel," Nancy said to Madame Chambray. "I'm terribly sorry."

"I'll go and call the water department. I'm sure they can fix it." She went inside and returned shortly. "Someone is coming right away. But what should we do in the meantime?"

Instantly George jumped down into the hole and tried to hold her hand over the opening in the pipe.

"It won't work," she said, disappointed. "Bess, why don't you sit on it?"

"Very funny," her cousin replied.

Less jovial, Nancy watched the slow buildup of water. If this keeps up, she thought, it will saturate the entire garden and prevent us from unearthing the hidden treasure!

Within fifteen minutes, however, a repairman arrived, carrying a bag of tools. He turned the water off, then worked rapidly to replace the damaged section of pipe.

"That ought to do it," he said at last, shaking mud off his feet as he stepped on the stone path that circled the statue.

"How long do you think it will take the ground to dry?" Nancy asked.

"We're looking for buried treasure," Bess cut in.

The man looked surprised but did not inquire further. "Well, it will take a day or so for all the water to drain," he replied.

"Gracious!" George said. "We can't wait that long!"

After the repairman left, Nancy told the others about the spy whom she had noticed by the garden wall. "He may have been Frieden or Bergère. I'm pretty sure I'd recognize him if I saw him again."

"Maybe he wanted to steal my beautiful statue!" Madame Chambray declared.

"Well, we are going to catch him before he pulls a stunt like that," Bess said bravely.

Nancy grinned at her friend. "You always come through in a pinch!" she said.

The girls figured the suspect must have approached the garden from the back steps that led down to the canal. They followed the towpath, hoping to find evidence of the stranger. Was he hiding among trees or had he left in a boat?

Chugging some distance away was a small craft. The man at the wheel had sleek black hair. For an instant he shot a glance back at the house.

"That's the spy!" Nancy exclaimed, squinting to read the name painted on the boat. It was *Wit Bloem*.

"I wonder what it means," George said.

"Madame Chambray can tell us," Bess declared, following her friends back to the house.

When asked, the woman told the girls that *Wit Bloem* meant white flower. "But why do you wish to know?" she added.

Nancy explained about the man in the boat, prompting her hostess to call the police. She reported the incident and at Nancy's suggestion, requested the name and address of the boat's owner.

It seemed like hours before the *politie* telephoned back.

"The craft belongs to a man named Theo Schlinger," the voice said and gave the man's address.

Nancy suggested they ask Hilda to go with them to meet the man. "We may need a translator," she said.

"You mean we may need the police! Besides, Hilda's going to a concert with Joseph," Bess reminded Nancy.

"Well, maybe she can squeeze in one more favor beforehand, and anyway, I think we can handle Mr. Schlinger. We don't have to accuse him of anything." Hopeful, the young sleuth telephoned the girl and after several minutes of conversation put down the receiver, beaming.

"She can go with us if we don't stay long!" Nancy exclaimed.

An hour later the girls arrived at Mr. Schlinger's home, and, exchanging nervous smiles, knocked on the door. A moment later an elegant gentleman, not the thief, appeared. He proved to be as delightful as his home, which was filled with nautical souvenirs, pictures of old sailing ships, and a photograph of Mr. Schlinger in a boatman's cap.

"Do you speak English?" Nancy asked him.

"A little," he replied. "Why, are you interested in finding a tour guide?"

"Oh, no," Nancy laughed. "Miss Permeke has already taken us sightseeing. It was wonderful."

Hilda blushed at the compliment and said she would translate any of Nancy's questions that Mr. Schlinger did not understand.

"Sounds like you mean serious business," Mr. Schlinger said. "Perhaps you would like to rent my boat?"

"N-no," Nancy said. "But we'd like to know who was using it today."

"His name was Bergère," Mr. Schlinger said. "He took the boat for an hour or so, then brought it back."

"Bergère!" Nancy cried out. "That's the man we're looking for!"

"You are? Is there a problem?" Mr. Schlinger asked

"Yes," Nancy replied. "We believe that man is a thief!"

"Oh, dear," Mr. Schlinger said, running his hand through his hair. "If I had known that, I would never have permitted him to—"

"Did he by any chance give you his address?" Bess interrupted.

The boatman shook his head. "No. But he did tell me that this was his last day in Brugge, and that he was flying back to New York tonight."

Mr. Schlinger did not know anything else about Bergère's plans, so the girls thanked him and left.

On the way home they discussed their next move.

"Now I'm convinced that Matey Johnson showed Bergère the letter Madame Chambray wrote to Mrs. Marvin," Nancy said. "That's why he came here."

"But it wouldn't make sense for him to leave Brugge before finding the treasure, would it?" George spoke up.

"Unless he stole the diamond cross and figures that's enough to bring home for now," Bess suggested.

"True," Nancy said. "He could even be planning to return to Brugge after we leave." But her mind took another turn. "Still, I don't believe he would return to America and then fly all the way back to Belgium. He probably lied because he figured we saw the name on his boat and would trace it to Mr. Schlinger. Perhaps he had already given Mr. Schlinger his name and was afraid we would find out."

"Good thinking!" George praised her friend. "So he told the fib about returning to New York hoping we'd stop looking for him."

Hilda was glancing worriedly at her watch. "I really ought to be on my way," she said finally. "Where are you going now?"

"That's the big question," Bess said. "The airport or home?"

"Home," Nancy said decisively. "I want to meet that impostor when he shows up."

On the way, they passed by a series of shops, including a quaint bookshop. "I guess this will be our only chance to buy gifts to take home," Bess pointed out, ducking inside.

The girls selected beautiful books about Belgium for each of their boyfriends.

"Maybe this will get them to come with us next time," George said.

As they paid for their purchases, Nancy glanced at a glass display case. In the reflection was a large cowboy hat.

It was the young man from Texas who fit Mr. Drew's description of François's great-grandson!

19

The Capture

Nancy whirled around to face the young Texan. "Cody Vaughan?" she asked, smiling broadly.

He flashed a grin at her and the other girls. "Mighty nice to see you all again," he said, "but how do you know my name? I never told you what it is."

Nancy introduced herself and her friends, then explained briefly, adding, "We've been hoping to run into you again. We're staying at a house that belonged to your great-grandparents."

"No kidding," the cowboy said. "I knew my family was originally from Belgium. That's one reason I decided to make this trip. It's my first time here, you know." He breathed in deeply. "Gee, I'd love to see that place."

"You will." Nancy sparkled. "Just wait until Madame Chambray meets you. She'll be so excited. She's been searching for a descendant of the Vonderlicht family."

"Who is Madame Chambray?" the fellow asked, puzzled. "And why on earth would she want to meet me?"

"She owns the Vonderlicht house now," Bess pointed out. "Shortly after she moved in, she found a beautiful antique cross wrapped in a piece of cloth that bore the name Antoinette Tissot—your great-grandmother."

"I think you folks have me mixed up with somebody. My great-grandmother's name wasn't Tissot. It was Warrington—Elaine Warrington."

Prompted to reveal the romantic story of Antoinette and François, George told how they moved to Brugge and changed their names.

"And they lived happily ever after," Bess finished.

"There's one small problem," Nancy put in soberly. "The diamond cross was stolen. But I have a hunch you can help us get it back!"

"Oh, I don't know, Nancy. I'm not much on catching crooks," Cody said. "On second thought, though, maybe it's not such a bad idea after all. I might get an acting part someday as a detective."

"Then you'll go to the house with us?" Nancy asked. "It's not very far from here."

She noticed that the young woman with whom she had seen him on the previous occasion was not in the store.

"Okay," Cody said, "but I'd like to call my hotel first. I have a date with somebody. Can she come along?"

Nancy hesitated, uncertain of the danger that might lay ahead of them. "Why don't you suggest meeting your friend a little later? You can call her from the house," Nancy said.

"I don't know how that'll set with her," the man said, "but I'll tell her."

By now, a haze of twilight covered the town, and there was a forbidding stillness in the air as the group reached the old stone house. To their surprise only one or two of the lamps were lit.

"Somebody's inside," Nancy said, seeing the outline of a man's head in the window.

"Should we knock?" Bess asked fearfully.

"No," Nancy replied, "we might scare off Madame Chambray's visitor."

She turned the door handle slowly, hoping it was not locked. The door clicked open. Signaling everyone to remain quiet, Nancy tiptoed inside. A murmur of words and laughter drifted into the hallway.

"Oh, Monsieur, I am so pleased to meet you at last," Madame Chambray was saying. "But, to tell the truth, I am very troubled."

"How could such a lovely lady be so troubled?" The man's voice oozed sweetly. It sounded vaguely familiar. "You know my grandfather had terrible troubles—romantic ones mostly. Women pursued him constantly. One girl from Brussels in particular literally forced him to move here to Brugge. She was simply too ardent."

"But," Madame Chambray said, "didn't he marry her?"

"Oh, no. He met somebody else."

Nancy's thoughts now fell clearly into place. That man was telling the story she had entered in the magazine contest! He was either Paul Frieden or André Bergère! She paused long enough for Bess to tug on her arm.

"I heard something upstairs," Bess whispered.

Was there another intruder in the house—a partner perhaps of the man seated inside? the girls wondered.

"What should we do?" George asked.

"You and Bess check the top floors while I introduce Cody to Madame Chambray," Nancy said.

Cautiously, Bess and George tiptoed to the second floor while the Texan trailed Nancy into the living room. The visitor was hidden from view in a high-backed chair.

"Excuse me, Madame Chambray," Nancy said politely, "but I'd like you to meet the great-grandson of François Lefèvre—"

"That's impossible!" the other man spouted angrily. He rose to his feet and turned sharply toward Nancy.

He was tall and slender, with a narrow face, thin lips, and a pallid complexion.

"Mr. Rocke!" Nancy cried out.

Furious, the man bolted past the girl, shoving her aside. "I don't know you," he growled.

"Grab him, Cody!" Nancy cried, but the agile impostor slipped out of the cowboy's reach.

He tripped on the carpet, causing a small, glittering object to fall out of his pocket. "It's the diamond cross!" Madame Chambray shouted.

Before Rocke could retrieve it, however, Nancy dived for it. He flew through the hallway, out the door, and down the steps to a waiting boat. Before Nancy or Cody Vaughan could catch him, he sped away.

"That's the last of Mr. Ghost," Nancy said, noticing the man's boots. "The only time he didn't wear those boots was when he followed us to the *Gruuthuse* and stole the lace!"

At once, the girl called the authorities and described Rocke and the boat he had escaped in. "He went up the canal in an easterly direction," she added.

"We'll look for him at once," the officer on duty promised. "We will also alert the airport. In case

he tries to leave the country, his passport will be flagged down."

Bess and George, in the meantime, were unaware of what had occurred below. Nothing was out of order on the second floor so they climbed to the third.

"I definitely heard something," Bess said, "and it's too far for mice to climb."

She and her cousin poised themselves outside the attic panel, then slowly slid it open. Except for the soft glow of streetlamps that traveled through the skylight, the room was completely dark.

"Stick close," George whispered.

"Don't worry." Bess shivered, beaming her flashlight toward the trunk and boxes.

"If someone was here," George observed, "I'm sure he left." A chair stood under the skylight. "And that's how he went."

As she swung her light to another corner, Bess noticed an antique bureau. All the drawers had been pulled out, revealing lace-trimmed garments and lots of books that resembled the leather-bound diary in the trunk.

"I don't recall that we ever opened those drawers," George said. "They don't have handles so we probably didn't realize they were drawers. The intruder must have pried them open."

"What about François's red jacket and the lace

çuffs?" Bess murmured. "I wonder if they were stolen?"

She hurried to the box near the trunk. The jacket was still there but the cuffs were gone! Obviously, the thief had mistaken them for the ones containing the secret message!

Suddenly the girls sensed that someone was behind them. Indeed, the hunched figure of a man was shuffling toward them, ready to pounce. In his hands were the missing lace cuffs.

"Help!" Bess cried aloud, as George gathered up all her courage and lunged toward the man.

Help, however, was on the way for the two terrified girls. Nancy and Cody leaped into the room, tackling the intruder. They pushed him to the floor within seconds.

"Let go of me!" he bellowed angrily.

"Not until the police come," Cody said, twisting the man's arm out flat.

"You're André Bergère, aren't you?" Nancy accused him, recognizing his face and sleek black hair. "I suppose Paul Frieden is around here as well."

Their captive laughed bitterly. Then, thinking he had everything under control, Cody loosened his grip a bit. Bergère took advantage of the movement, punching Cody in the ribs.

"Ow!" the Texan sputtered, allowing the prisoner to free himself in a sudden quick turn.

Nancy, however, grabbed his arm while George hooked another one, ready to heave him in a judo flip!

20

A Double Surprise

Once again Cody joined the struggle, weakening their prisoner at last.

"Quick, call the police, Bess!" Nancy told the girl.

"Oh, don't do that! I beg you!" the man pleaded in exhaustion as Bess ran downstairs. His arms sank limply in those of his captors. "Just let me sit down a minute."

"Don't you try anything funny," Cody warned.

"I won't, I promise I won't," The intruder gulped for air. "What do you want to know?"

"Are you or are you not André Bergère?" Nancy questioned. Nervously he ran his bony fingers through his sleek black hair.

"I am and—"

"And what?" Nancy prodded.

"And Paul Frieden."

"What!" She stared at him in surprise. "You mean, Frieden is only a fictitious character?"

Bergère nodded.

"So when Rocke intercepted my manuscript," Nancy continued, "he passed it on to *you!*"

Bergère shrugged. "We're friends."

"Was the contest prize worth so much to you that you decided to plagiarize my story and submit it yourself?" Nancy asked, feeling a twinge of disgust for the man.

"We knew there was an unsolved mystery in Brugge, that's why we ran the contest," Bergère grumbled. "We figured if Miller accused *you* of plagiarism, you'd stick around New York until you convinced him otherwise. Meanwhile, we could come here and search for the treasure mentioned in the letter."

George chuckled. "You must have been surprised when you found out from Rocke that Nancy was going ahead with her travel plans."

"So you waited for me to arrive at the airport and then stole my luggage!" Nancy added.

"No. That was Rocke," Bergère protested. "He borrowed an airport worker's jacket so he could get past the guards with your bag."

"He wanted to stall me in Brussels for a while," Nancy said, "but when that didn't work out the way he planned, he decided to scare us. Rocke played ghost in Madame Chambray's house—"

"I also kept close watch on everything you did," the prisoner interrupted with a self-congratulatory smile. "I watched you in the garden and through the skylight and—"

"How did Rocke ever get the key to the tunnel?" Nancy went on.

"The first time he went there the door was open and the key was inside," Bergère replied. "He had a duplicate made."

"Once Rocke came when the door was locked from the inside," Nancy said, remembering the time she had left the key in the lock.

"He pushed it out with a stick, then used his duplicate," Bergère said. "These locks aren't hard to tamper with."

"Did Rocke have fun riding in the procession?" George asked. "You didn't really think that dagger trick would frighten us, did you?"

Bergère shrugged. "We were desperate. Unfortunately, nothing worked. You girls spoiled everything!"

Just then Madame Chambray and Bess appeared in the doorway with two policemen.

"Here's the man who sent you that threatening

letter!" George piped up. "Or are you going to blame that on Rocke, too, Mr. Bergère?"

"No, I did it. But it was his idea."

The officers stepped up to handcuff him.

"You can't do anything to me!" Bergère shouted. "I'm an American citizen!"

"But you have committed a serious crime in our country," one of the policemen told him. "We shall arrest you and try you for theft!" With that they led him away.

Madame Chambray, meanwhile, went over to Cody and kissed him on both cheeks.

"I am so pleased to meet you," she said warmly. "I have something that belongs to you—or rather Nancy does."

The girl detective pulled the diamond and lapis lazuli cross from her skirt pocket and folded it into the Texan's hand.

"Too bad Rocke didn't drop the linen wrapping," Madame Chambray murmured. "It said, 'God protect you wherever you go.' "

Cody gazed at the gleaming cross. "Oh, but I can't keep this," he finally said. "You deserve it more than I do."

"Don't be silly," Nancy replied. "It was meant to bring luck to the Vonderlicht family."

"I know you have a date," George interrupted, "but—uh—"

Seeing the glint of interest in her cousin's face, Bess turned to Cody. "Our search isn't over yet, you know. We're still hunting for the treasure François—I mean Friedrich—mentioned in his will. Please stay. After all, whatever we find most likely belongs to you."

Cody smiled boyishly at George, who shifted her gaze in embarrassment. "Where should we start?" he asked.

"How would you like an old birdcage?" Bess giggled and darted behind the silk screen.

"Now I'll have to buy a bird." The cowboy laughed when he saw the cage.

Nancy stared at it openmouthed. It was a magnificent birdcage, and beneath years of tarnish was gold!

"I'm positive this is the geometric figure represented in the lace cuff!" the girl detective exclaimed.

"You think so?" Bess asked in amazement. "That never occurred to me."

Suddenly aware that the ceiling beams crossed to form open triangles like the other pattern in the cuff, Nancy scanned them slowly.

"Look!" she cried, pointing to a broken hook in one of the beams. "That's where the cage used to hang. I'm sure it was a marker of some sort."

"Here," George said, handing Nancy a chair

which she placed directly under the beam and climbed up on.

"The cage must've fallen years ago," Nancy surmised. She pulled on the hook, finding it loose but unwilling to budge. Disappointed, she started to step down from the old chair, when suddenly one of the legs gave way. Nancy grabbed for the hook, desperate to find something to help her regain her balance. The small section of wood tore away from the ceiling, and Nancy toppled to the floor while the onlookers attempted to break her fall. As they bent down to help Nancy to her feet, Bess noticed a ruby-studded pin and necklace on the floor. Looking up at the hole, Bess exclaimed, "François's fortune!"

"And yours now, Cody!" Nancy added as she pulled over a stool that was standing in the corner, again stepping up to inspect the beam.

"Is there anything else?" George asked, helping Bess pick up the additional fallen treasures.

"I'll say there is!" Nancy cried in happiness. She produced the missing lace cuffs. "I never dreamed we'd ever find—"

Gleefully, the girl detective jumped down from the chair and displayed the long-hidden, delicate clue.

Just as in Gelder's painting, one cuff bore the figure of a birdcage under a pattern of baseless triangles and the words *Je vous aime*.

"What's the message in the other cuff?" Bess asked eagerly.

Nancy examined it closely, repeating the words out loud. "It's *Épousez moi, s'il vous plaît*.

"What does that mean?" Bess asked.

Nancy translated, "Please marry me."

"And that's precisely what François did!" George said.

"Except no one in his family or hers ever knew it. It was their secret!" Nancy declared. "Antoinette changed her name to Elaine Warrington when she left home, and I gather that after her husband's death, she moved to the States."

"But she never told anybody who she really was," Cody said. "Just look at how little I knew about her."

"Well," Bess sighed, "Antoinette—Elaine really got what she wanted—François—Friedrich!"

Her listeners laughed, then George remarked, "The ending of your story, Nancy, was a bit different. This turned out to be a double surprise!"

"But that's because the beginning wasn't accurate," Bess pointed out. "Your hunch about François's move to Brugge, though, was right on target!"

As she spoke, Madame Chambray sailed cheerfully into the room. She blinked tearfully when she saw the jewelry and money. "I can't believe it. You found all this?"

Cody slipped his arm around her shoulder. "Please pick out something—anything—from here you would like to keep," he said to each one.

"Oh, we couldn't," George said.

"But I insist," the young man replied. "It would make me very happy."

Reluctantly, George selected a plain but beautiful gold necklace. Cody smiled.

"I would have chosen the same thing for you," he said, causing a flush of red to spread along George's neck.

"Thank you," she murmured.

Bess decided on an old-fashioned bracelet, while Madame Chambray selected an enamel and gold pin. When Nancy's turn came, she picked a delicate chain with a beautiful locket on it. Inside were two photographs. She used her magnifying glass to decipher the faded wording underneath them.

"These are pictures of Friedrich Vonderlicht and his bride," she said. "I can't take this. Cody, you must save it for someone special."

The cowboy shifted from one foot to the other. "Then you choose something else," he said.

Nancy settled on a ruby ring. "Red will always remind me of François's jacket." She chuckled.

Madame Chambray, in the meantime, spoke quietly with Cody concerning arrangements to pick up his family possessions.

"Do you realize," George turned to Nancy, "that the mystery is no longer a mystery?"

"Yes, I do, if you mean the mystery about François. But what about my manuscript?" Nancy replied. "I've got to talk to Dad about it."

When she telephoned the Drew home later that day, Hannah Gruen answered. Mr. Drew was out of town, she said.

"What's your news?" Hannah asked the girl detective.

Nancy related what had happened during recent days. "It seems that Matey Johnson heard enough of our conversation to trigger off a lot of interest in Madame Chambray's letter. Then his pal intercepted my manuscript to keep me from flying to Belgium. Can you imagine that?"

"I can." The housekeeper laughed. "Of course, he didn't realize that no one can keep you from doing anything you want to."

The next day Hilda and her parents gave a farewell party for the young sleuths and their hostess, Madame Chambray. Cody and Joseph were also present.

"Can't I convince you to stay longer?" the woman asked the girls.

"I'd love to," Bess said, trying hard not to glance at Joseph who hovered near Hilda.

"So would I," George admitted, "but Nancy—"

"My tour doesn't finish for a whole week," Cody interrupted. "Why don't you change your mind?"

Nancy winked at her friends. "Well, I would like to see Ned before the summer is completely over," she said.

Now Dr. Permeke offered a toast to his guests. "It is amazing to think that such an old, old mystery has been solved," he began, "but that it took three American girls to do it—ah—that's even more wonderful!"

"And we loved every minute of it!" Nancy answered. "Thank you very much for all of your help!"

The following day the girls flew back to New York, then on to River Heights. Mr. Drew and Hannah had just greeted Nancy when the phone rang.

"I'm sure it's for you, dear," Mr. Drew told his daughter.

To her surprise, the caller was John Miller, the editor-in-chief of *Circle and Square* magazine. "So you're home," he said. "Well, I have some wonderful news for our girl detective. You won first prize in the contest!"

Nancy was almost breathless. "I did?"

"Yes. I received word from the Belgian police last night that Herbert Rocke was arrested at Brussels airport when he tried to fly back to the

States." He paused. "I sincerely regret he was one of our editors and I apologize to you for—"

"That isn't necessary," Nancy interrupted. "I'm just so thrilled about the contest." She gulped back tears of happiness as she realized her immediate challenges had finally come to an end.

Where would Nancy's next adventure take her? She would find out soon when she solved *The Greek Symbol Mystery*.

"Mr. Miller," the young detective went on, "now that I've found the real solution to the puzzle would you like me to write a new ending to 'The Secret in the Old Lace'? "

"Indeed, I'll publish it!" Mr. Miller said with a chuckle. "Deep down I was sure you would solve the mystery!"